Black Soldiers
in Jim Crow Texas,
1899–1917

Number Fifty-seven:
Centennial Series
of the Association
of Former Students,
Texas A&M University Press

Garna L. Christian

Black Soldiers in Jim Crow Texas, 1899–1917

Texas A&M University Press

College Station

**Library of Congress
Cataloging-in-Publication Data**

Christian Garna L.
    Black soldiers in Jim Crow Texas, 1899–1917 / by
Garna L. Christian. — 1st ed.
        p.   cm. — (Centennial series of the Association of
Former Students, Texas A&M University ; no. 57)
    Includes bibliographical references and index.
    ISBN 0-89096-637-0
    1. United States. Army—Afro-American troops—
History—20th century. 2. United States. Army.
Infantry Regiment, 24th. 3. United States. Army.
Infantry Regiment, 25th. 4. United States. Army.
Cavalry, 9th. 5. United States. Army. Cavalry, 10th.
6. Race discrimination—Texas—History—20th cen-
tury. 7. Texas—Race relations. I. Title. II. Series.
UB418.A47C48   1995
355'.008996073—dc20   94-42428
                                                      CIP

And dost thou yet, ungrateful land
Expect my blood and kin to stand
In cowered silence, while thy hand
Continues to despoil our band?

— Cpl. Charles Frederick White
" Plea of the Negro Soldier"
February 16, 1907

Contents

Illustrations

Introduction

Hollywood discovered the black soldier in the 1980s. The film successes of *A Soldier's Story* and *Glory* more than a century after African Americans had become a permanent part of the U.S. Army gloomily emphasized the nation's belated coming to terms with a people who had fought in virtually every American war, from the shot heard round the world to the gunfire that pinned Manuel Noriega inside the Vatican Embassy in Panama, to Desert Storm that chased Saddam Hussein's troops from Kuwait.[1]

White historians barely beat the movie moguls to the scene. Although fifty-three black soldiers and sailors had received the Medal of Honor between 1863 and 1899, an American scholar could state in 1928: "The American Negroes are the only people in the history of the world, so far as I know, that ever became free without any effort on their part." Demonstrable evidence to the contrary abounded in print. A white officer, Col. Thomas Wentworth Higginson, recorded for an unremembering posterity his admiration for the 1st South Carolina Volunteer Regiment, which he commanded in the Civil War. "As to the simple general fact of courage and reliability," Higginson wrote of his men, "I think no officer in our camp ever thought of there being any differences between black and white." The first regiment of former slaves mustered for the Union represented, in its valor and dedication, the more than two hundred thousand blacks who rallied to the call: "Who Would Be Free, Themselves Must Strike the Blow!"[2]

An abundance of reportage covered black participation in the Spanish-American War. While their role in taming the West attracted less public notice, quintessential Rough Rider Teddy Roosevelt lauded the African Americans' heroics at San Juan Hill, the press trailed their movements in Cuba, and an outpouring of literature by black and white authors bid to immortalize their actions. The attainment of true freedom and equality, promoted by Civil War recruitment posters, appeared at hand.[3]

Immortality proved fleeting. The constructive image, even the memory of early black combatants, ebbed with the passage of time and a government policy that severely limited the deployment of black troops in two world wars. Despite the scholarship of adept black historians, a negative perception of their abilities took root. General histories ignored the contributions of the four regiments or scathed the use of black soldiers and militiamen during Reconstruction in the pro-Southern Dunningite interpretations of the day. Students, and in many cases their teachers and professors, occupied a world in which George Washington Carver's experiments with the peanut constituted perhaps the sole contribution of blacks to Western civilization. As a Depression-born southern white writer, I shared in the collective ignorance. As recently as 1971, historian John M. Carroll lamented that "the story of black contributions to American military history amounts to one of historical omission." For years prior to publication of his influential collection of readings, *The Black Military Experience in the American West*, he gathered articles on the subject to nourish his students in the textbook void. Five years earlier, William Leckie, disturbed by the paucity of published material on black soldiers, whom he had learned to respect during the Second World War, introduced to the reading public documented proof of "the true character and contributions" of *The Buffalo Soldiers*.[4]

An outpouring of monographs, articles, and collections in the 1970s eroded, at least with scholars, the Errol Flynn and John Wayne bluecoat stereotypes of the white winning of the West. Floodgates could scarcely contain the writings of Leckie, Carroll, Jack Foner, Arlen Fowler, Marvin Fletcher, William Katz, Frank Schubert, Willard Gatewood, and a legion of whites who joined black pathfinders, such as Benjamin Quarles, Rayford W. Logan, and others, in the academic vacuum. Fueled by energy from the civil rights movement, implementation of black studies programs, the rise of revisionist Reconstruction history, the reprinting of neglected regimental chronicles, and the military selection controversy over Vietnam, there appeared a significant body of writings that placed the American black squarely in the ranks of military tradition, particularly in the army.[5]

The professional black soldier was born in the aftermath of the Civil War, though his ancestors fought in the Revolution, the War of 1812, and the Seminole wars. After initially refusing to enlist the black, a practice reminiscent of earlier and subsequent conflicts, the Union deferred to black pleas. They viewed the war as an opportunity to validate their rights of citizenship, denigrated by the recent Dred Scott decision. Black abolitionist Frederick Douglass summed up these sentiments with the exhortation, "Once let the black man get upon his person the brass letters, U.S., let him get an eagle on his button, and a musket on his shoulder and bullet in his pocket, and there is no power on earth which can deny that he has earned the right of citizenship in the United States." White Sen. Henry Wilson, assuming that black service would hasten the Union victory and enhance black acceptance by society, concurred: "I do not say carry the war into Africa but carry Africa into the war!" The valor shown by black troops at Port Hudson, Milliken's Bend, Fort Wagner, Chapins Farm, and elsewhere clearly justified their inclusion.[6]

The creation of postwar regular army units constituted for American blacks both a promise and a fulfillment. The Wilson Act of 1866 established six black regiments, the 9th and 10th Cavalries and the 38th, 39th, 40th, and 41st Infantries. In March, 1869, commensurate with an army-wide reorganization, Congress combined the infantry units into the 24th and 25th Infantries (Colored). Disappointment and disillusionment, however, quickly set in. The army appointed white officers over the units, impeding black upward mobility. West Point graduated only three African Americans during the remainder of the century, and each faced some degree of service discrimination. Most white officers accepted their assignments with trepidation, imbued with the racial biases of the general population or chastened by colleagues such as George Custer, who refused to lead black troops. Those accepting commands often saw their assignments primarily as a fast path to promotion. Purportedly, officers developed an admiration for their charges, as with John J. Pershing, whose nickname Blackjack dated from his command of 9th Cavalry troopers. Even so, officers represented an authoritarian system that hardly viewed itself as an engine for social reform, and many praised their men while attributing to them childlike qualities. In all, the army proved a stern taskmaster for the freedman.[7]

Moreover, blacks drew the least attractive posts in the military itinerary. A chorus of protests from eastern communities at the thought of garrisoning blacks, coupled with the demands of the Indian West, led the War Department to deploy the new regulars beyond the Mississippi. All four regiments guarded Texas and other outposts in the 1870s, bringing order to desolate locales. Besides tracking marauding Plains Indians, who out of respect dubbed them "Buffalo Soldiers," they patrolled the Mexican border, built and maintained post roads, strung telegraph lines, and escorted wagon trains. Between bursts of excitement stretched endless hours of tedium, marked by incessant drills, inspections, rigid discipline, and maintenance of forts that they erected against the unforgiving countryside. Nearby communities, ordinarily the soldier's self-indulgent respite from danger and boredom, cast a cold eye to their dark-skinned protectors, often confronting them with threats and even violence. Yet, the blacks in most instances maintained their composure and rarely deserted. For all their tribulations, the men found more opportunity and security in their restricted garrison life than in most civilian trades open to them. Beyond fundamental considerations, the uniform represented a status previously unknown, a symbol of the United States and its protective arm. Little wonder that bigots bristled at the sight of a uniformed black and sought to humiliate him. Sadly, the camptowns of the frontier contained their share of such people.[8]

The black regulars withstood indignities on virtually a daily basis but sporadically returned vengeance in like manner. While the unreturned transgressions attracted little comment, retaliation created "incidents" and an outcry from residents, the press, and political leaders. At San Angelo, Texas, in 1881, Tenth Cavalry troops at Fort Concho threw a scare into the the town after a local rancher shot to death a soldier who was entertaining in a saloon. It was the second blatant killing of a black soldier within ten days, and irate troopers scattered handbills around the community protesting the unpunished murders and warning: "If we do not receive justice and fair play . . . someone will suffer, if not the guilty, the innocent. It has gone far enough." The signature stated simply and proudly, "U.S. Soldiers." When some of the men mistakenly identified the suspected culprit in town, a group from the fort unleashed a volley of gunfire, slightly wounding one civilian. Intervention by the Texas Rangers and the decision of the army to remove the companies and punish the leaders ended the threat to peace.[9]

Sturgis City, Dakota Territory, witnessed a similar event in 1885. The lynching of a black soldier inflamed a squad of 25th Infantrymen from Fort Meade. Soldiers fired into a saloon, killing a customer. In this instance the War Department resisted public demands to remove the troops after charging four soldiers with the shooting.[10]

Such isolated incidents of black retaliatory violence prefaced a series of violent episodes that erupted between the Spanish-American War and World War I. By the end of the century, the black military had matured to a state of supreme self-confidence. Over a period of time, the grateful, obedient freedmen had given way to free men who had never experienced slavery but suffered impatiently the surviving racial restrictions. They took pride in having pacified the West, while attempting to contain their anger at the continuing denial of Constitutional guarantees. The war with Spain in 1898 acted as a catalyst that converted impatience into retaliation. The United States bestowed six Medals of Honor and twenty-six Certificates of Merit on their members, and all four regiments inspired laudatory press coverage. African Americans believed they had clearly fulfilled all contractual terms that lay between them and the promise of full citizenship extended during the Civil War. The new assertiveness coincided with the strident philosophy of W. E. B. DuBois, who challenged Booker T. Washington's accommodationism.[11]

The expectations of the black soldiers collided head-on with the thickening wall of racial separation described by C. Vann Woodward in *The Strange Career of Jim Crow*. Bolstering the Texas Constitution of 1876, which racially separated schools, Texans added legislation in 1891 and 1903 that mandated separate seating on railroads and streetcars, respectively. Lynchings claimed the lives of between three hundred and five hundred black Texans in the late nineteenth century. As segregation struck deeper roots in the South, southern sympathies expanded northward. Uniformed, self-assertive blacks produced savage backlashes in Florida before and after the Cuban campaign. But the most notorious clashes occurred in Texas, at Brownsville in 1906 and Houston in 1917. Ironically, the state had first hosted the black regiments but had not witnessed serious confrontations beyond the San Angelo affair. The Brownsville and Houston incidents received extensive and highly negative news coverage, inspiring detailed studies more than half a century later. While they strengthened the most alarming stereotype of the armed black and inspired rationalization of racial discrimination, the encounters actually formed part of a pattern of behavior among whites and blacks that stretched back to 1898. Lesser-known, and until now undetailed, clashes occurred in the same state between 1898 and 1917.[12]

By no means peculiar to the state of Texas, these little-remembered episodes from a state steeped in military tradition offer in their repetitious patterns a deeper insight into conditions that produced the Brownsville raid and the Houston riot. Moreover, they illuminate the collision of racial discrimination with racial pride that portended the urban riots during and after World War I. It is a grim tale of petty biases, institutionalized prejudice, and mutual recriminations that perhaps irreparably divided American society. But it is also a story of lofty aspiration too long delayed, of the transformation of an obsequious race into a self-confident people, and the righteous attempt, sometimes mistaken in its approach, to realize the American Dream.[13]

Black Soldiers
in Jim Crow Texas,
1899–1917

One

The Road Back to Texas

On the road back from Cuba to Texas, ostensibly from war to peace, the 10th Cavalry encountered rocky terrain in Alabama and Mississippi, bastions of white supremacy in the former Confederacy. In a somber continuation of racial harassments the regiment had encountered in Florida before embarkation to the combat zone, incidents pitted the 10th against white soldiers as well as hostile civilians. On an October morning in 1898, the unit, under command of Lt. Col. T. A. Baldwin, detrained at Huntsville, Alabama. Scarcely had the men rubbed the sleep from their eyes when some of the more adventurous decided to inspect the town's red-light district. To their consternation, the early sojourners found this time-honored military prerogative closed to their race. An altercation prompted a call for the military police.[1]

The appearance of the white 16th Infantry provost guard fueled the fire. The detachment apprehended a Private Stevens of F Troop only to face several of the prisoner's comrades, who attempted to free him. The guards momentarily drove back the assailants by employing their rifle butts as clubs, but one of the black soldiers wrested a weapon, which discharged in the scuffle and wounded a guard in the thigh. According to the report of the provost commander, blacks then opened fire from their train, some one hundred yards distant. An exchange of shots mortally wounded two guards. Three cavalrymen fell wounded from the barrage, and a hospital attendant narrowly escaped harm. Several troopers were taken into custody.[2]

Various white witnesses joined the provost commander in condemnation of the black troops. The manager of the saloon in which the fighting erupted blamed the cavalrymen for the disturbance. Several employees of the Nashville, Chattanooga, and St. Louis Railroad accused the blacks of instigating the shooting spree, the conductor claiming to have observed a soldier fatally striking a guard. The violent fray could not have been better calculated to reinforce southern white stereotypes of armed blacks or to fashion an image of the entire regiment that would accompany it into South Texas.[3]

The bloody encounter also affected the relationship between the 16th Infantry and the 10th Cavalry for the remainder of the black regiment's tenure at Huntsville. When a circus opened in the city several weeks later, guards of the white regiment arrested and then released several troopers during a weapons search at the entrance to the big top. Although the rest of the evening at the amusement site passed peacefully, the tense confrontation raised the ire of a 10th Cavalry officer, whose official complaint spawned a series of missives that carried the interregimental dispute into higher military echelons.[4]

Capt. S. L. Woodward of Camp Albert S. Forse accused the provost guard of "annoying and imposing upon men . . . behaving in an orderly manner." To the adjutant general of the Fourth Army Corps, Woodward stated that a provost sergeant had admitted enforcing orders to search all 10th Cavalry members on the presumption that they were concealing carbines beneath their coats. Labeling this a "preposterous proposition," Woodward noted that only black soldiers had suffered the indignity and asked for the selection of military policemen "who are without prejudice and with sense and discretion."[5]

Responding to the allegation of racial discrimination, Capt. S. W. Dunning, provost commander, defended the actions of his charges at the circus midway. He insisted that all soldiers suspected of carrying arms had been inspected and that guards had taken pistols from three cavalrymen and a black teamster before a lieutenant halted the procedure. "My orders," Dunning reiterated, "are to arrest any soldier who is carrying weapons not on duty and no distinctions have been or could be made."[6]

The discovery of weapons on off-duty servicemen stirred the adjutant general's office to turn Woodward's complaint back on him. The superior officer directed his junior to justify the presence of weapons on his men or to discipline them accordingly. In a lengthy response Woodward acknowledged his men's absence of authorization to carry weapons, but he emphasized that only one of the three arrested men had possessed a pistol and that witnesses had sworn he found it in the wagon en route to the city. The captain lamented the three men having to spend the night in the guardhouse before delivery to camp. He stated that other members of his command had reported intimidating behavior by the military police, even after a weapons check at camp had accounted for all issues. Woodward condemned "the untrained . . . Provost Guard" for "not reflecting credit upon the army" and endorsed the deportment of his men:

> There need be no fear that the 10th Cavalry will behave more disorderly or require more watching than other organizations, and I sincerely trust that none of them may appear in the streets of Huntsville, mounted, drunk, falling from horses, and vomiting over themselves as was the case yesterday (Sunday) with men of another regiment.[7]

The experiences at Huntsville would follow the 10th Cavalry and other black units beyond the next decade, as they struggled for a place in a society that both admired their military prowess and obstructed acceptance. These contradictory forces bedeviled the regiment as it completed its duty in Alabama. The provost commander's assertion that black soldiers were responsible for the gun battle at the train station lacked verification from eyewitnesses capable of making positive identification or reaching agreement on the actual number involved. Even Captain Dunning raised the possibility that the guards might have unintentionally wounded the hospital attendant. The conflicting versions of the weapons search at the circus underscored the divergent perspectives of blacks and whites who shared a common military experience. Small wonder that white civilians, possessing no commonality with uniformed and armed blacks, united in their belief of black instigation. Far from ending, the drama continued as the troop trains transported the 10th Cavalry toward various destinations in Texas.[8]

Four regimental troops came under sniper attack while en route through Mississippi. Troops C, D, F, and M reached Meridian, in the eastern sector of the state, on the afternoon of January 30. When the horses refused to drink the water at the stop, the commander ordered the stock cars reloaded to proceed to New Orleans. The two trains departed at designated intervals, the first about nightfall. While nothing at Meridian signaled the slightest likelihood of trouble, a barrage of gunfire struck the lead car before it had moved beyond city limits.[9]

When 2nd Lt. H. B. Dixon heard the shots through the dark, rainy night, he speculated that friends of the regiment had decided to give the troops a rousing send-off. As he stepped to the platform, the whizzing of bullets and smashing of windows dashed that notion. A hasty inspection revealed shattered door locks and jambs and broken panes, with entry and exit holes clearly visible on either side of the coach. Luckily, a dozen shots of various calibers pierced the car but missed the guard posted near the door. Casualties were limited to scratches from broken glass. Afterward, the shaken soldiers drew little consolation from a trainman's observation that the shooting "was probably done by reckless men for no other reason than mere sport."[10]

Unapprised of the bizarre Mississippi reception accorded the smaller contingent, eight trainloads of 10th Cavalrymen crossed the Red River the following morning. Just ahead lay Texarkana, Texas, a community struggling both for modernity and retention of tradition.[11]

Like countless towns across the nation, the locality at the Texas-Arkansas line believed itself on the threshold of greatness. Boasting a population of about twenty thousand—when counting its Miller County, Arkansas, namesake—the Texas city hosted four rail lines, a medical and a business college, two federal courts, and a thriving lumber and cotton trade. "It is believed," stated a booster, "that the very favorable location of Texarkana will soon make it a leading manufacturing center." Moreover, "moral and religious conditions throughout the country are of a high order."[12]

Typical of the public relations hyperbole that often passed for factual description in guides of that time, the essayist omitted any references to matters not deemed in the community interest. While later generations would marvel at the existence of Caddo mounds and other traces of Indian civilization, publicists at the turn of the century saw no advantage in noting heathen Indian trails traversing the area. In like fashion the writer ignored the state of racial relations in the region of Texas most closely identified with the lost cause of the Confederacy. For example, when a young black minister and teacher, A. M. Gregory, had attempted to organize a black militia in Marshall, less than a hundred miles from Texarkana, in 1883, white resistance united across East Texas. Protests arose in Longview, Daingerfield, Tyler, Palestine, and even Shreveport, Louisiana. The Galveston *News* charged Gregory with embezzlement, allegations that the organizer heatedly denied. According to a chronicler of the episode: "Reactions of whites reached their greatest intensity in rural East Texas counties where blacks were a majority or a large minority of the population." Fifteen years later, a seriously perceived black challenge to white authority returned with the appearance of the 10th Cavalry at the Texarkana station.[13]

The recent incident at Huntsville was reenacted almost identically at the Texas border. Unidentified 10th Cavalrymen used the scheduled rest stop to patronize the Belmont House, in what polite society called "the restricted district." As in Alabama, the troopers discovered that the word *restricted* also conveyed racial connotations. A frightened, partially clothed resident of the Belmont managed to elude the intruders and rush to the courthouse, where she related the event to her surprised audience. A peace officer, accompanied by several other local officials, overtook a soldier hurrying toward the depot from the direction of the disturbance. As Constable J. F. Rochelle attempted to arrest the man, a group of cavalrymen crowded around the pair, jostling the prisoner free. The wanted soldier concealed himself on a crowded train while a number of his regimental fellows allegedly intimidated the officials and townspeople by pointing rifles from the coaches' windows. At the request of civil authorities, military officers delayed departure of the trains for several hours to effect a search. Several witnesses claimed they could identify the suspect and his rescuers, but a prolonged examination proved fruitless.[14]

By the next morning, residents across the Southwest read of the excitement in East Texas. Enjoying a news monopoly, a publication of the time could, if desired, publicize, neglect, or skew a story in consonance with its editorial views. An exclusive account picked up by other organs presented an especially inviting possibility of shaping public thought. Subscribers at Houston and Galveston, hundreds of miles from the scene, formed their first impressions of the entering regiment largely from the special submitted by a Little Rock correspondent.[15]

A story of a decorated black unit involved in a disturbance potentially posed a dilemma for a southern editor. Many warmly supported the military, particularly in garrison towns, where federal construction and payrolls enhanced local revenue. Prior to the Brownsville raid, the press more frequently associated black army units with heroics in Cuba than with destructive behavior. On the day following the Texarkana fray, the Galveston newspaper ran an article extolling the 10th Cavalry's record at Santiago. "It is a well known fact," stated the writer, "but that for the[m] . . . Roosevelt's Rough Riders would have been utterly annihilated."[16]

The southern military predilection, however, met with more than its match in the virulent obsession with white supremacy. Although Texas lynchings had declined in the late 1890s, pursuant to antilynching legislation that prosecuted offenders and required dismissal of negligent law officers, the toll still stood at a horrifying ten per year. The majority occurred in East Texas. Newspapers extended wide coverage to black crimes and punishment, often depicting mob actions as a necessary evil. They delivered the message that black soldiers, like others of their race, must not overstep boundaries, the more so since uniforms and bearing connoted authority.[17]

With racial considerations foremost, the coverage of the Texarkana incident allowed enthusiastic editors to introduce the account with such headlines as "The Tenth Cavalry Made a Rough House Out of Texarkana" and "The Texarkana Outrage." While essentially concurring with later official reports, the dispatch brimmed with emotionally charged descriptions. "When they arrived," the correspondent wrote of the troops, "they were a drunken mob and an effort was made by them to tear up the town." At the arrest of the soldier, "every car window held a drunken negro with a cocked rifle and after the guns had been stuck in the officer's face the negroes escaped into the cars." The assertion that all soldiers were drunk and participated in the freeing of the suspect contradicted subsequent investigations. The statement that "irate Texarkanans . . . armed with dynamite" had coerced the troops to agree to turn over their comrades lacked substantiation. In truth the identity and location of the wanted man and his liberators remained unknown.[18]

Accurate or not, the news story set into motion official machinery. Three days later, the Bowie county attorney, Horace W. Vaughan, sent a fuller and less passionate narrative of events to Gov. Joseph A. Sayers, requesting an investigation. Simultaneously, Vaughan released a copy of the communication to the press, guaranteeing continued public interest in the matter. The army showed sensitivity to the concern by retaining the troops on the trains overnight after reaching San Antonio. When a trainload of the soldiers passed through Laredo in the afternoon, a reporter felt compelled to calm his readership: "The troops were orderly and were given a reception by the colored population on their arrival."[19]

Vaughan's report, based on personal knowledge "except where stated on information," moderated the published account in some particulars. He stated that during the six- or seven-hour stopover in Texarkana the troops behaved "very well" save for the incident involving the arrested man. This appraisal contradicted the assertion that the soldiers were drunk aboard the train, tossing whisky bottles and lumps of coal at bystanders. While omitting any reference to civilians who supposedly collected dynamite to defend themselves from the troops, the county attorney denied any threat of explosives. He praised the actions of army officers in restraining their charges. "A tall yellow officer" stood between the cars and the crowd, commanding his men to hold fire. Vaughan lauded the "entirely proper conduct on the part of those officers of the regiment with whom we came into contact." The local official even gently reproached the constable, who "under the circumstances and excitement attempted to arrest the man in view of the regiment without having demanded him of the commander after spotting his man."[20]

In other essentials Vaughan's story constituted a searing indictment of the cavalrymen's deportment. At approximately 1:30 in the afternoon, "one of the inmates of a house of ill fame" rushed in a disheveled state into the courthouse while court was in session. To Vaughan, Constable Rochelle, Justice of the Peace P. G. Henry, and Deputy Sheriff L. C. Lynch, she attested that about ten blacks "had broken into their house" and threatened to kill the women, all of whom were white, if they refused them sex. When the officers of the court hurriedly arrived at the brothel, they learned that the men had left and that they were members of the 10th Cavalry. According to the matron, the soldiers had demanded that she "trot out her God damned whores" or face death. They turned on the black porter when he protested their presence. Reportedly, one drew his gun on the black employee but held his fire at the behest of his comrades.[21]

The county attorney depicted the tense scene at the depot much as the press, although acknowledging that Rochelle drew his gun as soldiers approached the arrest scene. Immediately, a trooper "ran up to Rochelle and started to shoot him in the back," but Henry Rochelle, the constable's brother, snatched the weapon. In turn, some of the men wrested the piece while others hustled the prisoner into a coach. Vaughan confirmed that soldiers inside the train leveled rifles on the civil officials and the gathering crowd. That action coupled with the servicemen's abusive language "almost precipitated a race riot. . . . They used language that was calculated to fire up the blood of any white man on earth."[22]

While Vaughan obviously felt disdain for the soldiers, he stopped short of condemning the entire unit. He directed his response toward "ascertain[ing] the names of the squad who went to the house of ill fame, so that they can be properly indicted . . . and surrendered to Civil Authority for punishment." To this end, he asked the governor "to demand of the proper authority in the proper way, an investigation into the transaction."[23]

Governor Sayers, a Confederate veteran just beginning his term, required little prodding. He assured the local officer, "I will do everything within my power to carry out what you desire" and fired off identical telegrams to Secretary of War Russell A. Alger and U.S. Sens. Roger Q. Mills and Horace Chilton of Texas.

> Soldiers of the Tenth Cavalry in passing through Texarkana acted in a most outrageous manner violating the law, insulting citizens and putting their lives in jeopardy. Please see President at once and obtain from him an order directing a trustworthy officer to proceed immediately to Texarkana and inquire into the matter, first conferring with Honorable Horace W. Vaughan. . . . Also obtain an order directing Colonel of the Regiment to furnish every facility to civil authorities for identifying and ascertaining the names of the soldiers. . . . Please answer.[24]

Meanwhile, the press exposed differences of opinion between some military and civil authorities, tending to place the latter in a better light. When a 10th Cavalry captain expressed skepticism at the reports of the regiment's conduct, a reporter disparaged his comments as "regarded as a huge bluff by the people of Texarkana." News items quoted Texarkanans as believing the army to be uncooperative and partial to the soldiers.[25]

Newspapers ran daily stories on the most emotional points, sustaining the heated controversy. Several days after the event a correspondent alleged, "Every railroad station from Little Rock shows signs of the soldiers' depredation. The sign board on every depot designating the colored waiting rooms was demolished." Interestingly, in this offhand and accusative reference to firing from trains, the press came as close as it ever would to reporting the shooting incidents of which the military complained at Meridian and, later, Houston.[26]

Four troops of the 10th Cavalry detrained in Houston, destined for South Texas, in an apprehensive mood. The experience at Meridian and the sensational reporting on Texarkana had clearly unsettled the commanding officer. When a reporter posed a routine question to Colonel Baldwin, the agitated officer turned him back with the reply: "I have absolutely nothing to say. You would print whatever you wished, any statement of mine to the contrary notwithstanding." On reflection, Baldwin attributed his bad humor to the East Texas controversy rather than any action of the local newspaper. An accompanying junior officer voiced the sentiments of his superior and doubtless other army officers who had commanded black troops. "They fought like tigers before Santiago," exclaimed the lieutenant, who had sustained a stomach wound in that campaign, "and I cannot bring myself to believe that they could commit such acts of lawlessness as have been attributed to them."[27]

The Houston journalist displayed more sympathy for the black soldiers than had many of his colleagues. "The men were given their liberty all during the time they were here [approximately three hours]," he observed, "and it can be said to their credit that they conducted themselves in a manner which elicited nothing but commendation from those who saw them." Extolling their recent war record, the writer described the troops as "a fine, lusty looking set of fellows" and accepted an invitation from Colonel Baldwin to visit their headquarters at Fort Clark.[28]

The newly optimistic mood at Houston dissipated in the adjoining countryside as the troop movement resumed that evening. When the train bearing Troops C and D chugged past Harlem, shots rang out from the darkness. In what must have seemed a recurring nightmare, Lieutenant Dixon heard reports from a .44 or .45 caliber single-action pistol at ten o'clock, while most of the men slept in the dimly lit or darkened coaches. By now a hardened veteran of sniper attacks, Dixon calculated the attackers to be "a more considerable party" than at Meridian. He judged the shooters' position at twenty or thirty yards from the track, occupying two hundred to three hundred yards along both sides of the rails. Perhaps a dozen rounds followed the initial bursts. Dixon acknowledged that troops from the targeted coaches returned fire, the crack of their .30 caliber carbines "plainly distinguishable" from the sounds of the other arms. The lieutenant raced through the cars, ordering his men to cease firing. He estimated the duration of the exchange at a minute to a minute and a half. His inspection of the destruction recorded a dozen broken windows and scarred woodwork. Fortunately, none of the command suffered injuries more serious than cuts and scratches about the face and hands. Dixon attributed this remarkable effect to the reclining position of the soldiers, asleep in their berths, at the time of the attack.[29]

The officer's personal investigation of the incident prompted conclusions that he presented to Colonel Baldwin. Despite the comment of the brakeman, who sought cover during the shooting, that reckless individuals often fired at lighted trains, all the bullets shattered darkened coaches. This suggested an attack on the sleeping soldiers rather than a sporting effort to douse the lights. Because of the darkness and the motion of the train, no passenger could see, much less identify, the snipers. The officers, earlier criticized by some East Texans as ineffective or uncooperative, "used their best endeavors" to control the agitated soldiers.[30]

Although the attack occurred only a few miles from Houston, the local press ignored it except for a terse item and an angry letter to the editor in the *Post*. An entry datelined Richmond, Texas, described "outrageous conduct" on the part of soldiers, whose alleged target practice from trains left "houses all along the line filled with bullets." Under the headline "Bad Conduct of Negro Soldiers," a resident of Harlem complained of troops firing "indiscriminately in every direction" from their coaches on the night of the attack. The writer protested that shells struck several houses, narrowly missing tragedy, and ended the correspondence on a sardonic note: "If such conduct can't be stopped, as I live very near the railroad, I would thank anybody who would let me know that they are coming, so we can escape with our lives, and will leave them our house and furniture and consider ourselves lucky."[31]

Unknown to the public, informed only of accusations against the soldiers, the military filed complaints of its own. Upon receipt of Lieutenant Dixon's report, Colonel Baldwin forwarded the account to the adjutant general at Washington with the comment: "I would respectfully state that I make this report to show how the colored troops have been treated while changing station and request that some steps be taken to enable them to pass through the country which they are sworn to protect without danger from hidden assassins." Secretary of War Alger dispatched copies to the governors of Mississippi and Texas and requested the U.S. Attorney General "to ferret out the perpetrators of these outrages and to prevent their reoccurrence."[32]

The exchange between Washington and Austin conformed to diplomatic correctness, masking any sentiments that might have accompanied the communications. Secretary Alger begged of Governor Sayers "such consideration and action, with a view to discovering the parties engaged in the outrage, as may seem to you to meet the ends of justice." The state executive responded that he had "taken the necessary steps to secure a thorough investigation of the affair" and promised to advise the cabinet officer "fully" of the results. Despite the cordiality, the two men represented quite different constituencies: Alger, the well-being of the soldiers, and Sayers, the safety and happiness of the Texas citizenry. The fact that the governor and other state officials owed their careers to favorable public opinion heightened the friction in the awkward military–civilian relationship.[33]

In compliance with Special Orders No. 36, Capt. B. H. Byrne, 6th Infantry, drew the assignment of investigating the Texarkana affray. He departed Fort Sam Houston, San Antonio, on February 9 and arrived in the East Texas town the following day. There he contacted the county attorney, Vaughan, for "a detailed account of the alleged misdeeds" of the troopers, only to have presented to him a duplicate of the letter that the local official had sent to the governor. Vaughan insisted that the communication contained the entire story. Wishing to probe further, Byrne asked that Vaughan and Constable Rochelle, also present, introduce participants or eyewitnesses.[34]

The attendants of the Belmont House described the abrupt arrival of six or seven soldiers, an estimate slightly at variance with the ten first reported, on the day of the disturbance. A tall mulatto and a short dark man attracted particular attention by their actions. One woman recalled that the former placed his foot in the door when she attempted to prevent their entrance and shouted, "Open that door and open it damned quick you God Damned Whores, bring your white bitches or we will tear the house to pieces." The other tenants and the black porter corroborated the narrative, the latter having distracted the soldiers sufficiently for one of the prostitutes to escape. The porter reproved the intruders, "You are in the wrong country to do any thing like that," provoking two of the men to threaten to "blow [him] . . . to hell." The mulatto intervened, according to the custodian, exclaiming: "He is a colored gentleman like ourselves, don't hurt him, it is the white sons of bitches we are after."[35]

Other witnesses recounted the attempted apprehension of the soldier and his flight, with some confusion on detail. Some disagreement arose on the point of the contact between the arresting officer, Rochelle, and the wanted man. One witness remembered the constable escorting the prisoner to the depot, others repeated the majority view that Rochelle arrested him at the station. There was also a lack of unanimity on whether the constable spotted the subject, apparently the mulatto in question, or was directed by an accuser. Witnesses presented the investigating officer a rather wide estimate of soldiers involved in freeing the fugitive, but all bystanders at the depot asserted that the troopers had pointed rifles from the train windows during the confrontation. Constable Rochelle, unquestionably the central witness, depicted his role essentially as reported in the press.[36]

The inspecting officer hoped that an internal military investigation might yet disclose the missing information. The testimony suggested that the second section of three troop trains had carried the disruptive soldiers. Accordingly, Captain Byrne shifted the focus of the inquiry to the 10th Cavalry command. He quickly discovered a striking contrast to the civilians' statements in the level of emotion and degree of certainty.[37]

On the essential matters of identification and responsibility, the officers commanding the troop movements contributed negligibly. Maj. J. L. Fowler, in charge of the suspect second section, claimed to have learned of the incident only after noticing a crowd gathering on the platform. He admitted having to place a sentry under guard for inebriation, but insisted that the man had exercised commendable restraint and courtesy toward the indignant citizenry. "He only said repeatedly, 'Please, gentlemen, keep back . . . now, keep back— please.'" The major quoted civil authorities as satisfied with the army's cooperation in the train search. Fowler observed no evidence of general drinking and heard less noise aboard the troop train than customarily. He doubted that men in his command had precipitated the conflict because of the briefness of time between the arrival of that section and the beginning of the disturbance.[38]

The regimental commander, Col. S. M. Whitside, also claimed no first hand knowledge of the matter. Traveling aboard the third section, he noticed "nothing to attract attention" at his arrival and took lunch at the depot dining room. While the colonel ate, "the sheriff," probably Constable Rochelle, entered the restaurant and approached the table. The peace officer appeared so little agitated that he insisted upon waiting for Whitside to complete his meal before telling him of the trouble. The colonel immediately appointed Capt. L. P. Hunt to assist the civil officers in a search of the trains. The regimental commander, like Major Fowler, saw no indication of intoxication on the part of any soldier.[39]

Captain Hunt, assisting in the search, first learned of the excitement by asking some soldiers the cause of a gathering crowd. They replied that "two citizens had disarmed a soldier and . . . some of the latter had resisted and threatened to shoot." While Hunt made no comment on the statement, the men's choice of words might well explain the soldiers' sharp reaction to the arrest. A perception of the civil authorities as merely armed "citizens" intent on harming, perhaps killing, one of their comrades would account for their hostile behavior. Hunt's statement contradicted a news account that described blacks taunting Rochelle by name. The captain felt "sure" that the fugitive was not a member of his command.[40]

Capt. Charles G. Ayres, leader of the first troop section, discounted the theory of some officials that the suspect had fled on an early departing train. Like the other officers, he denied direct knowledge of the incident that prompted the delay and search, commenting that no mention of trouble arose until after the two other sections had reached the depot. "All were sober and quiet," he said of his men, adding: "Men under my orders and control have yet in my career to make a disturbance as is herein described." Ayres's energetic defense stemmed from speculation that time constraints would have placed the offenders on the first section. The fact that Ayers's section also left Texarkana first fed the conjecture that the escapee had stowed away with his contingent.[41]

There the matter lay. A subsequent army report concluded: "From the tone of the accompanying endorsements it would seem that no special effort has been made to ascertain the identity of the men who made the visit to the house of ill fame and who were responsible for the consequent conditions, although such inquiry may have been made." Indeed, the tenor of each officer's response seemed primarily designed to release that commander and his unit from any share of culpability. No such frank appraisal accompanied the unrecorded efforts of the governors of Mississippi and Texas to locate the attackers of the troop train at Meridian and Harlem. Given the circumstances, one may doubt that the undertaking manifested much zeal.[42]

The reentry of the battle-hardened 10th Cavalry into Texas in January, 1899, both challenged and stiffened racial sentiment in the former Confederate state. At Texarkana and Harlem, whites and blacks brandished arms against each other, in the latter instance resorting to their use. Yet, unlike the situation at Huntsville, Alabama, no physical injuries resulted. The spectacle of a half-dozen enlisted men scurrying from depot to bawdy house during a rest stop would not have merited mention in other circumstances; nor would the attempt by a hunted soldier, with the aid of friends, to avoid arrest. Neither was the practice of shooting at trains "for sport" as unusual as rail employees would have liked. The racial factor turned obnoxious, if unsingular, actions into potentially devastating events. The memory of armed whites demanding a black soldier and the recollection of black troops leveling rifles at civilians overpowered subsequent gestures at comity between garrisons and communities. In that stark moment at the Texarkana depot, the approaching violence at garrison communities became possible.

After the Texarkana incident, army and state governmental reports on black military–civilian clashes in Texas would no longer enjoy the luxury of indifferent inquiry.

Two

South to the Rio Grande

After the shocks at Huntsville, Texarkana, and on the outskirts of Houston, sites where racial antagonisms ran deep, a young 10th Cavalry recruit might have viewed the approaching South and West Texas destinations as infinitely more promising. There, after all, people of Mexican descent composed the underclass, and the smaller numbers of blacks posed less of a target for discrimination. Headquarters unit, band, and Troops A, G, H, and L detrained at Fort Sam Houston in multicultural San Antonio, while B, C, and D Troops drew Fort Clark. The remaining five troops were parceled among Forts Bliss, Brown, McIntosh, Ringgold, and Camp Eagle Pass. Despite tensions and some incidents, decorum and indeed boredom proved the rule until the regiment returned to Cuba as an occupation force in the fall of 1899. The replacement units at Laredo and Rio Grande City, however, fared less tranquilly in the garrison communities.[1]

Laredo, the largest town and seat of Webb County, had reclined on the sun-baked left bank of the Rio Grande since 1755. It represented the last and northernmost settlement of José de Escandon's colonization of El Seno Mexicano, a barren region stretching from the Panuco River to the Nueces. Hot, dry, and virtually uninhabitable, the Mexican Gulf Coast had offered little enticement but to the boldest settlers. Isolated at one end of this vast desolation, Laredoans early developed a penchant for surviving adversity. Chaotic changes in government and nationhood, invading armies, revolutionaries, Indians, and defiant outlaws constantly tested their mettle. Cattle production, one of the few economic pursuits congenial to the harsh terrain, inspired rustlers from both sides of the river from a multitude of nationalities and races. With complete equality of opportunity, lacklaw Anglos, Hispanics, Lipans, Kickapoo, and Comanches treated themselves to beeves from inviting area ranches.[2]

Instability along the post–Mexican War border contributed to the construction of Fort McIntosh in 1849, linking a chain of army installations across the outer reaches of Texas. Perched atop a bluff one mile from the town, the star-shaped redoubt witnessed a parade of military notables in its prime, with the likes of Robert E. Lee, William H. Emory, John "Rip" Ford, Randolph B. Marcy, and architect Egbert L. Viele serving or visiting. To a man they deemed it incommodious. Captain Marcy described the cramped quarters as "of the most wretched character." Troops complained of slow mail and supply deliveries and meager gardens, making McIntosh hard duty. Lydia Spencer Lane, whose extensive travels with her officer husband enabled her to draw meaningful comparisons of posts, pronounced the location dismal, "where nothing lived but Indians, snakes, and other venomous reptiles."[3]

Necessity, rather than aesthetics, retained the fort at Laredo. With the border less tumultuous, the army reduced the garrison to twenty-six men in 1858 and abandoned it altogether the next year. Buildings and land reverted to the city, which auctioned off most of the structures. Within a few months, the depredations of Juan N. Cortina and his band forced McIntosh's reactivation. Troops again withdrew from the bluff in 1861 by order of the Department of Texas, but Confederates under Santos Benavides filled the void, staving off Indian, Mexican, and Unionist assaults. At the end of the Civil War, the United States replaced the site with one half a mile away, which the city conveyed for a consideration of $1,000. The new McIntosh displayed a look of permanency, as construction over the next two decades exceeded $50,000.[4]

The military construction coincided with one of the most lawless periods in the history of the border region. Postwar demand for Texas beef in northern markets contributed to intensified cattle theft in South Texas. Prominent rancher-rustlers such as King Fisher of Maverick County dominated local lawmen and intimidated jurors. Lacking political clout, Indians and Mexican nationals thinned the herds for profits or vengeance. Cortina and other raiders fueled Anglo antipathy of Mexicans, resulting in indiscriminate shootings of suspicious Latinos. Legendary Leander H. McNelly and his Special Force of Texas Rangers sought pacification through a gun barrel, ignoring restraints binding the U.S. Army. Mexican President Porfirio Díaz, en route to a thirty-year dictatorship, kept controversy swirling as political opponents in the northern states carried their grievances across the Rio Grande. Yet Díaz, in the opinion of critical Americans, appeared reluctant to use the full force of his authority to quell them, perhaps withholding cooperation as a tool for diplomatic recognition. As Washington warmed to Díaz, combined efforts of Rangers, South Texas garrisons, and energized Mexican *federales* reduced border chaos by the late 1870s.[5]

In the 1880s Laredo attained a prosperity and recognition that exceeded anything in its past. The new respectability arrived on the sleek rails of the International–Great Northern and the Texas-Mexican, which finally connected this hinterland to the world beyond, north and south. Shortly thereafter, the Rio Grande and Eagle Pass line linked the community to the coal fields above it. Promising access to markets and resources, while enabling security forces to reach the town more rapidly, the railroads alchemized the local economy. Land values and commercial outlets increased, with the population escalating from several thousand in 1880 to above thirteen thousand by the end of the century. The introduction of barbed wire and expansion of irrigation through power pumps modernized ranching and farming in the vicinity, with agriculture thriving on the newly adopted Bermuda onion.[6]

Economic growth failed to bring total peace to the border, though the ravages of the 1870s diminished considerably. Resistance strengthened to Díaz's tightening rein, creating disturbances on the left bank that would inundate South Texas early in the next century. Although the Plains Indians no longer presented a threat, Anglo and Hispanic renegades still shared a lucrative business. Political rivalry, which divided Laredoans into factions of Botas and Huaraches, frequently heated to combustible levels. Progress, in short, had not ended the need for military protection, though a parsimonious defense posture at Washington kept frontier forts at minimal operation strength and emptied their garrisons of regulars during the short-lived Spanish-American War.[7]

Troop E of the 10th Cavalry, which unpacked its equipment for garrison duty in early February, 1899, scarcely represented the typical racial types at Laredo. Census figures for the following year showed Webb County with only 205 black residents in a population of 21,851. This number reflected a reduction of nine from the previous count. Yet, even though the four black regiments had not served in Texas since the early 1880s, older South Texans could remember black soldiers as a common, if not always welcome, sight. The Corps d'Afrique and the 62nd U.S. Colored Infantry had bolstered Union forces during the Civil War against invasions of the region. Reconstruction had brought the controversial state police, which included blacks, as well as black occupation troops. Units of the African-American regiments had manned McIntosh and area posts on a regular basis during the Indian campaigns of the 1870s, often accompanied by black Seminole Scouts.[8]

During that time South Texans had noted the contribution of blacks toward border security and generally accepted them, but tensions always lay near the surface. Laredo leadership, both Hispanic and Anglo, had defended the Confederacy, and a residue of bitterness remained in the aftermath of the war. Disdain for blacks openly demonstrated by state officials and Texas Rangers reinforced racial bias, as did any actions of black soldiers or civilians that supported negative stereotypes. Lower-status Hispanics, the bulk of the population despite economic and demographic growth, often associated soldiers with repressive governmental policies that punished their folk heroes as bandits or revolutionaries. Many of them, through emulation, convenience, or conviction, shared the southern white prejudice against blacks.[9]

The introduction of Negro troops into a border community such as Laredo upset the existing tenuous relationship between Anglo and Latino. This balance rested on an accommodation, reminiscent of a medieval society, in which the Mexican masses deferred to whites and a few Hispanic leaders who mixed freely with the Anglos in return for toleration or political or economic protection. A workable modus vivendi had emerged from the early ranching stage but was now threatened by land development and commercialization, which submerged and embittered many Hispanics. Race relations acquired a new edge. In a candid moment a white attorney blurted, "These Mexicans are an inflammable people and . . . would rather revolute than work." The ease with which Cortina and other insurrectionists found solace among the Hispanic population indicated disfavor with the ruling elements. Black soldiers—uniformed, armed members of a widely disparaged race—destabilized the system merely by their presence. Whites desired the protection of a garrison but disliked the new occupants, while Latinos feared the further loss of their meager prerogatives. Accordingly, all eyes in the spring of 1899 turned to the familiar fort with the unsettling defenders.[10]

The army itself was not reconciled on the racial issue. Officers in command of black soldiers frequently displayed a condescending attitude toward their charges. These officers in turn drew allegations of opportunism from their counterparts who refused to command black troops. Above all, garrison commanders wished a harmonious relationship with the surrounding community and avoidance of incidents that attracted the attention of superiors. The stationing of blacks in former Confederate states threatened no end of possible mischief, but the War Department saw no alternative. Budgetary restrictions, military downsizing, and the Philippine insurrection against American occupation combined to thwart alternatives. Border unrest demanded active forts in South Texas, whatever the consequences.[11]

The interplay of relationships among the army, the local populace, and the state acted out a bizarre scenario for the 10th Cavalry. Smallpox, which had driven up the mortality rate to 57.5 per thousand in 1831 and ravaged the area periodically, revisited Laredo in March, 1899. It devastated poor Hispanics. Nevertheless, a quarantine imposed by the local health officer failed to contain the infected, who resisted transfer from their homes to the pesthouse. Embittered by negative experiences with government, an angry armed crowd gathered to prevent the removal of the ill. City officials summoned a contingent of the Texas Rangers, whose mythical prowess melted before the defiant assemblage.[12]

In the best Hollywood tradition, save the pigmentation of the troopers, the U.S. Cavalry rode to the summons. At the behest of Gov. Joseph D. Sayers, a critic of the unit since Texarkana, Capt. A. G. Ayres led two officers and thirty-five men with a Gatling gun primed to reinforce their old nemeses. The success of the collaboration drew praise from Mayor L. J. Christian. Conversely, the action presented disgruntled Hispanics another grievance against the occupants of Fort McIntosh.[13]

In September, 1899, Troop E joined the other Texas-based contingents of the 10th Cavalry en route to Cuba. Garrison duty at Laredo revolved exclusively on Company D, 25th Infantry, which had shared the post with the departing troop since the previous April. A widely praised unit in the Spanish-American War, the 25th had dispersed over the Rocky Mountain states after returning to the mainland. At the time Company D assumed sole control over McIntosh, two other regimental members rotated to Texas, one each to El Paso and San Antonio, while a single company remained in Arizona. The majority of the ranks steamed to the Philippines, where the "little brown brothers" showed no signs of deserting Emilio Aguinaldo's uprising.[14]

As subsequently occurred at El Paso, Waco, Houston, and elsewhere, hostility between the garrison and police triggered a crisis. In Laredo, Hispanics of working-class origins made up the constabulary. Soldiers complained of arrests at the slightest provocation and of excessive fines, assertions echoed by their superiors. Lt. John M. Campbell, the white commanding officer at Fort McIntosh, complained of police harassment to the inspector general shortly after his men took possession of the post. Paydays brought such an increase in arrests and fines that Campbell prohibited his men from going into town for three days after the first of the month. Shortly after the lifting of the ban, Officer José Cuellar beat and jailed an enlisted man arrested in the company of a Hispanic woman. The incident aroused the members of the garrison, some of whom endeavored to purchase revolver ammunition, apparently unsuccessfully, at various local stores.[15]

Against this volatile background, a relatively minor incident inflamed the garrison. On the evening of October 18, a peace officer named William Stoner attempted to arrest a soldier for carrying a knife into town. A number of the enlisted man's comrades threateningly surrounded the policeman. At that tense moment, a noncommissioned officer appeared, took the knife from the soldier, and promised to confine him to the post and present the prisoner to city court the next morning. Viewing no alternative, Stoner agreed. About 11:00 or 11:30 on the same night, an undetermined number of soldiers armed with rifles attacked Stoner as he approached them. Perhaps confusing Stoner, of Mexican descent despite his name, with the hated Cuellar, they viciously assaulted the officer with rifle butts and then fired their weapons in the streets.[16]

Lieutenant Campbell, a young officer recently commissioned for bravery at San Juan Hill, was relaxing at the Laredo Casino and contemplating his approaching marriage when the city marshal informed him of the attack. Hurrying to the reported site, he found it deserted but heard distant rifle fire. Unable to locate the source, the lieutenant returned to the fort, placed a cordon around it to prevent either entrance or exit, and mustered his troops. Noting everyone present, Campbell discovered the ordnance-room door broken, though no weapons were missing. He surmised that the culpable had returned to McIntosh before him and replaced their rifles, although no member of the company, under questioning, admitted knowledge of the matter.[17]

Whether the soldiers knew anything of the assault remained a moot point, but the wire services informed virtually every other interested party by the next morning. The Galveston *Daily News*, the state's leading newspaper, carried several stories under the eye-catching headline, "Barbarous Negro Soldiers." The first article, datelined Laredo, presented a less florid account than the riveting introduction suggested. Even so, the writer declined to spare readers the gory particulars, as when the soldiers "stamped . . . [Stoner] with their heels, fired several shots into the ground near his body, took his pistol, and stripped him of his police badge." The indiscriminate firing, upsetting but hardly unfamiliar to long-embattled Laredoans, "creat[ed] for the time a great terror among the women and children." A shot supposedly wounded an eighteen-year-old bystander, an assertion initially repeated by Campbell but uncorroborated in later reports. The estimate of "at least forty" assailants doubtless emanated from the victim Stoner, who may have overestimated in his fatigued condition.[18]

An accompanying Associated Press account tended more toward the sensational. The undetermined number of shots totaled "at least one hundred," one of which killed a C. Nunzio in his tracks. The reporter disparaged the post commander as "a very young man for the position he holds" and cited the numerous previous arrests of the black soldiers. Contrarily, the news release acknowledged the bravery of Campbell and his men in Cuba, noting that every member of the company wore a souvenir ring awarded at their return to Montauk Point, New York.[19]

The reports probably depicted accurately the surly mood of the populace, considering the growing public outcry against the troops. "There was a bitter and ugly feeling in the city this morning," stated one, "when the outrage became fully known." "The citizens are much incensed," observed another, "but all is calm tonight." An almost simultaneous bulletin from Rio Grande City swelled Laredo's consternation as it told of black soldiers from Fort Ringgold creating a gambling den disturbance that claimed one life and injured seven.[20]

A cooperative effort struck between the lieutenant and local authorities calmed the citizenry. Campbell had hoped to muster diplomatic skills to match his military talents. A corporal in the 71st New York Volunteers, his heroism in the Cuban campaign had earned him a second lieutenancy in the regular army and command of Fort McIntosh at the lowest possible rank. Aware of the public indignation at Laredo, Campbell assured city officials that he would render all possible aid toward identifying the guilty and turning them over to civil authorities for prosecution. Sheriff L. R. Ortiz, for his part, strengthened security at the jail to discourage a possible mob action against a black soldier charged with assault on a black woman. The district judge summoned a grand jury to investigate, with Campbell as one of the first witnesses. After hearing his testimony, the grand jury agreed to postpone its deliberations until the arrival of the inspector general.[21]

Campbell maintained a hectic pace, in the days following the assault, in multiple roles of post commander, the only commissioned officer at McIntosh, and the liaison between the army and the community. His frenzied schedule competed with earlier arrangements to marry Ruth Tompkins of New York City and to take an exam for promotion. He fired off three telegrams to his superiors on the first day, asking for a military investigation and presenting fragmentary information. The acting adjutant general, at San Antonio, cautioned Campbell: "Avoid controversy with civil authorities, assure them that guilty parties will be punished."[22]

On the second day the garrison commander submitted a fuller report of two typed pages. Adding little to the known story, Campbell explained the misconduct unacknowledged in the news accounts. "There has been some friction between the police and the soldiers for sometime past . . . but I have worked along with the civil authorities and tried to keep matters as easy as possible." The officer assured the adjutant general that he had "done all in my power to find the guilty parties."[23]

The city and the post then awaited the inspector general, whose impending arrival contributed to the outward calm of Laredoans. Lt. Col. Chambers McKibbin, commanding the Department of Texas, at San Antonio, dispatched Maj. W. H. H. Crowell to the South Texas community with instructions to conduct a thorough investigation and submit a special report. In the continuing spirit of military-civilian cooperation, McKibbin urged Crowell to "Consult freely with civil authorities and obtain names of witnesses." He authorized the inspector to send the "ringleaders under guard to Fort Sam Houston for confinement if circumstances warrant."[24]

Crowell met with the grand jury on the day after his arrival. The foreman recounted the known information and stated that the victim, Stoner, could positively identify some of the assailants if given the opportunity. Accordingly, the major ordered the troops paraded at McIntosh in the presence of Stoner, Sheriff Ortiz, grand jury foreman Albert Urbhan, policeman Salomé Mendez, Campbell, and himself. Following the review, Stoner pointed out three privates, Joshua Nichols, Benjamin L. Hover, and Robert Earl; and two corporals, Jason King and Edward Robertson. An hour later, however, Stoner recanted his identification of the corporals and asked their release. Under questioning by Crowell, the noncommissioned officers disclaimed any knowledge of the incident and swore that they had been at the post when it occurred. Campbell transferred the custody of the three privates to the sheriff on the assurance of the prisoners' safety.[25]

The orderly and courteous procedure belied the resentment of the community toward the black garrison. On the very day of Major Crowell's inspection, Laredo Mayor A. E. Vidaurri penned a two-page letter to Governor Sayers complaining of the incident and requesting intercession by the War Department. In a tone substantially different from his predecessor during the smallpox crisis, Vidaurri scored the soldiers' "riotous and belligerent conduct" as "a menace to the peace and quiet of our city and [a danger to] the lives of our citizens." While the official's depiction of the assault coincided with accepted fact, he omitted references to the garrison's complaints of exploitation and police abuse. In the eyes of the mayor, as with countless other South Texans, the violence sprang from single-minded malice "with the avowed purpose of attacking the police . . . and did attack and beat up the first policeman they met." Vidaurri warned "of something serious" if the situation remained unchanged, "because it is not to be believed that American citizens will have the patience to submit longer to [such] conduct." The arguments bolstered the mayor's plea for Sayers "to use your influence with the War Department for the removal of this company from this post."[26]

Vidaurri found a sympathetic ear with Sayers. In a message to Secretary of War Elihu Root, the governor asserted, "the soldiers . . . have given, without cause, the people of Laredo a great deal of trouble and annoyance." In a condemnation of Campbell previously unaired, Sayers charged, "I am reliably informed that they are under no discipline whatever, and that the officer who is in immediate command, even if he should desire to do so, does not and cannot control them." Although enclosing Vidaurri's letter, Sayers stopped short of seconding his demand for removing the troops: "I have to request that you will direct the General commanding at San Antonio to immediately inquire into the matter and to take such steps as will relieve the citizens of Laredo of the trouble which they are experiencing from the members of this company."[27]

Governor Sayers continued to involve himself in the matter. Ten days later, on the occasion of a scheduled trial of two of the enlisted men, he wired Colonel McKibbin: "Please maintain a watchful oversight over the troops stationed at Laredo, Texas. [I] am apprehensive that possibly some trouble may occur." Lt. Col. Cyrus S. Roberts, acting adjutant general, at the order of McKibbin, passed the governor's concern on to the commander at McIntosh. "Keep all men in post not required as witnesses and take all possible precautions to prevent any disturbances," Roberts instructed Campbell, telling him to report conditions at the fort.[28]

Sayers declined to state why he expected trouble. In fact, none had arisen since the original disturbance. The calm enabled Lieutenant Campbell to proceed with his examination for promotion, though McKibbin sent two officers to McIntosh during his absence. The acting post commander, accordingly, responded to Colonel Roberts, "Conditions quiet and no reason apparent why anything should be anticipated on part of soldiers." As it turned out, Sayers's concerns went for naught. The district judge at Laredo granted the defendants a change of venue to San Diego, Texas, to ensure an unprejudiced trial.[29]

Meanwhile, Mayor Vidaurri's request for removal of the black troops continued through government channels. Although Sayers had not specified a course of action to the War Department, Secretary Root interpreted his complaint as asking "remov[al] or proper discipline" and referred the matter to McKibbin. Root left the decision to the colonel, stipulating only "prompt action" and "reporting the result to this office."[30]

In a decision that surprised and perplexed Laredoans, McKibbin ordered a temporary evacuation of McIntosh rather than the desired transfer of Company D. He reached the conclusion on the basis of Major Crowell's report and Laredo's expressed dissatisfaction with the garrison. Crowell harbored no doubts about the attack, satisfied with sworn testimony and the discovery of government-issue shells and cartridges in the street. He was disturbed, however, about the community's treatment of the soldiers prior to the assault. "While there can be no justification of the conduct of the soldiers who were engaged in the unlawful acts," Crowell reported, "the testimony of . . . reputable citizens [confirmed] . . . that the causes which led to the trouble were the frequent and unjust discriminations against the soldiers in arresting and subjecting them to confinement, and fining them without cause."[31]

The inspector cited special policeman Cuellar as a particular source of agitation. Crowell described the plight of the soldier arrested only a few days before the assault on Stoner: "brutally beaten, his scalp laid open to the skull, confined in a dirty jail and his wounds left undressed for twenty-four hours for no offense other than . . . being in company with a Mexican woman, who . . . sought the soldier's society."[32]

Due to the antagonistic community attitude, Crowell recommended that McKibbin undertake drastic changes at McIntosh. He defended

Campbell from criticism, citing the lieutenant's identification of the guilty and prevention of further trouble. Nevertheless, the major judged the post commander "too young and inexperienced for the responsibility devolved upon him," reluctantly agreeing with Campbell's detractors. Consequently, he suggested that an older officer, if available, replace him; that another unit relieve Company D; or that the government withdraw the garrison and leave the public property with an ordnance officer until a captain could accept the command.[33]

Colonel McKibbin's report to the War Department relied heavily on Crowell's findings, including the observation on the racial climate at Laredo. After summarizing fifteen messages that had passed between Texas and Washington, D.C., McKibbin concluded that irate soldiers had attacked Stoner mistakenly, confusing him with Cuellar. "The trouble at Laredo," attested the Department of Texas commander, "is due, primarily, to race prejudice between the Mexican residents and the soldiers, and the association of these soldiers with Mexican women." Independent of Crowell's investigation, McKibbin attributed the rashness of the soldiers partly to their youth and inexperience, lacking "the habits of discipline which come with long service . . . and act as a restraint in periods of excitement."[34]

McKibbin took aim at Sayers's disparagement of Campbell and the garrison, though he agreed with Crowell's assessment of the lieutenant. He judged the governor's remark on Campbell's lack of discipline "obviously unfair and unwarranted," in light of the quietude at the fort since the incident. "Unanticipated disorders cannot always be guarded against," the colonel reminded, "as riots often take place in better regulated communities."[35]

The colonel opted for Major Crowell's last-noted option, the evacuation of McIntosh. As his reasons, he enumerated "the easy communication" by rail from San Antonio to Laredo in the event of an emergency, the dissension between the soldiers and a large portion of the community, the improbability that any black troops would be acceptable to that element, and the increased expense of supplying the garrison. McKibbin therefore requested the secretary of war to move the garrison to Fort Sam Houston and place an ordnance sergeant in care of McIntosh pending further instructions. Anticipating the acceptance of his recommendation, McKibbin directed the suspension of expenditures at McIntosh for repairs and all other items except those already received or contracted.[36]

The publication of McKibbin's withdrawal order and approval by the War Department caused confusion and consternation at Laredo and the surrounding area. The ambiguity of the wording created the impression to those most interested in retaining McIntosh that the army intended permanent abandonment. The outcry unleashed the usually subdued anti-Mexican bias of many of the Anglos. U.S. Sen. Charles A. Culberson expressed this sentiment to Secretary Root: "Considering the character of the Mexican population at and near Laredo, with the tendency to outbreaks of lawlessness . . . this post . . . should not be abandoned."[37]

Washington's assurances to Culberson that "it is not the intention of the War Department to abandon the post," merely to withdraw the present garrison, failed to placate the alarmed. The departure of Company D for San Antonio with a 9th Cavalry lieutenant in command of the eighty-two enlisted men left only a small detachment under Campbell to deactivate McIntosh. This action, seeming to validate the worst fears of white Laredoans, moved a local attorney to send a candid communication to Maj. Gen. Nelson A. Miles, commander of the army:

> The Americans here at Laredo protest against the removal of troops from Fort McIntosh at this place as it is reported is contemplated by the authorities. These Mexicans are an inflammable people and are liable to catch fire at any time and do no telling what . . . [T]he state officials are all Mexicans themselves; we need U.S. officials—soldiers . . . I trust that you will see that the negro troop that has been taken away are replaced by white soldiers. . . . The cause of these negro-Mexican disturbances were that the negroes were given *too many liberties.*[38]

The press shared the Anglo uncertainty as to which ethnic group constituted the greater threat. A newsman at Laredo denounced actions of black soldiers from McIntosh and Ringgold as outrages: "These . . . posts have been continually garrisoned by United States troops since 1848, and . . . in no instance have the soldiers ever come armed into town and terrorized the people by firing guns until [now]." He reported "bitter feelings here" over the army supposedly taking the side of the assailants and punishing Laredo by "dismantling Fort McIntosh and shipping off everything that was movable and abandoning the post." Like the protesting lawyer, the journalist desired a white garrison, an unlikelihood in light of the personnel shortage created by the Philippine insurrection.[39]

Ironically, while combating rumors of the abandonment of Fort McIntosh, the army confused even Colonel McKibbin, the author of the withdrawal order. On November 25, McKibbin telegraphed the adjutant general, at Washington: "Am I to continue packing and shipping stores from McIntosh, Telegram from Surgeon General not to ship medical until definitely decided. Post will be abandoned, valuable stores cannot be left there in safety in care of Ordnance Sergeant."[40]

McKibbin's own garbled message resulted from an equally tortured communication that passed between the surgeon general and the chief surgeon, leading the departmental commander to suspect a permanent closure of the Laredo installation. Adj. Gen. H. C. Corbin felt perplexed at the developing comedy of errors. He assured McKibbin of no policy change from the colonel's own recommendation of temporary evacuation. Corbin informed McKibbin that an officer and twenty men, not associated with the 25th Infantry, would be sent to McIntosh.[41]

To allay any residual misunderstanding, John A. Johnston, assistant adjutant general, elaborated the War Department's position to McKibbin several days later. He confided that "international considerations" would indefinitely necessitate a garrison at Laredo, but that "bad feeling between the soldiers and citizens" had demanded the removal of Company D. The army had always intended to reoccupy the fort when additional troops became available. The War Department now enjoyed the opportunity to transfer four 10th Cavalry troops from Santiago de Cuba to the Department of Texas, while rotating three 9th Cavalry units to the Department of Colorado. This move freed one 10th Cavalry troop for duty at Laredo.[42]

Accordingly, Troop E of the 10th Cavalry returned to Fort McIntosh in mid-January, 1900, a year after taking charge of the post. Laredoans and soldiers alike must have experienced an intense feeling of history repeating itself, but in actuality the civilian-military relationship at the South Texas city had deteriorated in the past twelve months. Viewed apprehensively at their arrival in 1899, Troop E, while not party to the ensuing controversy, drew more critical public scrutiny in 1900. Grimly aware of the rancor, Colonel McKibbin summed up the army's embattled policy:

> The question of race prejudice is doubtless a factor, but the wishes of such a class of population can hardly be consulted in assigning troops to station. The expenditures of the Government for supplies, etc., as well as the money spent by troops is the real desideratum. . . . It is needless to add that the strategic importance of Fort McIntosh is better understood in the War Department than at Laredo.[43]

Colonel McKibbin's dour assessment of Laredo applied equally to his opinion of Rio Grande City, where the 9th Cavalry at Fort Ringgold in 1899 experienced an even stormier relationship with the Hispanic population. Located approximately one hundred miles down river from Laredo, diminutive Rio Grande City shared much of the history and sociopolitical environment of the larger city. Also carved from the Escandon grant, Rio Grande City sprang from Rancho Davis, named for American adventurer Henry Clay Davis, in 1847. It developed into an important port for river freighters after the Mexican War and, under its new name, became the seat of Starr County.[44]

The town failed to match Laredo as a major border crossing, however, and its population barely passed two thousand by the end of the century. Lacking the rail connections and commercial markets of Laredo, the river front community largely served agricultural and livestock interests. River traffic from as far away as Brownsville, a hundred miles to the south, promised potential business growth, and a small furniture industry persisted despite timber scarcity. The isolation and limited development persuaded a resident to acknowledge, "More than nine-tenths of the population . . . are Mexican, speaking mainly Spanish and addicted to the old ways of their people."[45]

With its counterpart at Laredo, Fort Ringgold had guarded South Texas since the end of the Mexican War. Antedating McIntosh by several months, Ringgold initially bore the designations of Camp Ringgold and Ringgold Barracks. In 1850 the War Department granted the installation permanent status, but did not attach the title *fort* until 1878. Its history, marked by Indian and outlaw campaigns and late-century improvements, paralleled that of McIntosh and other border redoubts. When frame and brick structures replaced the original adobe dwellings in the mid-1880s, Ringgold emerged as one of the most attractive posts in the state. Still, the isolation and absence of area social life continued to create tedium for the enlisted men, particularly when blacks garrisoned the fort.[46]

Components of the 9th and 10th Cavalry returned to the border point following the Spanish-American War. Troops B and M of the 10th served briefly in early 1899 without incident before moving on to Cuban garrison duty. In early May, Troop D of the 9th unpacked its gear at Ringgold, anticipating routine duty.[47]

In an ironic manner the brief and turbulent interlude at Ringgold corresponded to the regiment's service in the Lone Star State after the Civil War. The first of the four black regiments to enter Texas, the 9th also departed earliest. From 1867 until 1875 its troops fought to restore law and order from Brownsville to Fort Stockton. Many times the civilian population under their protection posed a threat to the soldiers' safety. For example, in 1870 a settler near Fort McKavett murdered a black trooper and then killed two others sent to apprehend him. When the killer finally faced the court, the jury freed him.[48]

Alleged collusion between civil officials and unsavory elements at Rio Grande City early made that community particularly difficult for the 9th Cavalry. In 1873 Maj. John Hatch established his headquarters and five troops there. Recognizing the appearance of professional gamblers at the post on paydays, he ordered one off the reservation. To his chagrin, a Starr County grand jury indicted Hatch, forcing the officer to enlist a defense attorney. On another occasion, an armed gang attacked a cavalry patrol, killing two soldiers while sustaining casualties of its own. The grand jury indicted nine Hispanics, some still bearing telltale bullet marks, but the court tried only one, finding him innocent. In the process local law officers arrested three soldiers for murder and, in a bizarre turn of events, held over Major Hatch and a junior officer for burglary. Such brazenness moved Secretary of War William W. Belknap to threaten Gov. Richard Coke with closure of Ringgold, despite the unsettling border conditions. Although the government stopped short of deactivating the post, it hastened the rotation of the regiment to New Mexico and grew increasingly critical of South Texas garrison towns.[49]

The intervening twenty-four years failed to mellow the residents of Rio Grande City toward black servicemen. Shortly after the new troop had readied the fort, the commanding officer reported the presence of gamblers and other unscrupulous types near the post. The men of Troop D, 9th Cavalry, soon complained of racial slurs, refusal of service at some businesses, and harassment by the largely Hispanic constabulary. For four months minor incidents accumulated and tensions built between town and fort. On October 17 the powder keg ignited at a gambling house, where a row between soldiers and locals resulted in the shooting of two troopers and the knifing of three.[50]

People beyond the riverfront town received bits of information in the major dailies for several days before a fuller version emerged. Initially, the Galveston *Daily News* carried within its coverage of the Laredo assault a cryptic line on a "disturbance . . . at Fort Ringgold" that "intensified the feeling" against the black soldiers at McIntosh. Below that story, bearing an earlier dateline, appeared the brief but inflated account: "Reports from Rio Grande City state that a party of negro soldiers . . . started a disturbance in a gambling house . . . with the result that one was fatally shot and seven others more or less wounded by the gamblers and citizens."[51]

"First details" reached the reading public five days after the incident. Datelined San Antonio, an article recounted "A Mexican deputy sheriff" shooting three soldiers and arresting three others. This account omitted the undocumented fatality and scaled down the number of arrests, though the total of gun shot victims remained higher than the ensuing investigations revealed. The story followed the tone of the previous two, placing blame squarely on the soldiers. According to the writer, "a body of negro soldiers armed with pistols" entered the casino and gathered at various tables. After losing most of their money, one of the men fired his weapon at the ceiling and others raided the games to seize the betting stakes. The deputy sheriff, evidently at hand, shot a soldier who aimed a pistol at him. Two other troopers lunged at the peace officer, receiving "serious wounds." Irate civilians cut several soldiers with knives during the melee. The following day the justice of the peace fined the three blacks sixty-five dollars each, a considerable sum at that time. The *Dallas Morning News, San Antonio Express,* and *Houston Post* carried the story on the same date under similar dramatic headlines.[52]

The soldiers presented a quite different version of the events. One of the casualties, Pvt. William Turner, had served five and a half years in the army, almost half that time in Troop D. Shortly after arriving at Ringgold in May, he was arrested for carrying a pistol into town and fined $34. Allowed to pay the fine in installments, Turner stated that he went into Rio Grande City on October 17 to make a payment to the sheriff. He denied visiting the gambling hall, insisting that a policeman in the company of other Mexicans stopped him on the street and spoke something unintelligible to him. When Turner failed to respond, the officer struck him on the head with a club and shot him in the arm as the soldier attempted to flee. Managing to escape, Turner ran to the post hospital for treatment.[53]

The other gunshot victim, Pvt. Thomas Nicholson, admitted observing the brawl but denied participation in the fracas. An enlistee with almost five years service time in Troop D, Nicholson reported walking by the gambling den while the fight was in progress. A number of people suddenly rushed into the street, causing the private to run for safety toward the fort. A group of men surrounded him, as one of the members shot Nicholson in the shoulder. Like Turner, he succeeded in eluding them and raced for Ringgold. "I hadn't been in the building or gambling or doing anything out of the way," Nicholson insisted. "I was quietly standing outside."[54]

The suspected combatants found no sanctuary at Fort Ringgold when confronted by the young commanding officer. Erubian Holland Rubottom, born twenty-six years earlier in Indiana, had graduated from the University of California in 1899, immediately receiving a commission as a second lieutenant. Rubottom had taken command of the post only five days before the incident, though he had joined the garrison the previous month. En route to a distinguished military career that would elevate him to the rank of lieutenant colonel before retiring in 1920, the junior officer acted quickly to enforce discipline. After learning of the disturbance, he conducted a bed check about 2 A.M. "and found a number of men absent including some non-commissioned officers." Rubottom placed these men under arrest later that morning and punished them by summary court. The lieutenant then issued a general order forbidding anyone from leaving the fort, an edict that remained in effect for nearly two weeks. The wounded at least received succor; Nicholson's wound, which penetrated his lungs, required prolonged treatment.[55]

The embargo imposed by the post commander appeared effective. Rubottom believed his men in strict compliance but worried about the consequences of eventually lifting the ban. "Several prominent citizens to my knowledge . . . made threats that they would shoot any nigger they saw in town on any day," he later reported to a superior. The approach of payday, November 20, brought him increased concern. Accordingly, before leaving the post on November 17 to collect the funds, Rubottom augmented the sentries and instructed them to prohibit the entry of any person to the quarantined reservation, except those on official business. The guards carried out the order to the letter, turning back even the sheriff and the county attorney during the lieutenant's absence.[56]

Soldiers and civilians awaited November 20 with some anxiety. Rumors circulated in both sectors that the other faction intended to attack on that day. Enlisted men reported sightings of suspicious persons throughout the day. Rubottom initially paid little attention to the stories but strengthened the guard anyway. Immobilized by a recent injury during mount exercises, he grew more alarmed as "reports came in from all sides of Mexicans patrolling near the garrison and hiding in the bushes . . . waiting for the night." In the most disturbing incident, the post mail carrier claimed that someone shot at him an hour or so before noon between the reservation and the town. Stating that the bullet passed within six inches of him, the carrier "turned quick and saw a Mexican darting into the bushes." Although shaken, he continued his assignment and joined the guard near the hospital and post exchange that evening.[57]

The level of apprehension moved some town women to seek safety at Ringgold during the day. Several black women swore that they had heard of a plot to attack the fort that night. A white woman testified that she entered the post twice after seeing armed civilians. The wife of a 5th Cavalry sergeant imprisoned in Florida relayed her fears to the post engineer, who informed Rubottom.[58]

The rumors and sightings set the post commander on edge by the evening. He cautioned the men to remain "quiet and sober," to maintain readiness in case of attack, and "not to fire a shot unless . . . attacked and . . . necessary to protect the garrison." Somewhat before 7 P.M., the guard at Post #3, near the stables about six hundred yards directly in front of town, insisted that two shots were fired at him from nearby bushes. He returned a shot toward "three Mexicans" crouching in the brush, missing them, and summoned the corporal of the guard.[59]

Pvt. Albert Brodie's round set off an exchange of fire that resembled battlefield conditions before the end of the night. A number of his garrison mates corroborated hearing gunfire outside the reservation and spotting civilians near the post, though not actually viewing the attack. Pvt. George Harcoumbe, the sentry at Post #4, near the hospital and post exchange, testified that fleeing Hispanics fired in his direction, a bullet striking a fence post near him. Percy N. Barnesby, the acting surgeon general and only officer other than Rubottom assigned to Ringgold, counted several bursts of gunfire near the hospital within the next half hour. The medical officer, like other members of the garrison, claimed to distinguish the sounds of the shots from those of military weapons. Subsequently, while checking unfounded rumors of wounded soldiers, Barnesby saw shadowy figures firing from the chaparral at distances of forty to seventy-five yards from the reservation.[60]

Acting on sentry alarms, Rubottom adopted more extreme measures. He ordered his first sergeant to place the entire troop on guard, dividing the men into four sections, each under a sergeant, to cover the flanks. Rubottom warned the first sergeant to keep the men in position to prevent an attack from an unguarded quarter, not to allow anyone to fire in retaliation, and "to remain inside the garrison and act only in the defensive." The lieutenant rationed each soldier one

hundred rounds of carbine ammunition, limited pistols to the ordnance room, and readied a Gatling gun. Hearing an exchange of
gunfire behind the hospital, on the town side, Rubottom hastened to
the scene as fast as his condition allowed. "Bullets were flying thick
and fast all around me," he observed, ". . . striking on the tin roof and
on the parade ground." Arriving behind the medical officer and the
first sergeant, he told the latter that the men's rapid firing wasted
ammunition.[61]

Rubottom assessed the chaotic situation and decided on further
action. He attempted to wire the department headquarters at San
Antonio, only to learn that the lines were down at Laredo. The officer
provided shelter for the various women on the post amid sustained
firing. Considering the post under siege, Rubottom sent for additional
ammunition and directed fire ineffectively toward the distant flashes.
"As a last resort," the beleaguered post commander ordered up the
Gatling gun and placed it at the front gate, trained toward the arroyo
slightly to the left of town. This was the location of heaviest armed
activity. The ordnance sergeant issued, by his own testimony, "not
more than 40 rounds" of .45 caliber ammunition.[62]

The maneuver proved deftly effective. Warning his men to hold
their fire to a minimum, Rubottom later recalled, "[They] fired only a
few rounds which was sufficient to silence fire from the outside." The
lieutenant then inspected the lines in the company of two sergeants,
satisfying himself that all soldiers had remained inside the reservation
at their posts. When the danger of attack appeared lessened, Rubottom allowed half the men to draw blankets and turn in for the night,
while the remainder continued on alert. "There was no more trouble
during the night," the officer reported.[63]

Trouble of a different nature awaited the young commander and
his troop at first dawn. Unlike the gambling brawl, which attracted
belated and minimal news coverage, the gun battle captured the front
pages, even though the army had commandeered the telegraph lines
and restricted the flow of information. Below headlines proclaiming
"War on Negro Troops," "The Negroes Terrorized the Place," and
"They Smiled on Senioritas," the *Galveston Daily News* described a
"report of a pitched battle last night . . . between a company of the
Ninth United States Cavalry (colored) . . . and several hundred citizens who attacked the post shortly after dark." The lead paragraph,
essentially the army's interpretation of events, contrasted both with
the headlines and the tone of the accompanying articles.[64]

A story beneath a San Antonio dateline attributed the clash to widening resentment between black troops and Hispanics along the border. The reporter explained the animosity in the narrowest terms, sexual rivalry. Disregarding deeper implications of stationing black soldiers amid economically inhibited populations, the writer stated:

> When at the close of the Spanish war, the Department sent the colored regiments . . . to garrison Texas posts, a general protest went up. The Mexican population at the frontier posts at once made a fight upon the negro soldiers because of the social attentions which the colored men in uniform paid the Mexican girls, and which the latter did not repel. The tension . . . resulted in a fight [with] the police in Laredo some weeks ago . . . [causing the abandonment of Fort McIntosh]. The Mexican population considered this a victory for them, and the news spread up and down the Rio Grande.[65]

From the viewpoint of the author, Starr County Hispanics, which included most of the constabulary, hoped to force the War Department, through indignities to the servicemen, to remove the black garrison, as supposedly had occurred at Laredo. Reportedly, members of Troop D had written friends at San Antonio, detailing name-calling and even occasional firing into the reservation. Indeed, a line from an earlier article on Fort McIntosh referred to "Fort Ringgold, where the negro soldiers bitterly complain of continued insults." The correspondent believed the rounds fired by the soldiers had been directed toward the hated saloons and gambling houses, locations of previous conflict.[66]

The one-dimensional assessment, which at least attempted an explanation beyond mere black malevolence, found little support in Rio Grande City. Local officials and residents denied any provocation on their part, dismissing as worthless prostitutes the women who associated with the soldiers. They circulated exaggerated reports that the troop had fired fifteen hundred rounds from every vantage point on or off the reservation, killing one person and wounding others. On the morning following the shooting, townsmen reportedly moved women and children into the countryside while they collected weapons and ammunition for defense.[67]

Meanwhile, the injured and weary post commander worked to alleviate the situation. After several unsuccessful attempts to reach San Antonio by telegraph, Rubottom managed to contact the commander at Fort Brown for reinforcements. With communication to department headquarters eventually reopened, he reported conditions hourly and, with departmental approval, assumed control of the wires. The lieutenant "held back several false communications from certain citizens . . . [knowing] that if any further trouble occurred it would be brought on by civilians and not soldiers." He conferred with local officials, who promised cooperation, after warning the county judge "that a second attack would meet with extreme measures." By the end of the first day the situation appeared under control, with troops en route to Ringgold from Brownsville and San Antonio.[68]

An exchange of telegrams among civil and military officials signaled peace while portending a growing separation of the two sectors. On November 21 Rubottom sketched the circumstances to the adjutant general of his department, recalling rumors of people "gathering in the country," a condition that would require additional troops. Colonel McKibbin assured him, "[I] am taking every possible precaution to prevent further trouble." Meanwhile, Governor Sayers, learning of the incident from McKibbin, asked Sheriff W. W. Shely, boss of the Red Club, or Democratic party, in Rio Grande City, to wire full particulars "and do everything within your power to maintain order and to preserve the peace."[69]

The Texas governor's reaction to the events of the previous night hardened as he received additional advisories from the affected area. After the initial notification, Sayers dispatched his adjutant to the site, although he felt "inclined to believe the affair is greatly exaggerated." A telegram from Starr County Judge T. W. Kennedy, however, deepened his concern. The future Republican county commissioner claimed the soldiers had fired fifteen hundred rounds into the town, resulting in "one citizen . . . wounded in his home" and houses "all over town" suffering defacement. Expressing fear of public retaliation, the judge accused Rubottom of "direct[ing] this cowardly act." Kennedy urged Sayers to beseech Washington and Departmental Headquarters for a "searching investigation and removal of troops at once."[70]

Governor Sayers seized on the demand for an investigation and troop removal. Repeating Kennedy's report, he asked the secretary of war to conduct an "immediate impartial and searching investigation" and to "issue an order for immediate removal of troops." Turning to McKibbin, Sayers requested "the most reliable officer you have" to investigate and to "have troops removed at once." The governor next apprised Judge Kennedy of his actions and asked the county official to "urge citizens to be quiet and to rely upon me to see that justice is done." He further advised Kennedy of the imminent departure of his adjutant for Rio Grande City.[71]

A communique from Chief Deputy Sheriff Gregorio Duffy, subsequently gunned down in a local political struggle, sounded the same note of alarm against the garrison. "The negro soldiers [opened] fire on the town without provocation," asserted the lawman. "Citizens are quiet, but authorities will be powerless to maintain order if the soldiers attack the town again," he warned. The message spurred Sayers to wire McKibbin a third time that day, repeating Duffy's statement and pressing the commander, "I shall depend upon your prompt and effective action in the premises. [I] am doing what I can to quiet the people."[72]

In response, two inspectors representing divergent constituencies approached Rio Grande City. Lt. Col. Cyrus Roberts, acting adjutant general and "the most reliable officer" requested by Sayers, left San Antonio by train on the afternoon of October 21 and completed the journey in a mule-driven escort wagon on the night of the twenty-second. Despite the arduous journey, Roberts, finding the area quiet, "immediately began an investigation of the disorders reported."[73]

His counterpart, Thomas Scurry, recently named Texas adjutant general, followed a similarly exhausting route. The forty-year-old Waller County native left Austin on the evening of the twenty-first, somewhat later than Roberts, and proceeded by rail and stage coach. He reached Rio Grande City "about noon on November 24." Closely observing their movements, a newsman surmised that the investigators would likely file quite different reports to their respective superiors.[74]

Perhaps surprisingly, in light of the excitement, Roberts and Scurry quickly struck a positive relationship of cooperation and mutual respect. Scurry, a major in the 1st Texas Volunteer Infantry during the recent war, approved of the quietness at both the town and fort, with the soldiers confined to the reservation. Upon arriving, Scurry sent word to Roberts, who had spent the night at the post, and arranged a meeting at the courthouse after dinner. The two investigators met with Capt. M. W. Day from Fort Brown, Lt. G. B. Pritchard, Jr., from Fort McIntosh, Judge Kennedy, Sheriff Shely, and County Attorney Knox Jones.[75]

The inspectors proceeded methodically. Roberts apprised Scurry of the progress of his own inquiries and invited him to study the testimony and conduct a mutual investigation. Scurry agreed, thereby eliminating the cumbersome prospect of separate inquiries and the discomfort of Roberts having to question hostile residents alone. For his part, Scurry handed the army officer a copy of evidence obtained in Robert's absence. "He worked with an earnest desire to get at the truth," the Texan said of his counterpart, "and rendered me valuable assistance."[76]

Meanwhile, news accounts combined new leads with speculation and gossip for a receptive readership. A press item two days after the shooting raised the estimate of rounds fired to two thousand. A civilian, Tomás Hinojosa, suffered a leg wound, according to the report, and various structures on the post showed signs of bullet damage. Striking a middle course, the writer thought the incident "a mutual misunderstanding, intensified by irresponsible tale-bearers" on both sides. "The immediate cause" he attributed to the firing of a pistol "by some lawless person . . . on the town space between the post and the town." The identify or motive of the person remained unknown.[77]

Speculation swirled around the future of the post and its commander, Lieutenant Rubottom. An item datelined November 23 stated the unwelcome expectation that Ringgold faced permanent abandonment. Although the War Department actually had reached no decision on the fort, the widespread belief of McIntosh's imminent closure fed the rumor. A correspondent at Laredo, lamenting the expected decision, expressed public anguish against Rubottom: "All feel here that the firing on citizens of Rio Grande City . . . is an act that . . . demand[s] that the officer who is responsible shall be held accountable."[78]

The critical assessment of the post commander and his probable punishment enjoyed wide support. A news item from San Antonio cited "military men" as predicting a court-martial for Rubottom. "They contend," according to the reporter, "that the young lieutenant will have to make out a very strong case for himself to come out of the affair with only a reprimand." Allegations of insobriety, repeated in testimony to the investigators, further damaged the junior officer's prospects.[79]

Disclosures of the testimony to the press kept the controversy alive. The media also focused on civilian witnesses. "It is admitted that the soldiers fired on the town with Krag-Jorgensens and a Gatling gun," summarized an observer. "The disputed point is who started the firing." According to the townspeople, the troop assaulted them "without provocation," and they returned "but eight to ten shots." Shells uncovered in the brush near the town challenged the soldiers' claim of not having crossed the reservation fence during the episode.[80]

Testimony of Rio Grande City's leading citizens proved particularly damaging to the garrison's contention of self-defense. Sheriff Shely acknowledged his absence from town on the night of the affray, but insisted that his fifteen years of familiarity with "every man, woman, and child" enabled him to refute categorically the possibility of a conspiracy to attack the post without his knowledge. Indeed, his indisputable influence in patronage and political decisions for the past five years lent credence to his claim. He denied the soldiers' charges of harassment by him or his deputies, offering court records to demonstrate that the men had not suffered disproportionate arrests or fines. Citing an example of the troop's duplicity and the commander's gullibility, he told of personally disproving alleged sightings of Mexicans in the arroyo near the fort. Shely asserted that "the first shots were fired by them with the object of having a plausible pretext for the outrage . . . the officers, being inexperienced in army life, and without knowledge of the negro character, were weak enough to believe them and to let them have their way that night."[81]

Chief Deputy Duffy, aspiring to the level of influence held by Shely, testified to rushing to the scene after hearing gunfire. Other deputies, already present, told him that soldiers were shooting from the reservation in their direction. Duffy observed several volleys from the post, strafing all parts of town. He saw no townspeople in threatening positions; on the contrary, women and children were fleeing and screaming. The chief deputy further repudiated the idea of a civilian conspiracy by arguing that residents had followed their usual routines that night, with shops remaining open and a typical number of people on the streets. He counted only five shots fired from the town, and those followed the initial bursts from Ringgold.[82]

Judge Kennedy traced the origins of the clash to the gambling den disturbance of the previous month and rebuked the post officers and the higher military command. He described the gambling row as a foiled robbery attempt by a soldier: "Since that time there have been rumors that the soldiers intended to get even with the authorities." While insisting that he had given little credence to the rumors, Kennedy admitted "some misgivings" about the youth and inexperience of Rubottom. The judge also believed the post commander "entirely under the influence of Dr. Barnesby . . . a very improper advisor." Kennedy considered "both addicted to the use of liquor." Describing himself as a defender of the Union during the Civil War, Kennedy condemned the rumored closing of Ringgold as punitive, leaving the town alone "to repel foreign invasion if any come. The removal of these troops will be no punishment [to the soldiers] for the violation of the peace and dignity of the people they have outraged."[83]

Deputy U.S. Marshal K. H. Merren essentially corroborated the testimony of Duffy and others on the scene who attributed the assault to the malice of blacks. Merren confirmed that "everything was quiet" early in the night, with no drunks or armed persons in sight. The sound of gunfire summoned him to the section where Duffy and other deputies had already gathered. Swearing that he had seen "no Mexicans between the town and fort," the federal officer insisted that "parties in the brush were firing toward town." Merren scoffed at the notion of a civilian plot to attack Ringgold inasmuch as "this town was absolutely unprepared for either attack or defense." Numerous people had begged him and other lawmen for the use of arms and ammunition to defend themselves while under fire. He discounted the assertion of bad feelings on the part of male Hispanics against the garrison on account of sexual rivalry: "I know that the negroes keep Mexican women or frequent houses of Mexican prostitutes. But in those cases the Mexicans generally classify such women as negro prostitutes and have nothing to do with them."[84]

Such testimony, emanating from more than twenty town witnesses, impressed Texas Adjutant General Scurry more than the statements of the dozen military witnesses. Even so, the state official submitted a temperate report. Although the post bore clear markings of an attack, Scurry considered the evidence "too conflicting for me to undertake to say by whom the shots from the outside were fired or, even what particular locality; nor can I say at what time the shooting in the direction of the post began . . . or the number of shots fired from the outside." He acknowledged giving "a wide range" to the townspeople in their arguments, as the Texan judged their contention more difficult to demonstrate.[85]

Scurry displayed greater certainty in denouncing Lieutenant Rubottom's actions. While assuming that inexperience underlay his behavior, he deemed the officer's orders ill-conceived and perilous: "When he became convinced that 'matters looked serious' it was his duty to notify the civil authorities of the probability of trouble." Granting Rubottom's suspicion of local officers, except for the absent Shely, various options still lay open to the post commander. He could have relied for factual information on his eleven Indian scouts, thoroughly familiar with the citizenry. If action were warranted, Rubottom could have deployed a squad or more of soldiers or scouts to clear the reservation of trespassers or arrest them. Scurry thought it incumbent on the lieutenant to have advised local officials of his movements, regardless of his distrust of them, and warn them of his intentions if attacked. In any case, Rubottom's responsibility included commanding the troop personally, not indirectly through the first sergeant.[86]

Scurry considered the alternatives followed by Rubottom indefensible. He issued ammunition to men "antagonistic" to the citizenry and requiring "very little, if any, provocation to make them begin firing." Evidence pointed to serious misconduct or misjudgment on the part of the garrison. The bullet mark that Private Harcoumbe had displayed as proof of an attack from the outside appeared caused by a ball fired within the reservation. Although a sergeant insisted that he had spotted insurgents at a distance of more than one hundred yards, other soldiers testified that "a man could not be distinguished fifty feet off." One enlisted man contradicted his own testimony. Believing Rubottom to have been "in position to prevent the trouble," Scurry judged him "primarily responsible" for the shooting and applauded his replacement by Lt. G. B. Pritchard.[87]

On the other hand, the adjutant noted several weaknesses in the civilians' case. The three boys claiming to have collected army rifle shells in the area between the reservation and the town could have gathered them at the target range previously. Duffy's assertion that every town resident except those in his party were hiding in their homes during the firing strained credulity. Scurry also doubted the witness's contention that the soldiers had shot to kill: "I am inclined to believe that . . . [they] intended to shoot over the town to scare the citizens and not to hurt them." With many questions remaining unanswered, Scurry urged a continuing investigation until "every individual who engaged in such a dastardly act . . . be prosecuted and punished to the full extent of the law." He concluded his report without comment, "November 20, pay day, was a very active day at the canteen in the post," the beer sales totaling fifty dollars.[88]

Colonel Roberts had investigated in tandem with Scurry and agreed with him on various points, but the army officer's report emphasized more strongly the community's early antagonism toward the black garrison. He shared the common view that the gambling ruckus had triggered the crisis, though he was "unsure of the facts concerning it." The fact that only the soldiers had sustained injuries strengthened the perception of police bias. He would not dismiss the rumors, largely carried by Mexican women, of a conspiracy to attack the fort. Intemperate language by residents and officials, including the U.S. commissioner, increased the soldiers' anxiety. "They were spoken of as niggers frequently in my presence during my inspection in town," Roberts observed, "and as a rule with profanity added." He discounted the numerous affidavits denying racial antagonism against the troop.[89]

The soldiers particularly resented Deputy Sheriff Duffy and Deputy

U.S. Marshal Merren, Roberts believed, for unfair arrests and severe treatment. Significantly, each insisted "that the firing was begun by the soldiers and continued by them and that practically no shots were fired from the town."[90]

The army inspector questioned the veracity of some town witnesses' testimony. After pointing out the site between the reservation fence and the town where they had discovered government-issue shells, one of the boys admitted picking up some on the post. From that admission, Roberts conjectured that "all were found there, or placed where they were found by parties interested in" misleading the investigators. The officer doubted the possibility of the men firing at the town from outside the reservation: "It is almost beyond belief that soldiers would remain not more than 150 yards in front of the fence while thirty men behind them were firing rapidly into the bushes where they were said to have been hiding." Roberts's incredulity extended also to the statement of the town baker, who claimed to have seen a black in a campaign hat running rapidly toward the post and firing.[91]

Roberts's assessment of Rubottom, though milder in its reproach, coincided with that of Scurry. The colonel approved of the junior officer's order restricting his men to the garrison prior to payday but criticized his defensive preparations without consulting civil authorities and personally supervising the guard. In the absence of casualties, Rubottom's authorization to return fire lacked "necessity" or even "legitimate excuse." Roberts took into account the excessive burden of responsibility that the numerous duties of the post placed on the young, inexperienced commander. Advising against "further proceedings in his case," the inspector proposed attaching Rubottom to an experienced senior officer. Roberts considered "unwarranted" the allegation of Judge Kennedy that the lieutenant and Dr. Barnesby employed "excessive use of intoxicants."[92]

To forestall future clashes, which he deemed inevitable, Colonel Roberts urged the closure of Fort Ringgold, a subject of speculation since the crisis. "I have little doubt the feeling against any colored troops would be the same," he said of the area Hispanics. "They consider themselves their superiors, whereas with white troops they accept their inferiority." Aside from Sheriff Shely, whom Roberts believed to be fair-minded but necessarily protective of his constituents, civil officials in Rio Grande City stoked the bias through their words and actions. The paucity of military replacements occasioned by the Cuban occupation and Philippine rebellion essentially precluded the garrisoning of white troops on the border.[93]

Roberts considered Ringgold expendable in any case. Conditions requiring its creation no longer existed, with the border more secure and rail transportation from San Antonio to Laredo and Eagle Pass assuring easier defense of South Texas. Contrarily, Ringgold remained "an expensive post to supply" because of its relative isolation. While Rio Grande City would suffer the loss of army payrolls and supply sales to the United States government, that consideration "would hardly justify the retention of troops." Civil authorities, including Texas Rangers, possessed the capacity to protect property interests and maintain order in the region.[94]

Like Scurry, Roberts enclosed a statement from the court records, indicating twelve cases involving fourteen soldiers from their arrival in May until the current date. Permitting various interpretations, the records showed four dismissals of charges and seven fines at the minimum level. Although the numbers appeared to substantiate the argument of civil officials that the punishments were not excessive, Roberts noted that court costs applied on all convictions, even with fines as little as one dollar.[95]

Colonel McKibbin, commanding the Department of Texas, forwarded Roberts's report to the adjutant general at Washington with strong support of the recommendations. "I cannot but feel impressed," he stated, "with the advisability of permanently abandoning the post of Fort Ringgold. It is, from a military standpoint, absolutely useless, and simply serves to keep up a disreputable frontier town. It has made little difference in past years whether the troops . . . were white or black, the state system of fees in criminal cases made then, as now, the United States soldier the easy victim." McKibbin blamed racial prejudice, "fostered by a class of county officials" to enhance "their political following among the Mexican population," for the crises both at Laredo and Rio Grande City. He further endorsed Roberts's defense of Rubottom against charges of intoxication and recommended no formal proceedings.[96]

McKibbin publicly aired his misgivings about Rio Grande City to reporters at Galveston. Reiterating his support for closing Ringgold, he denounced "the class of people" who "simply live off the soldiers." The colonel dismissed assertions of an anti-southern or anti-Texas bias in the War Department, commending it for prompt action on the matters.[97]

The outspoken officer and the impatient Texas governor soon locked verbal horns over the state judicial process. Amid conjecture that the Starr County grand jury planned to indict Rubottom and other military personnel, McKibbin wired Sayers:

[I] am informed that State Court intends to issue warrants for arrest of Lieutenant Rubottom and all the non-commissioned officers at Fort Ringgold for occurrences which took place on [the] reservation. This the military authorities cannot permit as it would destroy all control over troops at post. [I] fear that civil authorities are taking this action with deliberate intent of causing additional friction at Post.[98]

Although McKibbin later described his missive as only informal, the governor treated the curtly phrased note as a challenge to state authority. Sayers turned for a legal opinion to the attorney general's office, which buttressed Sayers's states-rights philosophy. Assistant Counsel R. H. Ward cited various precedents to conclude that a crime committed on a military reservation against the community fell under state jurisdiction. He quoted the 59th Article of War to justify state process:

When any officer or soldier is accused of a capital crime, or of any offense against the person or property of any citizen . . . which is punishable by the laws of the land, the commanding officer [and other officers] . . . are required, except in time of war, upon application duly made . . . to aid the officers of justice in apprehending and securing him, in order to bring him to trial.[99]

Armed with legal ammunition, Governor Sayers delivered an extensive and warm rebuttal to the commander of the Department of Texas. Depicting McKibbin's position as "untenable," Sayers accused him of proposing the commission of a felony. Of the garrison he rankled, "If the troops at Fort Ringgold cannot be controlled should a judicial investigation be had. . . the sooner those troops be discharged the better it will be for the service." Their actions the governor attributed "in no small measure . . . to the incompetency of the officer in command." While acknowledging no information of proposed prosecutions, he sardonically appraised the wartime exemption clause, not mentioned by McKibbin: "Surely, by no fiction of the imagination can the hostilities now existing between the United States and . . . the Philippine Islands be so construed as to embrace the territory in and around Fort Ringgold." Pledging "to do everything within my power to secure the arrest and trial of all persons" involved, the governor prepared to send the correspondence to the president, "that he may take such action in the premises as he may deem advisable."[100]

A chagrined Colonel McKibbin presented his version of the legal controversy to the adjutant general in Washington the following day. "The result of the arrest of the officer in command and of all the non-commissioned officers of the post," he submitted, "would not fail to create a feeling which would be extremely difficult to control at a post . . . in a community like that in which Fort Ringgold is situated." His department, attested McKibbin, had complied with every request of the civil authorities to date, yet Sayers chose "to inject into this matter the old question of state sovereignty, which is hardly an issue, except by forced consideration." The colonel wryly added, ". . . Governor Sayers' letter was read by me in the public press before the original was received."[101]

Fortunately, the jurisdictional issue remained only academic, as the grand jury in mid-December failed to return indictments against any member of the garrison. The report, which like the McKibbin-Sayers exchange received press scrutiny, cited "the reticence of witnesses and the suppression of material facts" as barriers to the establishment of "a conclusive case against any party or number of parties." The document placed "moral" responsibility on Rubottom and his non-commissioned officers for an assault "without the slightest provocation." Summarizing testimony of the most vehement witnesses against the soldiers, the jurors dismissed the allegations of a civilian attack as "entirely and absolutely without foundation and support." Lamenting their inability to bring the culprits to trial, the signers stated:

> If this is the discipline and control of the United States army . . . God help us and all others thus at the mercy of such irresponsibility. . . . It is a sad commentary . . . that its negro troops can assault a town . . . with no notice to remove the helpless, the sick, and the women and children; yet it was confessedly done, by the statements of the army officers, and no one disciplined or punished for it.[102]

As the harsh rhetoric waned, conditions along the Rio Grande reverted to a strained normality. Intermittently revitalized by foreign revolutions and wars, Ringgold and McIntosh remained active despite threats of abandonment until 1944 and 1946, respectively. The disorders of 1899 merely led to an exchange of units of the 10th Cavalry for components of the 9th Cavalry and 25th Infantry. The year had sorely tried the garrisons and the South Texas communities, although none experienced the anguish of serious injuries and litigation. But soon even that consolation evaporated hundreds of miles to the west after the 25th Infantry entered the desert town of El Paso.[103]

Three

At the Pass of the North

To an isolated, enterprising western town of the late nineteenth century, the arrival of a new year occasioned less stock-taking than lauding the real and fancied virtues of the community. Local news publishers, more conspicuous for their imaginative press agentry than for permanence in a particular location, hailed their modest municipalities as desert metropolises. El Paso, Texas, warming to recent growth and recognition, received the twentieth century as a clarion to glory.[1]

The previous two decades had witnessed the metamorphosis of El Paso from an adobe village to a bustling, undisciplined young city. Incorporated in 1873 at the extreme western tip of the state, the Rio Grande community dated from an early eighteenth century Spanish land grant to Juan María Ponce de León. Invigorated by the California gold rush, which drew prospectors and pioneers through the Pass of the North, the lowest all-weather route across the Rockies, the neglected village undertook a steady surge of growth. The entry of the Southern Pacific, the Texas and Pacific, the Santa Fe, and the Galveston, Harrisburg, and San Antonio railroads in 1881 assured the border town's success. The county seat dutifully transferred from Ysleta two years later. As the old century waned, El Paso claimed a population of 22,500 and considered itself a railroad, mining, and cattle center. It financially dwarfed the countryside within three hundred miles in any direction. A writer enthused, "El Paso is a cosmopolitan city and destined to be in a few years the greatest city in the Great Southwest."[2]

The scribe might have added that no small part of the city's economic fortune rested on a military base. Fort Bliss had grown up with the civilian community after Maj. Jefferson Van Horne led several companies of the Third Infantry to the future site of downtown El Paso in 1849. Initially a border post in the vein of Davis, Hancock, and Quitman, the fort developed a permanency unmatched in neighboring installations. Situated in a series of locations in the West Texas town, Bliss provided security, income, and culture to El Pasoans throughout the second half of the nineteenth century. Indeed, no other Texas city save San Antonio enjoyed such a symbiotic relationship with the army. In 1893 the fort moved to its new and final site at Lanoria Mesa on a spacious location guaranteeing future expansion. Townsfolk raised thousands of dollars to purchase property for the War Department, considering the transaction a wise financial investment. The expected benefits of a permanent army post melded with the anticipated introduction of industry to create the collective sentiment of optimism that greeted the twentieth century.[3]

The arrival of Company A, 25th Infantry, in late April, 1899, reunited the city with a black garrison, continuing a relationship that dated intermittently from the end of the Civil War. Two companies of the 125th U.S. Colored Troops garrisoned Fort Bliss immediately after the resumption of peace, while a company of the 24th Infantry occupied Camp Concordia within two years of the relocation of the fort to that site in 1868. Units of the 25th Infantry and 9th Cavalry subsequently replaced the 24th. Black soldiers continued to occupy the fort until the end of 1881, the year of the establishment of the Hart's Mill post. The relationship proved congenial: not only were there no confrontations between the town and black garrisons during the entire period, the final sixteen months in which the white 15th Infantry shared the reservation produced no racial incidents among the soldiers either.[4]

Various factors encouraged the renewal of harmonious race relations in 1899. Doubtless, many El Pasoans still recalled the decisive role played by the 9th Cavalrymen from surrounding areas in quelling the "Salt War" rioting at San Elizario twenty-two years earlier. Civic leaders, distressed by the recent depletion of Fort Bliss during the Spanish-American War, necessarily welcomed the soldiers in order to maintain a garrison. Accordingly, the local press reported the presence of black troops courteously, even enthusiastically. Commenting on the passage of the 9th Cavalry through El Paso en route to New Mexico and Arizona, a reporter described the troopers as "a splendid set of men physically" and lauded their faultless behavior. By the spring of 1899, El Pasoans had reaccustomed themselves to the sight of ebony-skinned soldiers moving quietly among leathery faced Anglos and Mexicans on the sunbathed city streets.[5]

No half-remembered local episode threatened racial strife. When black troops had occupied Fort Bliss and other western posts in the 1870s, El Paso counted only several hundred inhabitants, most of them racially indifferent Latinos. In recent years the city had tied its star to regional commerce and federal installations, institutions less obsessed than others with race. Years later a newsman could truthfully state that El Paso had never witnessed the lynching of a black.[6]

El Paso's African Americans comprised less than 3 percent of the city's residents and enjoyed high status in comparison to blacks elsewhere in the state. "The Four Hundred," a term newspapers used in referring to the black community, received favorable, if infrequent, mention from the press, which often railed against Chinese opium dens. The sizable Hispanic population filled menial jobs ordinarily associated with blacks in most southern communities. Consequently, the black sector included an inordinate ratio of businessmen and professionals, who enhanced the prestige of the group without challenging white leadership.[7]

Still, the Confederate orientation of El Paso posed a potential obstruction to the further assimilation of blacks, both civilians and soldiers. Many whites, particularly of the Democratic establishment, shared the racial perspectives of southern society in a period of deteriorating race relations. The old biases surfaced when their preeminence appeared threatened. The Republican preference of the blacks often drew criticism and ridicule from Democrats in election years. As elsewhere, insecure El Paso Anglos viewed the uniformed black as an authority symbol challenging white supremacy. Accordingly, mixed emotions vied for expression at the Pass of the North as Company A detrained from brief service at Fort Huachuca, Arizona Territory, on a spring day in 1899.[8]

Six months in the western desert had rested the foot soldiers somewhat from their grueling experiences in Cuba. The regiment had actively engaged the Spaniards at the blockhouse at El Caney, whose surrender hastened the end of the campaign. In appreciation of their role, regimental commander Lt. Col. Aaron Daggett wrote:

> Formed in battle array, you advanced to the stone fort against volleys therefrom and riflepits in front, and against a galling fire from blockhouses, the church tower and the village on your left. You continued to advance, skillfully and bravely directed by the officers in immediate command, halting and delivering such a cool and well-directed fire that the enemy was compelled to wave the white flag in token of surrender.
>
> Seldom have troops been called upon to face a severer fire, and never have they acquitted themselves better.

. . . You may well return to the United States proud of your
accomplishments, and if any one asks you what you have
done, point him to El Caney.[9]

While El Paso turned an optimistic face toward the celebrated unit,
the facade harbored forebodings. Newspaper disclaimers of military
misconduct, in themselves a reflection of deepening apprehension,
gave way to items cataloging disorders. Two soldiers admitted in court
to having robbed a Chinese of twenty-six dollars after waylaying him
on the post road. Another wandered drunkenly into town and used
abusive language in the presence of several women. The commander
of Fort Bliss declared a postside saloon off limits after a series of
disturbances and shootings at the establishment. Such incidents had
occurred frequently when white troops garrisoned the area; but only
black soldiers held the fort at the end of the century, and each transgression certified images of racial instability.[10]

The press played down these matters in its tradition of supporting
the military presence. The drunken and abusive soldier, the *Times*
observed, had proven a model prisoner. When the 9th Cavalry crossed
the city bound for New Mexico, a reporter stated obliquely that the
troops "created quite an excitement during their stopover here, having started out to have a good time." In reporting that black soldiers
had shot up Rio Grande City, the writer observed that there were two
sides to the story. Meanwhile, newspapers campaigned for a local
volunteer guard unit to demonstrate the city's patriotism. They circulated the statement of Maj. Gen. Nelson A. Miles that El Paso could
expect a large military base when the Filipino rebels accepted American rule. Cognizant that most of the 25th Infantry had already been
dispatched to quell the insurrection, an editorial predicted, "Let Texas
get to the Filipinos and we will soon have the big post."[11]

Despite public professions of support for the black garrison, El Paso
bore criticism from some officers and enlisted men as "the coldest
community and the most unpatriotic community" they had witnessed. A military report of early 1900 offered an even more stinging
rebuke:

Soldiers from the post are arrested for infractions of police
regulations, or when intoxicated, or in the least degree noisy
or disorderly, when white men committing the same offenses
are not interfered with. . . . A negro soldier in uniform is frequently subjected to insult though behaving with perfect
propriety for no other reason than his color.[12]

Against this backdrop of increasing antagonism toward the servicemen, incidents involving comparatively minor offenses ballooned to alarming proportions. A soldier, identified in the press only as McCabe, carried a bicycle to an El Paso repairman, after which a local resident charged that someone had recently stolen it. Army authorities incarcerated the soldier in the post guardhouse. When the deputy sheriff and the repairman drove to the fort to transfer the prisoner to city jail, they encountered a group of at least forty soldiers who refused to let them depart with their comrade. As tensions mounted, a corporal ordered the prisoner back to the guardhouse, shouting "Damn the captain's orders," according to the repairman. The law officer whipped his horses away, with the prisoner aboard the carriage. However, the soldiers intercepted them via a shortcut and again demanded their fellow's release. The deputy sheriff trained a gun on the group until an army lieutenant appeared and, after issuing several orders, dispersed the men. Amid ugly murmurings on the city streets the following Saturday evening, Capt. Robert H. R. Loughborough, post commander, telephoned an apology to Sheriff James Boone, promising to punish the obstructors.[13]

Several days later, a soldier interpreted the events in a different manner. In a published letter he stated that the deputy sheriff would have avoided trouble had he not handcuffed the prisoner, who was not attempting to escape. Although the soldiers resented the arrest, he stated, they put up no physical resistance and the men returned peacefully to their barracks. The writer argued that a civilian employee at the fort could corroborate his version. Citing the service record of the regiment, he implored: "These men are United States soldiers and should receive the respect due those who wear the uniform."[14]

Subsequent news accounts of black violence increased. When other members of the 25th Infantry passed through El Paso destined for San Antonio, locals read items from Arizona newspapers charging them with lusting for Indian women and fighting with reservation police. The soldiers, in turn, claimed that some servicemen had fired at the police when the latter had attempted to arrest a few of the men. Evidently neither explanation calmed the nerves of the city fathers, for the fighting 25th remained aboard the train during the layover at the pass. Residents drank their morning coffee to the news that a local black, described as "a colored warrior," had tried to dissect a citizen with a hatchet. In the meantime, a soldier deserted Fort Bliss, triggering reported sightings along the valley and sending the sheriff in vain pursuit to Fort Hancock.[15]

The incidents served as prelude to the predawn violence of February 7, 1900. Under the banner "Day Breaks On A Battlefield At Our Very Door," the morning *Herald* told of two fatal shootings at the city jail, one of them Officer Newton Stewart:

> A brave and fearless officer, a popular young man and a gallant soldier of the Rough Riders dead amid the mourning of his bereaved parents, his comrades, and many friends.
>
> A negro soldier is dead, shot by Officer Dick Blacker, who amid a storm of bullets stood the ruffians at bay and defeated their attempt to storm the jail, though his comrade lay weltering in his own blood.[16]

Relying on circumstantial evidence and an account by Blacker, who admittedly witnessed only a portion of the tragedy, the press pieced together a narrative. The previous day the police had arrested two soldiers on charges of drunkenness and disorderliness in the red-light section. Around five o'clock the next morning, an employee of a meat market saw a band of a dozen or more soldiers in canvas clothing carrying rifles and at least one axe into town. He was unable to identify any of the figures, who apparently entered the police station in an attempt to release the prisoners.[17]

Blacker, the jailer, was asleep in the adjoining room. One news report stated that a scuffle awakened him, while another quoted Blacker as saying that he was unsure of what caused him to awake at that moment. In any case he attested that he saw a black soldier pointing a rifle at his breast. Blacker leapt from his bed, seized his six-shooter, and shot the soldier dead center as the latter erratically fired. The jailer and the soldiers briefly exchanged shots; then Blacker jumped to safety through an open window. When he returned minutes later, he found the station empty save for Stewart, lying unconscious on the floor from two rifle wounds. The officer died several hours later without gaining consciousness.[18]

Investigators found substantial evidence of the violence. Bullet marks pocked the walls of both rooms of the station. An examination showed that Stewart had been struck in the shoulder, apparently from a shot fired through an open window, and in the face at close range. A trail of blood extended a hundred yards from the station to the fatigue-clad body of Cpl. James H. Hull, in death clutching a rifle. A second rifle lay on a nearby street, as if dropped by someone in flight. But the assailants had disappeared into the night, and Blacker was as unable as the meat-market employee to identify them.[19]

The blood stained trail led to the fort on the mesa. Soon after the shootings, several townsmen joined a policeman in circling the post as a security measure, finding no trace of the fugitives. Several hours later, a peace officer and a member of the fire department rode to the base to apprise Captain Loughborough of the crime. The post commander expressed disbelief, exclaiming that he secured all arms at night. He then learned from the corporal of the guard that the keys were missing from beneath the pillow where the noncommissioned officer had placed them the previous night.[20]

Now believing some of his command guilty of the murder of Stewart, Loughborough termed the action "a disgrace on Fort Bliss and a discredit to the army" and promised to cooperate fully with civil authorities. This pledge failed, however, to dissuade the more hot tempered among the citizenry. To those who contended that Loughborough would protect the guilty, Mayor Joseph Magoffin defended the commander as "a West Pointer and a strict disciplinarian who will not let any guilty man escape if he can help it." Outside the jail, Police Chief Con Lockart dispersed a mob, which demanded the two soldiers whose arrests evidently had prompted the violence. Scattered exhortations of marching on the fort and "exterminating the negro soldiers" likewise came to nothing. Nevertheless, a number of distraught persons called for the transfer of Company A.[21]

Various civil officials joined the outcry against the garrison. "I have been opposed," declared County Attorney Wyndham Kemp, "to the policy of being lenient with soldiers who get into trouble in town." He charged that when offenders had been turned over to their commanding officer for discipline, they had gotten the idea that civil officers could not punish them. "I gave orders some time ago to the constables to hold for trial every soldier arrested," he stated. City Attorney Payton Edwards blamed the deaths on "the inherent meanness" of the black. "He is not fit to be a soldier," he reproached, "and should never be allowed to have a gun in his hands." Customs collector Moses Dillon termed the soldiers "breeders of trouble" and urged their departure from El Paso. "The negro is the same wherever you find him," asserted the federal official, whose superiors subsequently reprimanded him. "Put him in a uniform and he thinks he can run things to suit himself."[22]

Developments followed hard on the event. Captain Loughborough told his superior the day after the shootings that he had locked away all arms and ammunition, was not permitting anyone to leave the garrison, and was cooperating with the civil authorities. The departmental commander, Col. Chambers McKibbin, ordered an additional officer to Fort Bliss to undertake a thorough investigation and notified the adjutant general that he anticipated no further trouble. Within a day Loughborough wired Fort Sam Houston that he believed he had uncovered the leader and that the noncommissioned officer in charge of the barracks was among the culprits. An inspection of Hull's body had turned up the keys to the arms racks in his clothing. Local officers were "very considerate and cooperating." Hours later the captain wired tersely: "Everything quiet, have leader beyond doubt; believe I will have all the guilty parties shortly."[23]

El Pasoans hungered for the belated news reports, while the local press now resisted the temptation to further sensationalize. The *Times* beseeched its readers not to judge the company by the criminality of a few:

> Let no negro escape, but don't blame another soldier simply because he is black. The attempt of the lawless element at Fort Bliss to overpower the city jail must be resisted with energy but only by legal means.
>
> No El Pasoan can more keenly regret yesterday's tragedy than the officers of the 25th U.S. Infantry. They can be relied upon to help the law in its course.[24]

The evening newspaper directed its call for rational thinking and legal procedure toward a city awash with rumors and bitterness. When local authorities arrested the bartender of a saloon frequented by the military and suspected as the site of the conspiracy that led to Stewart's death, the man begged his apprehenders not to take him into town for fear of a lynch mob. Rumors spread as the adjutant general of the Department of Texas and an aide appeared at Fort Bliss. Although only one man sat in the county jail in connection with the investigation, stories circulated of undisclosed arrests of nine soldiers.[25]

In the first days following the jailhouse assault, El Pasoans fed on distant news items reprinted in local newspapers. The San Antonio *Express* first reproduced the telegrams making the rounds of Fort Bliss, Fort Sam Houston, and Washington. The organ supplied the lead that one of the suspects had confessed the entire story to Captain Loughborough. The Houston *Post* quoted a Washington source as shrugging, "Oh, it was nothing but a drunken row and it is wrong to make a race issue out of it." Recalling that black soldiers had served Texas for the past twenty-five years, the official promised punishment for the guilty, but he cautioned against withdrawing the black troops and abandoning the border until white soldiers returned from Cuba and the Philippines. Nevertheless, two days later the Houston paper reported that Rep. John H. Stephens had received a telegram from "Prominent parties" in El Paso asking their removal. Stephens assured the petitioners that he and both U.S. senators from Texas would carry their plea to the War Department.[26]

Less than a week after the shooting deaths, three peace officers rode to Fort Bliss to place in custody three soldiers whom Loughborough had incarcerated at the base. The prisoners were Sgt. John Kipper, age 25, Cpl. William Powell, age 27, and Pvt. Leroy Roberts, age 27. To preclude the possibility of company mutiny in support of the men, the police captain equipped the jail guards with Winchesters. "We will not be caught unprepared again," he warned, "as long as there is a negro soldier stationed at Fort Bliss." A policeman expressed hope that Washington would soon rotate the black troops. "I have a suspicion that every time a colored soldier comes to town there will be a military funeral at Fort Bliss the next day." The suspects appeared nervous at the prospect of an angry reception at El Paso, moving the mayor to allay their fears by suggesting that their capture alone would satisfy the citizenry.[27]

Lt. Col. Cyrus R. Roberts, acting adjutant general of the Department of Texas, filed a lengthy report of his investigation. In it he confirmed the general impressions of the news stories, while adding important details. Still he failed to establish uncontested guilt of the alleged participants. The report supported the published account of the arrest of the "more or less intoxicated" Cpl. Samuel E. Dyson, but placed the time at about 1:30 on the seventeenth. Dyson was with Kipper and Pvts. William H. Davis and Boyer Wright when arrested. The three men endeavored to obtain Dyson's release by paying bail or a fine, but the officer at the jail refused them on the ground that the person authorized to accept bail had left duty. Accordingly, Dyson would have to remain incarcerated until morning. The report did not indicate the tone of the exchange. It presumed that the soldiers, minus Dyson, returned to the post.[28]

Eyewitness accounts vaguely placed Sergeant Kipper and others at the scene of the murder several hours later. A sentry sighted Kipper bicycling into the post from town at about 2:30 that morning. Approximately half an hour later, a soldier stated that Kipper entered the former's squad room, awakened him, and told him to help release Dyson. A second soldier confirmed the version and quoted the first as declining because of illness. The noncommissioned officer in charge of quarters claimed that someone silently removed the keys to the gun racks from beneath his pillow during the night. Eight rifles and two fire axes were taken.[29]

Roberts's report incorporated Blacker's published account. However, it surmised that the jailer "was so much frightened that it is doubtful if he saw anyone or not." Other than Blacker, only the meat market employee, L. J. Stoltz, reportedly saw any of the assailants. Consistent with the press reports, he sighted a group of men dressed as soldiers carrying rifles and axes, but could not identify them.[30]

The men subsequently apprehended, Kipper, Powell, and Roberts, owed their arrests to circumstantial evidence. Several members of the hospital corps stated having seen Kipper, in company with another man, removing a pair of canvas trousers immediately before reveille. Shortly afterward, the musician of the guard spotted Roberts, followed by Kipper, entering the garrison. Authorities discovered a canvas suit imprinted with Kipper's name while inspecting a tile pipe in the rear of the bakery. A search of squad rooms in a vacant barrack turned up two rifles and two suits of clothing, one of the latter bearing the name Roberts. Later searches uncovered six rifles, leaving two at large.[31]

The three soldiers evidently made up less than the entire attack group. Suspects in confinement at the post were Cpl. Gardner Davis, guardian of the arms keys, and Privates Davis, Wright, and Elmore Sears. Military officials reportedly had two or three more suspects, although no tangible evidence connected others to the case. On the morning of February 23 Cpl. George O. McElroy, an unarrested suspect and noncommissioned officer of the guard, deserted with arms and equipment, which he cast aside near the military reservation. The best efforts of civil and military authorities failed to locate and return McElroy.[32]

Officials at the base and the city favorably impressed Roberts. He conducted no independent investigations, preferring not to interfere with Captain Loughborough and the civil officers, whom he described as "in thorough harmony." The colonel's interviews with the mayor, sheriff, district attorney, and various prominent citizens convinced him that Loughborough stood high in the esteem of the citizenry. They also assured Roberts that there existed no danger of lynch violence despite "the excited condition of the community" and that the defendants would receive a fair trial.[33]

Roberts reported that the evidence for the prosecution appeared "far from satisfactory" but he hoped further developments would strengthen the hand of the state. Although circumstantial evidence "strongly" connected Kipper with the murder, it was weaker in regard to the other men. In no case did he think the known facts "would justify conviction." The inspecting officer surmised that the state probably would need one or more of the soldiers as witnesses for the prosecution.[34]

He devoted a portion of the report to the issue of racial conditions in El Paso. Blacks as a group, he found, suffered less prejudice than in other border towns. Yet public animosity against black soldiers seemed stronger than elsewhere. Townspeople regarded the military uniform as a badge of authority and resented its use by the black. The officer predicted a continuation of racial incidents in army towns along the Rio Grande as long as blacks garrisoned the posts, regardless of the vigilance of military and civil officials. He graciously praised the El Paso press for its "studiously conservative" reporting of the shootings and contrasted the derogatory statement of Collector Dillon about black troops.[35]

The report commended the conduct of Company A for the previous eight months. During that time police had arrested only thirteen soldiers for disturbances in the city, while ninety-four men of the unit possessed entirely clean records. Considering that more than fifty soldiers had compiled less than a year of military service, Roberts thought the behavior "excellent." Nevertheless, he welcomed additional precautions by Loughborough to preclude the misuse of arms and ammunition. The colonel concluded by proposing that the military assign at least two officers to each company of black troops.[36]

Colonel McKibbin summarized Roberts's report and attached his opinions for the adjutant general at Washington. He described the arrest of Dyson as warranted, but deduced that the soldiers who conspired for his release "had no intention of adding murder to the crime of assault." Stating that the troops recently inducted demonstrated "less independence of character" than formerly, an assessment not expressed by Roberts, he endorsed the proposal to augment the number of officers at single company posts. Noting the existence of racial prejudice in El Paso against uniformed blacks, despite the fact that blacks proved less troublesome than white soldiers, McKibbin argued against their removal. "It cannot be expected that the government of the United States shall accept dictation upon the use to be made of them, or their stations."[37]

McKibbin decried the racial statement of the customs collector. Deploring federal officials who frequently aired their prejudice in public, the departmental commander lamented:

> While it is impossible to protect colored soldiers from insults from the hoodlum class, or unjust discrimination in border towns where the right of drunken cowboys and other white men to 'shoot up the town' upon occasions is tacitly recognized, it is submitted that the government is entitled to expect that the utterances of federal officials should tend to allay, rather than to intensify, local excitement and prejudice.[38]

On March 2 Captain Loughborough supplied details of the arrests to the Department of Texas. The frailty of circumstantial evidence had moved the post commander, somewhat reluctantly, to release several suspects. Then a friend of the incarcerated Powell approached Loughborough with the suggestion that the corporal might agree to aid the prosecution in return for "protection." The captain and Sheriff Boone agreed to the offer, and Powell handed over a sealed envelope identifying the participants in the slaying. The following day, the two officers heard Powell cite Sergeant Kipper as the instigator of the scheme to release Dyson. Powell described how the men slipped to the jail, avoiding contact with several persons along the route, and the manner by which Kipper directed the assault on the jail.[39]

Kipper assigned each man a duty, according to the informant. Three of the party rushed the jailhouse door, already open, while Corporal Hull called out, "Give up those prisoners." Powell heard two shots and saw Hull run out, leaning forward as if wounded. Powell believed that Hull was shot by "the man just inside the door" and thought either Hull, McElroy, or Pvt. Benjamin F. Carroll killed Stewart. The first two shots came so close together that he could not discern who fired first. All save the dying Hull then ran back to the post. Powell swore that Kipper admitted to having stolen the keys to the gun racks.[40]

El Pasoans eagerly followed the news releases. Local newspapers summarized the military reports, omitting the observations on racial prejudice. Knowledge of Corporal McElroy's desertion provoked no little excitement in the city. Overly zealous seekers or practical jokers placed the man in a sundry of locations and guises. A more alarming report had fifty armed soldiers descending on El Paso. A less imaginative observer spotted six black soldiers in the foothills near the smelter. Several children sighted two black troopers on a railroad bicycle in the eastern sector of the city. Sheriff Boone tracked one rumor to Odessa, surprising a very nervous Mexican.[41]

The news of the arrests of the alleged participants produced a calming effect on the civilian population. An editorial praised Captain Loughborough "for his prompt apprehension of the guilty men" in advance of any court decision. The police chief periodically expressed confidence in the imminent capture of the deserter. The relieved public warmed to the concerts of the new Mexican band, and two wagonettes of "merry young people" ventured to enjoy "a delightful dance at the post hall."[42]

But news items from other locations kept alive the specter of a racial clash. In Montgomery, Alabama, a young black was lynched after shooting a white man. A few days later, bullets sprayed the home of a black family. Reportedly, a thousand blacks were gathering at the site. A West Virginia mob lynched a black for criminally assaulting a white teenager. A Pueblo, Colorado, black male suffered the same fate on suspicion of killing two white girls.[43]

By comparison El Paso's racial news was mild. No reassurances or veiled warnings toward the local black community followed, as at other sites after a racial conflict. Still, the trial of Sergeant Kipper loomed, and none could predict its impact.[44]

Of the several forthcoming trials, Kipper's stood above the others in public interest. In addition to bearing the charge of the identified ring leader, he had compiled a splendid military record, which included heroism in Cuba, and was a personable and educated mulatto. A native of Galesburg, Illinois, Kipper had served four years of duty in Montana, Florida, Cuba, and Texas, receiving two promotions in 1898. Described as "something of a hero in the eyes of the colored people" of El Paso, his stature ironically resembled that of the victim Stewart, Spanish-American War veteran and son of a prestigious mining operator.[45]

The Kipper trial began in the state district court on May 1, 1900, attracting a large gathering of spectators. The prominence of the court officials enhanced public interest. Judge Anderson M. Walthall had earned the respect of the legal community and the citizenry while presiding over the 34th Judicial District Court for the past two years. Destined to become an associate justice of the Texas Court of Civil Appeals, Judge Walthall and his wife worked devoutly for the local Baptist Church. District Attorney John M. Dean brought a long legal and political record to the courtroom. First elected to that position sixteen years earlier, Dean had also served a term as state senator in the intervening period. Subsequent to the Kipper trial, he narrowly lost election to the U.S. House of Representatives. His propensity to seek a multitude of political offices once inspired a friend to remark,

"If he was to die and go to Heaven he would at once enter into a campaign with the Almighty for the throne of the Universe." At his death, nine years later, Dean was a prosperous rancher, had earned the accolade Judge from the press, and enjoyed a reputation as a Bible scholar. Although a native of segregationist Georgia, the prosecuting attorney refrained from fanning the racial issue before and during the trial.[46]

No record remains of what prompted defense attorney Marvin W. Stanton to accept such an obviously unpopular case. His flamboyant style and independence of mind, however, suggest that he probably relished the opportunity. Like Dean originally a Georgian, Stanton pioneered law at El Paso, coming to the mountain pass in the 1880s. A city alderman during the next decade, Stanton impressed an observer as "a stormy character in politics . . . and nobody ever had to ask where he stood. . . . no campaign was ever complete without M. W. Stanton in the midst of it." The noted "stormy character" eventually involved him in a disbarment proceeding, which featured accusations of unethical conduct, improper relations with a lady client, and fraud. Still the embattled Stanton retained his license and practiced law at the pass for another twenty years, drawing from his critics a grudging admiration of his abilities.[47]

Stanton opened the Kipper trial armed with motions for continuance and change of venue. Maintaining that his client had been allowed insufficient time to obtain witnesses on his behalf, the attorney accused Powell of antagonism toward his client and unreliability as a state witness. He based the appeal for change of venue on racial grounds. Contending systematic exclusion of blacks from El Paso grand juries, Stanton paraded twenty-five leading black citizens before the court who swore they had never been impaneled. The defense argued that racial antagonism precluded a fair trial for Kipper. Witnesses for the two sides disagreed on whether public feeling warranted a removal of the trial, though they agreed that sentiments had run strongly against the black soldiers at the time of the crime.[48]

Although the court denied the defense motions, impaneling the petit jury proved an arduous task. At the end of a full day of juror selection, attorneys had decided on only nine members. None was black and only one bore a Spanish name. The defense dismissed several veniremen who admitted bias against Kipper, while seating others who expressed racial prejudice against the black race in general. Stanton exhausted his peremptory challenges before the end of the process. The defense then objected to the absence of blacks on the jury, but the court refused the objection. Reporters described Kipper as appearing anxious and worried for the first time.[49]

The prosecution's star witness, Powell, did not testify the first day, but other soldiers submitted damaging circumstantial evidence against Kipper. One witness stated that the defendant had obtained ten cartridges from him the night before the shootings. Another claimed to have seen Kipper pulling off a pair of fatigues on the morning of the assault. He admitted under cross examination, however, that the figure had stood a hundred yards from the observer's vantage point inside the hospital ward. Another witness testified that Kipper had returned to the post initially at two o'clock in the morning, bolstering the charge that the sergeant had gone back to the fort to organize a rescue party after failing to release Dyson. The defense pinned Kipper's innocence on the inability of the soldiers to have walked the five-mile distance several times each way in the time at their disposal, but the prosecution contended that the use of bicycles facilitated their task.[50]

The eagerly awaited Powell appeared before a packed gallery on the fourth day. Powell swore that Kipper had awakened him and others on the morning of February 17 and told him "to come downtown and get Corporal Dyson out of jail." The eight men dressed in fatigues, carried rifles and axes, and kept to the shadows. At the jail Kipper instructed three men to enter the station by knocking down the door with an axe and then demand the cell keys. Kipper handed the arms rack keys to one of the three. Powell, on the outside, heard three shots and saw the soldiers scatter. He and Carroll returned to the barracks together.[51]

The defense failed to shake Powell's testimony in any significant respect. While admitting that he had confessed in order to escape punishment for his part in the raid, the corporal denied receiving any promises other than immunity. Although some of his statements appeared vague, the witness avoided contradiction throughout the cross-examination. Powell denied the defense's charge of soliciting money from various soldiers in return for not implicating them in his testimony.[52]

Blacker, the jailer, detailed his now-familiar story. He testified that Kipper had "kicked pretty loud" on the door after midnight when he attempted to bail out Dyson. Blacker told him to return later and speak with the police captain, but Dyson called out to Kipper, who then tried to enter the cell. At that point Blacker commanded the defendant "to get out." The events preluded the sergeant's later return.[53]

Kipper took the stand on the fifth day amid mounting public excitement. Relating his story publicly for the first time, he stated that he had spent much of the afternoon of February 16 on pass in Dunn's Road House. Dyson joined him later in the day and the two passed some time in another saloon. After the men parted in the early morning hours, Kipper went to a restaurant where he was eating when two soldiers informed him of Dyson's arrest. The sergeant denied formulating any definite plans with the men for the soldier's release.[54]

Kipper admitted attempting to bail out Dyson, but insisted that he never returned to the police station. He testified that he "went off" when told that he could "do nothing" about the ten-dollar fine in the absence of the captain. Kipper insisted that he walked alone to the barracks, fell asleep, and arose at reveille:

> I never stole the keys of the gun rack. . . . I was dressed in my blue uniform. I had no brown canvas clothes. . . . I knew nothing about the trouble until I was told that morning at breakfast. Captain Loughborough came to the quarters and questioned me, and I answered him just as I am answering the questions now.[55]

He denied any connection with the death of policeman Stewart. The defendant repudiated the testimony of five soldiers who placed him in questionable locations before reveille and the direct accusation of Powell. The sergeant acknowledged that his story had not convinced the post commander, who ordered him to solitary confinement pending removal to the city jail. He told of difficulties in obtaining counsel due to the army refusing to release his pay.[56]

The defense then called a series of witnesses in an effort to weaken the state's charges. A corporal testified that Captain Loughborough had offered him "protection" in return for a confession before the suspect convinced his commander of his innocence. Another soldier contradicted a hospital corpsman who claimed to have arisen early enough to witness Kipper's return.[57]

The efforts proved unavailing. After several hours of deliberation, the jury found Kipper guilty of murder in the first degree and sentenced him to life in the state penitentiary. "When he had learned his fate," a reporter observed, "Kipper manifested no joy or disappointment. He remained in his chair as calm and unconcerned as though he had no vital interest in the case." The spectators were so confident of a guilty verdict that they had remained in the courtroom for an hour after the jury retired, anticipating an early decision. Many of them expected the death sentence; a few thought he would be acquitted. The life sentence apparently surprised many in the gallery. Reportedly, the sentence constituted a compromise. On the first ballot ten jurors voted the death penalty and two judged the defendant not guilty. The decision of life imprisonment ultimately mollified both groups.[58]

The verdict ended the trial that had aroused more public attention than any witnessed in recent years. Spectators had occupied every available seat throughout the proceeding. Because of the inflammatory nature of the case, the state had withheld much of its evidence until the witnesses submitted testimony.[59]

The prosecution subsequently brought other alleged participants before the court. Pvt. Joel Elazer escaped conviction when Powell failed to place him at the scene of the crime. Private Carroll, purportedly the man who shot Stewart, seemed in more serious difficulty, "very nervous . . . and under a great strain." After asking to review evidence several times, Carroll's jury remained deadlocked, with two jurors favoring hanging and ten supporting life imprisonment. Eventually the majority ruled, and Carroll received the same sentence as Kipper.[60]

Although others continued under indictment, the state refrained from further prosecutions. The cessation marked a period of calm. White El Pasoans appeared satisfied with the results, and local blacks demonstrated no outward displeasure. Captain Loughborough accepted a promotion to major and prepared to join the 6th Infantry in the Philippines. The 25th Infantry also made ready to confront their "little brown brothers" in the islands. The El Paso press withheld editorial comment on the latter rotation and stated that the order bore no connection "with the recent troubles between the negro troops and the citizenry." A San Antonio release showed less restraint: "The welcome news comes from Washington that the negro soldiers will leave this city . . . on their way to the Philippines."[61]

But the issue persisted. The Kipper defense, already planning an appeal, drew inspiration from a U.S. Supreme Court decision that overruled the conviction of a Texas black, Seth Carter, because the grand and trial juries that determined his case had excluded blacks. Despite the denial of the state assistant attorney general that the verdict required blacks on every jury panel, a local editorial conceded, "The question of the negro's jury rights and privileges is one that has arisen in El Paso and all over the state." When Kipper appealed his conviction on the points raised in the Carter decision, the prosecution assumed that Carroll would follow. On April 10, 1901, the Texas Court of Criminal Appeals confirmed the mounting suspicion that the El Paso convictions had not written the final line on the Stewart murder.[62]

As anticipated, the high court ordered a retrial of Kipper. Referring to the Carter precedent, the tribunal stated, "Whatever this court or the trial courts of this state may think of the decision . . . [it] is conclusive and binding." The Texas court noted regular exclusion of blacks by El Paso jury commissions, with minor exceptions in county civil cases, "because they would be offensive to white jurors." Kipper had been allowed no opportunity to challenge the grand jury that indicted him. Further, the prosecution had erred in describing the assault on the jail as "perpetration of burglary" rather than conspiracy. One month later, the same court reversed the conviction of Carroll and ordered a retrial by the identical criteria.[63]

The legal delays frustrated El Pasoans who had awaited the departure of Company A. A gambol by a half score of black troops into the city made the newspapers. "There was a lively time at Fort Bliss Sunday night," intoned a reporter, prompting Loughborough to protest the decision at Washington to close post canteens. Under attack from temperance advocates and town saloon keepers since their implementation in the 1880s, canteens, according to those of the post commander's opinion, had disinclined soldiers "to wander off and get into mischief."[64]

Even the presence of black civilians grated on the sensibilities of some locals. "Negroes are becoming more numerous in El Paso every day," complained a news writer. "Last year there were only a few hundred Ethiopians here, while now the number has more than doubled." His impatience must have magnified the actual number of blacks, for the federal census of 1900 placed the percentage of blacks at only 2.9, with the 1910 number merely 3.7. Nevertheless, when sixty-nine members of the 12th Cavalry arrived at the depot in mid-May, townspeople stood agog at the soldiers' pigmentation. "The Twelfth Cavalry is white," blurted a spectator. "That is better luck than El Paso expected and there were many exclamations of surprise . . . this morning."[65]

Meanwhile, the military strained to accommodate the cumbersome pace of the legal machinery. District Attorney Dean, at the outset of the proceedings, had requested the War Department to retain Loughborough and other military witnesses within the jurisdiction of the district court "until the conclusion of certain suits." Washington, in turn, promised to keep the request "in view and . . . duly considered" despite Loughborough's impending promotion and possible transfer. When the department ordered the regiment to the Philippines, it allowed the Post commander and thirty-six of his men to remain at Fort Bliss and await the October term of the district court. The prosecution selected ten of that number as state's witnesses, and defense attorney Stanton chose the remainder.[66]

The fragile accord between civil and military authority began unwinding. The court released from indictment Pvt. George Simms, whom the army immediately dispatched to his regiment in the Philippines. As Simms waited at the depot, El Paso police arrested and bonded him as a defense witness. After a flurry of communications, the War Department revoked the soldier's orders. Colonel McKibbin voiced suspicions of unnecessary delays and ordered an officer to investigate. Accordingly, Colonel Roberts returned to El Paso early in March, 1901.[67]

G. H. Liebe, judge advocate of the Department of Texas, broached the issue of rendering unto Caesar a few weeks later. In a written opinion to the War Department, he affirmed the obligation of a soldier to obey state law insofar as practicable. In the performance of military duties, however, the soldier acted as an instrumentality of the United States government, and in this realm the state could not interfere. For example, a sentinel would have to resist disarmament by civil officials. Liebe believed the current controversy over courts impeding troop movements fell within this category. Nevertheless, he recommended compliance with the court orders:

> I am of opinion that states cannot by means of their governmental machinery obstruct or render ineffective the machinery of the United States. But we nevertheless recognize the importance of aiding the state law. . . . we should not remove to any great distance witnesses required in the trial of persons so accused, unless the necessity be urgent.[68]

Proceedings persisted at an elephantine pace. District Attorney Dean predicted the end of the trials by June 30, barring a change of venue. Defense counsel Stanton, however, anticipated removal of the trials. Colonel Roberts's investigations yielded no indication of "unnecessary delay." He agreed that public sentiment against the indicted soldiers demanded careful study of prospective jurors. "The defense insist that an impartial jury is impossible in El Paso, owing to prejudice," commented Roberts, "and I am inclined to agree with the proposition." He proposed that witnesses on both sides enter written depositions, thereby freeing Loughborough and his men for transfer to active duty.[69]

Attorneys haggled over the legality of deposition by witnesses. Stanton offered to wave his clients' constitutional right to face their accusers in court, but Dean argued that the recent *Marshall Cline v. Texas* decision disallowed the presentation of depositions by prosecution witnesses.[70]

The duration of the litigation also sparked differences between the sides. After the reversal of Kipper's conviction, Stanton estimated that the cases might require two years for completion. He blamed the delays on the prosecution's insistence on trying each defendant separately. "The district attorney will receive larger and additional fees if he tries each case separately," Stanton chided. Dean, in turn, accused Stanton of prolonging the issue by bonding an excessive number of witnesses. Promising to complete the trials within several months, the district attorney scored Stanton for attempting to create the impression in Washington of an interminable proceeding, "hoping that the war department will take hasty action and order Major Loughborough and other witnesses . . . beyond the jurisdiction of the Texas courts."[71]

The Philippine insurrection pressed so heavily on military resources that the army could not resist the temptation to add the Fort Bliss witnesses to the combat rosters. The Kipper reversal, while anticipated, determined the action. On May 11 the adjutant general's office notified Dean of the decision to transfer Loughborough and his men. The prosecutor, exclaiming that the move would jeopardize the case, appealed to Gov. Joseph D. Sayers for intercession. The Texas chief executive promptly wired the adjutant general of an impending "miscarriage of justice" and asked revocation of the orders. The official suspended the move "for the purpose of affording time for correspondence with Governor Sayers."[72]

William Carey Singer, acting secretary of war, followed with a letter to Sayers describing the military dilemma. Noting the time lapse since the commencement of the prosecutions, the necessity for increased personnel in the Philippines, and the army's desire to see justice served, his department requested the cooperation of the state government in speedily processing the trials. Dean assured Washington that he intended to dispose of the cases between June and "December next."[73]

Events now quickly fell into place. The jury commission created a grand jury for the June term of the district court, which featured one black, George B. Duvall, among a sea of whites. Since another black

sat on the jury commission, a newsman asserted "that little techni-
cality" which had reversed Kipper's conviction now stood eliminated.
In a matter of days the grand jury returned indictments against Kipper, Carroll, Davis, and Roberts. Each pleaded not guilty, and Stanton
moved for a continuance until October. Failing this, the defense asked
a change of venue on two grounds: inability of his clients to receive a
fair trial at El Paso; and depletion of the reservoir of potential jurors.
The court heard testimony on the venue motion and moved the trial
to Dallas County, noting that its criminal district court was nearly
always in session.[74]

Accordingly, the Fort Bliss contingent of the 25th Infantry moved
eastward to Dallas, rather than westward to embarkation. A number of
El Pasoans accompanied the troops. In all, thirty-five military and
twenty-five civilian witnesses, the county sheriff and his aides, and defense attorneys departed. The state shackled the prisoners and kept
them under strict surveillance. With the Davis trial scheduled first, the
cases opened in July, earlier than anticipated. Observers expected the
proceedings to continue for several weeks. Public interest in the prosecutions also moved eastward; spectators packed the galleries for the duration of the trials, though Dallas newspapers gave the cases short shrift.[75]

Despite mounting racial tensions in Cleveland and Chicago, areas
that had never known slavery, no racial incidents ensued in the Jim
Crow city of Dallas. Fort Bliss blacks demonstrated drill and sham
battle maneuvers for the benefit of St. James Church and marched
smartly at the Colored Fair. The prosecution, meanwhile, despaired.
The Dallas County district attorney dismissed the case against William
H. Davis due to insufficient evidence; a jury acquitted Leroy Roberts
less than a week later, after only an hour and a half of deliberations.
The court granted a continuance in the trial of Benjamin F. Carroll
because of the absence of material witnesses. The following day, the
court dismissed the case against Carroll on motion of the state. "Hope
dwindles," lamented a correspondent, "that the criminals will be
brought to justice, unless the state is saving its hand." Relatives of the
slain Stewart employed a private prosecutor to assist the state as the
Kipper trial approached.[76]

Charges of perjury against witnesses rebounded through the hall of
justice. An affidavit brought Pvt. Arthur G. Taylor before the grand
jury during Kipper's trial. Taylor testified that Pvt. Boyer Wright had
induced him to perjure himself during the previous proceedings.
Judge Charles Clint adjudged Wright guilty of contempt of court,
fined him one hundred dollars, and sentenced the soldier to three

days in jail. The exasperated presiding judge exclaimed, "The action of witnesses in these El Paso cases is unprecedented and unheard of and I intend to bring all perjurers if possible to justice. This indiscriminate disregard of the truth must stop."[77]

The most sensational perjury charge involved "Black Fannie" and Cpl. Samuel F. Dyson, whose arrest the previous year allegedly had triggered the slaying of Stewart. Judge Clint ruled Dyson guilty of contempt for having wired the woman to leave El Paso in order to avoid testifying against Kipper. El Paso police apprehended Fannie as she prepared to escape to Mexico and transported her and two other women to Dallas. "The action of Corporal Dyson shows to what extremes the negro raiders will go to thwart the ends of justice," complained a reporter. "Several have already been arrested for perjury, but it was principally on their evidence that the men under indictment were pronounced 'not guilty.'" Indeed, there was more to bemoan. Two days later, Pvt. William J. Hunter joined his comrades in jail on a charge of perjury.[78]

The Kipper trial, roundly considered the headliner of the series, bedeviled the jury. The prosecution's singular reliance on Powell's testimony, charges of perjury, and a parade of conflicting witnesses augmented the confusion. After extensive deliberation, the jury reportedly locked at eight to four for acquittal. Judge Clint discharged the panel and reset the case for the following Monday.[79]

On August 20 the second jury found Kipper guilty of murder in the first degree and sentenced him to life at hard labor in the state penitentiary. A peace officer confided that the jury deliberated but a short time on this occasion. The verdict required only two ballots: the first resulted in nine votes for hanging and three for a life sentence.[80]

Black Fannie's reluctant testimony produced grief for her and Kipper. She admitted that she had heard the defendant say on the night of the raid that he intended to obtain a gun and "kill the white ———— ———— ————" who had arrested his comrade. The judge charged Fannie with swearing falsely.[81]

Defense attorney Stanton, sighing that he had shed seventeen pounds during the trials, made out eighty bills of exceptions. "I propose to ask for a new hearing," he promised, "and if this motion is overruled I will appeal the case." Doubtful that his client would receive a new trial, Stanton thought an appeal had "a good chance to clear him." The Texas Court of Criminal Appeals reviewed the Kipper conviction on December 9, 1903, sixteen months after the transfer of the remainder of the 25th Infantry from El Paso to the Philippines.[82]

The high court struck down every bill of exception, excluding some as "absolutely unimportant" or decided frequently in the past. The court directed considerable comment to Stanton's contention that the jury erred in finding Kipper guilty of first- rather than second-degree murder, since no evidence proved him the actual murderer of Stewart. Citing a series of precedents the court panel, with one dissent, ruled that participants in a conspiracy shared responsibility for each other's actions. Evidence showed Kipper at the site of the shooting. To warrant a second-degree murder charge, the shooting must have lacked malice or deliberation. This the court rejected:

> The parties not only contemplated releasing the prisoner, Dyson, from the Jail, but they also apprehended opposition. . . . The conspirators contemplated the use of deadly weapons to overcome opposition. It cannot be said that their design was simply to slip into the jail and release the prisoner. . . . They had ample time to deliberate in regard to this . . . when the minds of the conspirators were cool and deliberate. . . . The judgment is affirmed.[83]

John Kipper served ten years in the state penitentiary. On June 20, 1913, Gov. O. B. Colquitt granted him a conditional pardon, reserving the right to revoke Kipper's freedom if later found "guilty of any misconduct or violation of the laws of this state" before the expiration of the sentence. A further condition relieved the state of the customary expense of purchasing railway transportation for the prisoner. The pardon described Kipper as a model prisoner, sufficiently punished.[84]

Four

The Brownsville Legacy

When Companies B, C, and D of the 25th Infantry detrained at Fort Brown on July 28, 1906, they completed a journey of more than sixteen hundred miles to make their first appearance at the oldest post on the Rio Grande. After hostilities broke out between the United States and the Philippine insurgents in early 1899, all regimental companies except four had shipped to the islands. Company A at Fort Bliss, G at Fort Sam Houston, and D at Fort McIntosh then garrisoned Texas, while C remained in the Arizona Territory. The following year they joined their sister units against the rebels. The regiment demonstrated the same combat proficiency in the Pacific tropics that had earned it accolades in Cuba. Brig. Gen. A. S. Burt unabashedly praised his men. "You are as gallant as the best, remember El Caney, O'Donnell, Iba, Arayat, and members of lesser fights in Zambales." The commander, still their defender in later troubled times, believed them genuinely respected by the inhabitants of all their stations.[1]

The movement of the regiment stateside began in late June, 1902, with all components reaching their destination by September 18. Headquarters, Band, and 1st and 3rd Battalions occupied Fort Niobrara, Nebraska, as the 2nd Battalion garrisoned Fort Reno, Oklahoma Territory. Over the ensuing thirty-four months, the companies performed essential routine duties of practice marches, maneuvers, and reservation patrol. The 1st Battalion, under command of Maj. Charles W. Penrose, took part in the National Rifle Competition at Fort Riley, Kansas, in the summer of 1904 without incident. The *Valentine* (Nebraska) *Republican* paid highest tribute to the African Americans as "the better class of their race:"

> A more gentlemanly or better behaved lot of men never garrisoned Fort Niobrara than they have thus far proven themselves to be, and it may be said to their credit, they show a dis-

position to create less disturbance and noise than did many white soldiers who have been stationed here.[2]

The "even tenor" of Nebraskan garrison life ended for the 1st Battalion with issuance of General Orders No. 98, which closed declining Fort Niobrara. Departing the midwestern installation by rail on July 24, the battalion, minus Company A, arrived at Fort Brown, via Fort Worth, four days later. The 3rd Battalion settled in at neighboring Fort McIntosh.[3]

Fort Brown, the southernmost continental military post, had shucked some of its traditional isolation and Spartanism by 1906. Only two years earlier, the long-awaited rails connecting Brownsville with San Antonio and Corpus Christi had not yet reached the Rio Grande. Until 1905 the journey necessitated long, overland marches or jolting wagon rides. Troops in residence even the previous year lacked the convenience of indoor plumbing. The sparse region had impressed a string of military occupants since the fort's earliest days. Col. Robert E. Lee, who served several tours of duty at the station in the 1850s, judged the adjoining settlements "out at the elbow." The wife of West Point graduate Egbert L. Viele, whose eclecticism designed both Fort McIntosh and Central Park, admired the post's "well kept fences and regularly placed barracks and buildings, with the vine covered cottages that form the officers' quarters." However, Mrs. Viele shared Lee's assessment of the drab countryside. "Vermin is the scourge of this country," she observed, and the area "the birthplace of the flea; those found in other parts are merely occasional wanderers from this, their native land!"[4]

Still, many had fought for possession of the fort since Gen. Zachary Taylor constructed an earthen predecessor in April, 1846, as Fort Taylor, or "the camp opposite Matamoros." The Mexican army attempted to dislodge the 7th Infantry under Maj. Jacob Brown shortly afterward, immortalizing the American officer with a mortal wound that rechristened the fort in his name. When the War Department abandoned the installation in 1859, Mexican folk hero Juan Cortina promptly seized it. The American army, with the help of Texas Rangers, regained the stronghold just in time to inaugurate a struggle for control between Union and Confederate soldiers. After the last shots of the Civil War died on the breeze at nearby Palmito Hill, the fort stood guard against ubiquitous border rebels and raiders.[5]

Construction of permanent buildings and settlement of title at first appeared to offer the post a new lease on life. William C. Gorgas attracted public attention to the site by experimenting with mosquitoes during the area's last major yellow fever attack in 1882. Despite the recognition, however, Fort Brown fell victim to the army's late-century entrenchment and consolidation policy, which closed redundant outposts. Notwithstanding Brownsville's affection for its economic and strategic presence, Fort Brown teetered on the brink of expendability as the white 26th Infantry exited in the summer of 1906.[6]

Although it continually linked its future to railroads and commercial agriculture, Brownsville, like its adjoining fort, had declined from earlier prominence. Located twenty-three miles from the mouth of the Rio Grande, the city of six thousand mostly Hispanic residents grew up around the Fort and under the shadow of Matamoros, its sister city across the river. Its founding father, Charles Stillman, had forsaken his native New York for a successful business career in the Mexican city. With the end of the United States-Mexican War, Stillman organized a partnership that purchased fifteen hundred acres of a Spanish land grant for a town site on the north bank. An invigorating land boom ensued, even though Matamoros continued to dwarf the younger community in population and economic importance. Immigration to Brownsville brought a cosmopolitan mix of Europeans and Americans alongside the Hispanic majority. Many of the latter comprised the laboring class, creating a subculture entrapped by tradition and entrepreneurship.[7]

The Civil War ushered in the glory days to the twin communities as Texas cotton passed to the Mexican port of the former town of Bagdad to circumvent the Union naval blockade. The population of Brownsville swelled to around twenty-five thousand with the massive influx of opportunity seekers. British and French ships lay anchor on the coast, supplying the river boats carrying merchandise upriver to Roma and beyond. The end of hostilities, however, spawned a lengthy decline, relieved temporarily by cattle drives to the Chisholm Trail. Banditry, hurricanes, and epidemics exacted a toll, but the rail extension from San Antonio to Laredo in 1881, bypassing the lower Rio Grande Valley, proved decisive. At the turn of the century, business leaders reinvigorated their campaign for a railroad, driven by visions of commerce, truck farming, and irrigated orchards. Like El Pasoans twenty years earlier, Brownsvillians charted the daily progress of the approaching line.[8]

As anticipated, the St. Louis, Brownsville and Mexico Railroad stimulated development and immigration. Brownsville finally eclipsed

Matamoros economically, and old-line merchants shifted their trade accordingly. The opening door to progress also signaled discontent within the ranks of an increasing underclass, early residents critical of change, and unsuccessful opportunists. The rumblings to the south, which would dislodge dictator Porfirio Díaz in a few years, also increased agitation along the Rio Grande. Into this tense mixture of frenzied enterprise, racial and class subjugation, changing fortunes, and a new window to the outside world marched the 25th Infantry.[9]

The first-time occupants of Fort Brown encountered conditions and treatment reminiscent of garrison duty at other Texas posts at the turn of the century. As other black units had found at San Antonio, Laredo, Rio Grande City, and elsewhere, elements of the town population resented their presence and freely expressed their feelings. In addition to the customary taunts from residents and racial exclusionary policies by biased proprietors, the soldiers again felt the wrath of law officers and federal employees. The border conflicts of five and six years earlier, widely reported in the Texas press, burdened the minds of both soldiers and citizens. The servicemen learned that their heroism in Asia counted for no more with local bigots than their acclaimed bravery in Cuba. A morbid sense of the remembered past settled over the military and civilian communities.[10]

Despite later testimony to the contrary, the soldiers must have resented the behavior of some Brownsvillians. Citizens wired Washington to complain about the troops even before their arrival. Departing white soldiers, sometimes the subject of abuse themselves, heard threats against the incoming blacks. The 1st Battalion entered Fort Brown in a somber mood, the War Department having rescinded its participation in maneuvers at Camp Mabry to shield them from biased Texas National Guardsmen.[11]

The city administration, hopeful of maintaining a constructive relationship with the army, could not prevent an escalation of tensions. Fred Tate, inspector of customs, pistol-whipped Pvt. James W. Newton for allegedly jostling Tate's wife and another white woman on a sidewalk. Another customs officer, A. Y. Baker, pushed Pvt. Oscar W. Reed into the river, claiming the latter had returned from Matamoros drunk and boisterous. Enlisted men reported racial slurs directed to them on the streets.[12]

Payday, August 11, passed peacefully, but the calm proved short-lived. The following night a report circulated that a black soldier had attacked a white woman, the motivation for countless southern lynchings. Mrs. Lon Evans, who lived near the red-light district, said that a uniformed black had seized her hair and thrown her to the ground. He then fled into the darkness. Cognizant of the explosive potential, Mayor Frederick J. Combe met with Major Penrose to defuse the situation. The post commander imposed an eight o'clock curfew on his men, which appeared successful.[13]

About midnight shots rang out near the garrison wall separating the fort from the town. According to testimony from various residents, a shadowy group of from nine to twenty persons charged up an alley toward town, firing several hundred shots indiscriminately or into lighted areas. Evidently dividing into two sections, the raiders gunned down a bartender, Frank Natus, and shot the horse from under police Lt. Joe Dominguez, shattering the man's arm, which was later amputated. A bullet grazed bookbinder and editor Paulino Preciado and barely missed other bystanders. The shooting ended within ten minutes, leaving an angry and armed citizenry roaming the city streets.[14]

Reminiscent of the episode at Rio Grande City six years earlier, the perceptions of the soldiers and citizens contrasted. The civilians, to an individual, insisted the raiders were soldiers. Some claimed to have seen them directly, others identified the shots as reports from military Springfield rifles. Endless repetition of the story established a kind of rote of certitude despite inconsistencies within the accounts. No one could identify a culprit specifically, leading a disappointed grand jury to drop charges against individual suspects. Ensuing investigations raised grave questions over what the witnesses actually saw or heard in a brief moment of panic on a dark night.[15]

From the sound of the first shot until the death of the last surviving serviceman three-quarters of a century later, the soldiers maintained their innocence. Pvt. Joseph Howard, the sentinel guarding the area closest to the wall, swore that the gunfire came from outside the reservation. He fired three shots into the air to sound the alarm, believing the fort under attack. Matias Tamayo, the post scavenger, was emptying ash cans when he heard the firing. Like Howard, he thought the shooting took place outside the wall and assumed an attack on the garrison.[16]

Major Penrose had not yet retired for the night when he heard two shots, which he judged to be pistol fire followed by rifle reports. Until confronted by Mayor Combe, Penrose shared the belief that the fort was under siege, perhaps in reaction to the alleged molestation. His company commanders called out the troops and noted all men present or accounted for. Noncommissioned officers in charge of quarters and arms vouched for the enlisted men's presence during the shooting and accounted for all weapons and ammunition. An arms inspection at dawn found the rifles clean and apparently unfired. A search of the post grounds uncovered no spent shells, discarded cartridge belts, or other signs of firing from the fort. However, the morning also brought the Brownsville mayor, who showed Penrose discarded rifle cartridges supposedly gathered from the streets. This evidence persuaded the major, for a time at least, of his battalion's guilt:

> Were it not for the damaging evidence of the empty shells and clips I should be of the firm belief that none of my men was in any way connected with the crime, but with this fact so painfully before me I am not only convinced it was perpetrated by men of this command, but that it was carefully planned beforehand.[17]

Virtually every interested party beyond the enlisted men's barracks accepted Brownsville's version of the facts. U.S. Sens. Charles Culberson and Joseph Weldon Bailey telegraphed Secretary of War William Howard Taft a day after the shootings:

> We are advised that negro soldiers stationed at Fort Brown have been guilty of most outrageous misconduct, and in the interest of the peace of the community, as well as the good of the military service of the government, we urge you to transfer the disorderly negro troops to some other point without delay.[18]

Two days later Culberson followed with another missive to the cabinet officer, reminding him of an earlier warning against garrisoning black troops in Texas. "The recent outrageous conduct of such troops there fully justifies the fact," he asserted. "Can not these troops be removed at once?"[19]

The senators responded to their own racial views, buttressed by demands from their constituents and the extravagant news coverage of the major dailies. The *Houston Post, Dallas Morning News,* and *Austin Statesman* ran almost identical front-page stories on August 15 in tones representative of southern journalistic norms. "A dastardly outrage was committed against the people of Brownsville," stories began, ". . . by a squad of about twenty negro soldiers . . . who came from Fort Brown armed with Krag-Jorgenson rifles for the purpose of raiding the town."[20]

The identification of the weapons would change in later news accounts with the revelation that the battalion had been issued the new model Springfields; the certainty of culpability would not. The reportage tracked the local version of the attack, listing the casualties and the involvement of citizens at a mass meeting. The public forum selected a committee to visit Major Penrose to demand the arrest and delivery of the guilty parties and sent telegrams to state and local officials. The accounts described Penrose as visibly moved when presented the evidence, "and said he would rather have lost an arm than have had his men commit such a crime." He promised the strictest security at the fort, while town leaders sought protective troops from the state adjutant general.[21]

News reports assessed the causes as "trivial." The soldiers reputedly resented the refusal of Brownsville saloons to serve them. The articles might have noted that some establishments in fact accepted their money and that a soldier and recent veteran had opened a bar directed toward their trade. The pistol-whipping incident supposedly sparked further hostility, augmented by a few reprimands and arrests of disorderly blacks. "This is absolutely all the provocation they had," opined a journalist, pending later assessments that included the Camp Mabry cancellation. A sympathetic army chaplain from Fort Niobrara believed the men guilty, but not from trivial provocation. He wrote his wife in New York: "The soldiers could get no redress, so they shot up the town. Our men are not rowdies, nor are they slaves with no spirit in them."[22]

The public demand for banishment of the black troops from Texas found support in the fourth estate. Beneath the headline, "Remove the Negro Troops," the Houston *Post* veered from its praise of the 10th Cavalry after the Texarkana ruckus: "If the war department be not conducted by a set of fools, the negro troops will be removed from Texas without delay." The editorialist attributed the raid to the anger of the soldiers at the refusal of "the white people of Brownsville . . . to treat them as equals." The blacks then "waited the opportunity to unleash their brutal and murderous propensities." Predicting "a further clash" if the troops remained in the state, the writer depicted a scenario in which whites would attack them, the very thing that critics claimed already had happened at Brownsville.[23]

The Austin *Statesman*, voice of the state capital, carried a similar editorial. It viewed "The Brownsville Happening" as demonstrating "to what . . . a brute strength arising from numbers can extend . . . especially when augmented by racial feelings." The soldiers, if permitted to remain, "should be treated as common curs and not men and when not under the eye of their masters they should be rendered harmless by the taking away of all arms and other instruments that would permit of them doing physical harm to their superiors."[24]

Events following the shootings led to a consensus of belief in the battalion's guilt. Major Penrose maintained the closest relationship with the town fathers as he interrogated his charges. Gov. S. W. T. Lanham, an outspoken critic of the garrison, considered security at Fort Brown adequate without dispatching state guardsmen. On August 18 Maj. Augustus P. Blocksom, assistant inspector-general of the Southwestern Division, arrived at Brownsville pursuant to President Theodore Roosevelt's order of an immediate investigation. He examined privately the five officers present when the shooting occurred, all enlisted men who had submitted affidavits, "all important witnesses," and the houses and buildings bearing bullet marks.[25]

Major Blocksom rendered his investigative report eleven days later, concurring in the guilt of battalion members. As motives for their destructive conduct, he cited omission from the Camp Mabry maneuvers, opposition of the residents to a black garrison, exclusionary policies of principal saloon keepers, incidents of physical abuse, and the cancellation of passes after Mrs. Evans's report of an attack. The officer entertained no doubts about the woman's story or the allegations of drunk and disorderly soldiers. He acknowledged that Tate probably had reacted too drastically in clubbing Private Newton "in the manner of the South," and that "facts were exaggerated on both sides." Unlike the inspecting officer at El Paso, who rebuked a customs official for uttering racial statements, the major suggested no reprimand of either Tate's or Baker's more severe actions. Nor did Blocksom criticize "the manner of the South," in contrast to investigators at Laredo and Rio Grande City. He remarked on the "many sterling people at Brownsville" and mildly chastised "others of a somewhat lower class [who] think the colored soldier should be treated like the negro laborer of the south." However, Blocksom softened even this modest observation with the statement, "It must be confest [sic] the colored soldier is much more aggressive in his attitude on the social equality question than he used to be."[26]

The assistant inspector general drew heavily on the testimony of the townspeople, essentially discounting the denials of the soldiers. He surmised that the firing began between B Company barracks and the adjoining brick wall bordering the town. Some soldiers fired into the air to create an alarm; then nine to fifteen or more jumped the wall and rushed through an alley to the streets. "No reliable evidence" showed firing from Brownsville, and no traces of bullets marked the barracks. The raiders first sprayed the house of Mr. and Mrs. Louis Cohen, miraculously missing the two women and five children within. Lieutenant Dominguez rode to the scene, meeting gunfire, which took his steed and arm. The attackers next peppered the Miller Hotel at the end of the second block, nearly striking a guest sitting by a window, and separated into two units. One group proceeded up the alley, killing the bartender Natus in John Tillman's saloon as he attempted to close the back door. The other group zigzagged to the Fred Starck home on Washington, riddling it within eighteen inches of two sleeping children, probably mistaking it for the Tate residence next door. From that point the men "probably" ran back to camp.[27]

Blocksom acknowledged the difficulties confronting eyewitnesses: "None of the individual raiders was recognized. Streets are poorly lighted, and it was a dark night. Those who saw them were busy trying to keep out of sight themselves." He also noted, contrary to his assertion of revenge as motive, that Tillman had served blacks, albeit on a segregated basis, and that Natus had never quarreled with troops. Still, he believed, "The evidence of many witnesses of all classes is conclusive. Shattered bullets, shells, and clips are merely corroborative."[28]

The major defended the officers from the criticisms heard in town and circulated in the press. Discounting retroactive suggestions that they should have doubled the guard and enacted other precautions, he believed canceling passes and dispatching patrols early in the evening was appropriate to conditions. The culprits deceived Penrose into believing the fort under attack and then returned in the confusion to assemble and secretly clean their weapons. Blocksom might have credited the testimony of the officers to vindicate the enlisted men, but preferred to view them as duped. It concerned him that Capt. Edgar A. Macklin, officer of the day, had slept through the incident and that Penrose had failed to incarcerate the men in charge of quarters and arms, sentinel Howard, and scavenger Tamayo, despite an absence of direct evidence against them. Blocksom recommended the discharge of all the enlisted men in battalion, with no opportunity for enlistment in any military branch, if they refused to identify the guilty by a date determined by the War Department.[29]

During the inquiry, Texas Ranger Capt. William J. "Bill" McDonald arrived with a few men to maintain order. Finding the area quiet, the legendary lawman joined the citizens' investigating committee, which, according to Penrose, practically delegated its authority to him. Con-

temptuous of the men and of the officers unable to detect the assailants, McDonald arrested and Penrose jailed twelve members of the
garrison: Sgt. George Jackson, B Company, in charge of quarters; Sgt.
Darby Brawner, C Company, in charge of quarters; Sgt. James Reid,
B Company, sergeant of the guard; Cpl. David Powell, D Company, on
pass; Cpl. Willie H. Miller, on pass; Cpl. Charles Madison, C Company,
on pass; Pvt. Joseph Howard, D Company, guard; Pvt. James Newton,
C Company, assaulted by Tate; Pvt. Oscar Reid, C Company, whom
Baker shoved into the river; Pvt. James Gill, D Company, companion
of Reid when pushed; Pvt. Charles Askew, C Company, a cap bearing
his name supposedly found in town; and Pvt. John Hollomon,
B Company, part owner of a Tenderloin saloon. Ernest Allison, an ex-
soldier and business partner of Hollomon, was also arrested and detained.[30]

McDonald's actions defied the absence of confessions and the statement of Gen. William S. McCaskey, commanding the Department of
Texas, that "there is no evidence that the majority of them were in
any way directly connected with the affair." Still, some of the Ranger's
suspects warranted examination. Blocksom previously had recommended arresting the noncommissioned officers on the grounds that
they would have been privy to any plot. Howard, close to the scene,
had reported the first shots. The other arrests raised more questions.
The story of Askew's cap apparently originated with the soldier himself, who thought incorrectly that he was arrested because of its
discovery in the street. Since McDonald had not charged him on that
account, his detention remained a mystery. Hollomon and Allison
drew suspicion merely because soldiers frequented their establishment. Newton and Reid were held for supposedly seeking revenge
against the customs collectors who abused them, an ironical form of
double jeopardy. Even more curious, Gill's crime was witnessing a
dunking.[31]

A state-military jurisdictional dispute, reminiscent of the Kipper
debacle at El Paso, followed the arrests. President Roosevelt, heeding
Texan demands, ordered the battalion to Fort Reno, Oklahoma Territory, and the suspects to Fort Sam Houston while the investigation
continued. Captain McDonald, fearing removal of the prisoners beyond the authority of Texas, attempted to block their departure. He
relented only when District Judge Stanley Welch withdrew the warrants. The awed Blocksom believed the captain "might have fought
the entire battalion with his four or five rangers[,] were their obe-
dience as blind as his obstinacy," and quoted an opinion that the

lawman would "charge hell with one bucket of water." The subdued battalion departed Brownsville at 6:30 A.M., August 25.[32]

No soldiers of the 25th Infantry garrisoned Fort Brown after late August, but their memory weighed on the minds of Brownsvillians. The Cameron County grand jury took up their case at the September session, but exhausted three weeks of investigation without returning an indictment. The judge, nevertheless, issued a scathing denunciation of the troops' "fiendish malice and hate, showing hearts blacker than their skins." The town chafed under the knowledge that white troops would not replace the African Americans as hoped. The War Department scheduled Fort Brown for temporary closure as soon as caretaker Company H of the 26th Infantry completed the transfer of supplies.[33]

Ironically, the angry Brownsvillians released their grasp on the twelve prisoners, whom they blamed for attacking their lives and property, while the United States government, employer and beneficiary of the soldiers, held tightly. The acquitted men remained under guard at Fort Sam Houston, with the remainder of the three companies confined to post at Fort Reno. Perturbed by his inability to uncover the guilty, Roosevelt ordered Gen. Ernest A. Garlington, inspector general at the War Department, to Fort Reno and Sam Houston. The unambiguous instructions directed Garlington to "endeavor to secure information that will lead to the apprehension and punishment of the men of the Twenty-fifth Infantry." The president, entertaining no doubts of culpability, authorized the general to inform the enlisted men, "If the guilty parties cannot be discovered . . . orders will be immediately issued from the War Department discharging every man in Companies B, C, and D, without honor." The punishment would prohibit reenlistment in the army or navy. Garlington himself could determine the deadline for the soldiers to come forward.[34]

The general's investigation, concluding with a report of October 22, ended as barren as the previous inquiries. He examined the suspects and other battalion members individually and in groups at the two bases. He encountered in every man "a wooden, stolid look" followed by absolute denial of any knowledge of the matter. Under close questioning, each man admitted awareness of racial discrimination in Brownsville and of the several incidents of physical abuse. They even acknowledged having heard the incidents discussed in barracks. However, Garlington "could extract no admission from any man that this discrimination and these acts of violence had caused any feeling of

animosity." Not even the threat of debarment elicited any cooperation from the men. Accordingly, the inspector recommended that
Roosevelt implement the dismissal plan first broached by Blocksom,
notwithstanding that "a number of men who have no direct knowledge . . . will incur this extreme penalty." As justification for such
harsh action, Garlington argued, "They appear to stand together in a
determination to resist the detection of the guilty; therefore they
should stand together when the penalty falls."[35]

Roosevelt's dismissal order, signed on November 4 and published
the following day, widened the scope of the controversy from Texas to
the nation. Critics accused the president of delaying the order until
after the congressional elections for fear of alienating black voters in
key northern states. The charge carried substance; African-American
newspapers and leaders attacked the decision, when known, as racist.
The Richmond *Planet* asserted, "The fact that he [Roosevelt] withheld
his decision until after the election emphasizes that he is about as
much of a politician as he is a statesman." The Atlanta *Independent*
concurred: "No self-respecting Negro man would have voted the republican ticket last Tuesday in the face of this flagrant violation of our
constitutional rights." Black ministers leapt into the fray, and rising
activist W. E. B. DuBois urged his followers to vote Democratic in the
1908 presidential election. The rebukes stung Roosevelt, who prided
himself on fairness, had served with black troops in the Spanish-
American War, and had appointed blacks to government office in his
administration. His insistence that he would have treated white troops
in the same manner met derision from most prominent African
Americans other than Booker T. Washington. The widely publicized
White House guest and instrument of patronage to the black community remained loyal to Roosevelt, thereby sharing in the criticism of
the president and heir apparent Secretary of War Taft.[36]

An interracial organization, the Constitutional League, first raised
the argument of the troops' innocence. The League, directed by white
Progressive John Milholland, condemned the findings of Blocksom
and Garlington as hasty and racist and hammered at inconsistencies
in the citizens' testimony. This campaign in behalf of the cashiered
troops caught the attention of Joseph B. Foraker, Republican U.S.
senator from Ohio.[37]

Foraker provided the political leadership, through committee hearings, speeches, and writings, which prompted sympathizers to com-
pare him to Emile Zola, zealous defender of Alfred Dreyfus. Probably
devoid of purely altruistic motives, Foraker no doubt relished settling

old grudges with Roosevelt while enhancing his presidential ambitions. A conservative Republican, the Ohioan opposed the administration's Hepburn Act, which strengthened federal railroads regulation, and other progressive measures favored by Roosevelt. Sharing a political base with fellow Cincinnatian Taft, Foraker realized the value of the disgruntled black constituency in turning the 1908 nomination to his advantage. The senator recognized Roosevelt's discomfort in boxing up the dismissal order and hastening off to the Canal Zone, leaving his vacillating secretary of war to suspend and then reissue the edict. Even the staid New York *Times* commented, "Punishment is supposed to follow a trial."[38]

As the Fifty-ninth Congress opened its second session on December 3, Foraker introduced a resolution for a Senate investigation of the raid. In strident language the measure called for the War Department to provide all evidence upon which it had acted to dismiss the soldiers. The successful resolution substituted a weaker White House version asking information "not incompatible with the public interests."[39]

Roosevelt's message embodied questionable assumptions. He omitted consideration that an outside band might have assaulted the town or that some evidence and testimony appeared dubious. Denying that the summary discharges constituted punishment, obviously intended to justify the absence of a trial, the president argued the propriety of his action. The accompanying official correspondence, designed to bolster the White House decision, excluded the judgment of Maj. C. J. T. Clarke, "doubtful" that the charges against the twelve soldiers had been "substantiated."[40]

Battle lines drawn, Roosevelt and Foraker dug in their heels as principal advocate and opponent, respectively, of the dismissal of 167 men of Companies B, C, and D. The president conceded only two points the remainder of his term. He authorized Secretary Taft to accept appeals for reenlistment from the debarred troops and he removed the ban on civil service employment. These glimpses of flexibility little diminished the intensity of the controversy. Roosevelt sent Blocksom and Milton Purdy, assistant to the attorney general, to Brownsville to elicit additional civilian testimony. Foraker followed with a series of Senate speeches in which he chided Ranger McDonald's behavior at Fort Brown, questioned how a soldier might prove his innocence for the purpose of reenlistment, and challenged the power of the commander-in-chief to exercise the congressional prerogative of regulating the military. The senator scored the punitive nature of the dismissal of the innocent soldiers: "I have not heard anybody contend that all the men in this battalion are guilty. . . . The lowliest citizens, the humblest man, is entitled to his day in court."[41]

Foraker argued that a trial would produce the murderers and the accessories, if the government's assumptions were correct. Citing shootings at Sturgis City and San Carlos, the Ohioan emphasized that attempted cover-ups had resulted in conviction of the perpetrators. By the unstated portion of this proposition, of course, a failure to convict would demonstrate the soldiers' innocence.[42]

The Senate Committee on Military Affairs began hearings on the Brownsville affray on February 4, 1907, suspended meetings during the summer and early fall, and continued until March 10 of the following year. Their length provided a constant rekindling of the issue but exhausted the remaining public attention. By the time of the hearings' conclusion, the election year was in full swing and most blacks had drifted back to the Republicans and Taft. At the Chicago convention the hefty secretary of war garnered the nomination with 702 votes, while Foraker's flagging candidacy mustered only 16. New accusations of "friendly relations" with Standard Oil cost Foraker his Senate seat the next year.[43]

The report of the Military Affairs Committee, published in March, 1908, reflected virtually every aspect of the controversy in dispute at that time. The nine-member majority, composed of five Democrats and four Republicans, including Roosevelt's old friend Henry Cabot Lodge, supported the administration's decision. The four remaining Republicans submitted two reports. All—Nathan B. Scott of West Virginia, James A. Hemenway of Indiana, Morgan G. Bulkeley of Connecticut, and Foraker—signed the first, which denied sufficient evidence. They cited witnesses' failure to identify any individuals; the inability of the grand jury to indict; lack of proof of a conspiracy of silence; contradictions in eyewitness testimony; and the exemplary records of the men, many with lengthy service. The report concluded that even the guilt of some battalion members would not justify dismissal of the entire garrison.[44]

Foraker and Bulkeley went a step further in a separate minority report, which argued the innocence of all the soldiers. Combing through thousands of pages of testimony, they pieced together a case for the soldiers that critics of the official decision echoed more than six decades later. The soldiers lacked motivation for the deed, the two Senators asserted, while members of the citizenry stood to gain from their disgrace and removal. Townspeople had protested the troops' transfer to Fort Brown even before their arrival, and various people reported threats against the men. Some boasted their tour of duty would end quickly. Although subjected to indignities, the men expressed no hostile feelings toward their hosts. The alleged attack on Mrs. Evans aroused the indignation of the residents, not the soldiers, and presented the former a strong motivation for action.[45]

No officer or enlisted man, they continued, reported any advance or later knowledge of a military plot. To a man they considered the firing an attack on the fort. Major Penrose and other officers first heard shots from pistols, weapons not issued the garrison, followed by high-powered arms fire, not necessarily Springfields. No one described firing from the reservation, the sentry Howard and the scavenger Tamayo in perfect position to observe. The short duration of the attack and the hastily formed ranks afforded little time for an assault, a premise strengthened by the accounting of all men, arms, and ammunition.[46]

The government, according to the minority, relied on discredited testimony from biased Brownsvillians. Nighttime experiments conducted at Fort McIntosh demonstrated that supposed eyewitnesses could not have seen the raiders clearly on that dark night at the distances described. Captain Macklin noted spent cartridges in the streets lying in a contrived configuration, suggesting tampering. The shells collected by Mayor Combe bore evidence of having been fired at the Fort Niobrara rifle range and transported to Fort Brown in easily accessible boxes. Bullets lodged at elevated heights in town houses, ostensibly fired from barracks balconies, struck at improbable angles, according to field experiments. At least one bullet pried from a wall did not match issued ammunition. The administration accepted the dubious evidence from prejudiced investigators who actually led the witnesses in their testimony.[47]

Aside from suggesting the culpability of residents, who either attacked the fort or their own town, Foraker and Bulkeley raised the possibility of outside assailants. Smugglers, for instance, bore grievances against customs collectors, and Tate's residence in fact suffered damage. Foraker summed up these arguments in the *North-American Review* a year later. They failed to persuade the administration, hopelessly antagonistic to Foraker, and passed into history as material for future research.[48]

During the Brownsville hearings, two courts-martial of prominent officers at Fort Brown fueled the issue of culpability. Approved by Roosevelt in his December, 1906, message, the War Department pressed charges against Major Penrose for taking inadequate precautions and Captain Macklin, officer of the day, for sleeping through the commotion. The trials at Fort Sam Houston consumed much of the first half of 1907 and found the officers guiltless of any punishable offense. Still, Penrose's tribunal criticized his failure to issue more specific orders to the captain. Both courts accepted the official view of the raid, ironically deeming the prosecuted officers innocent and the untried enlisted men guilty.[49]

The courts-martial generated yet more skepticism. Some who thought the soldiers culpable labeled the trials a whitewash; those sympathetic to the men contrasted their neglect with the officers' special treatment. Further unsettling matters, both Penrose and Macklin voiced opinions of the soldiers' innocence of the alleged rape attempt and the raid.[50]

The process played itself out in the spring of 1910, almost four years after the attack. Following more hearings, speeches, and testimony, the War Department ultimately allowed fourteen of the 167 dismissed soldiers to reenlist, never explaining the reasons for the selections.[51]

The controversy gradually faded as the actors of the drama passed from the stage. Roosevelt and Foraker retired to private life after the elections of 1908, and President Taft left office after one troubled term returning to Washington as Chief Justice in 1921. The debarred soldiers moved unnoticed among the forgotten of society. The official version of the raid solidified control of the public consciousness in the absence of debate. Race-baiting politicians revived the story to underscore black depravity or to rail against their use in wartime. Residents of Texas garrison towns feared a reenactment of their understanding of the attack. At length the riveting events of the Great Depression, a second world war, and the reshaping of the global order after victory eroded even the stereotype from the national memory.[52]

Historians showed little interest in the matter until mid-century. Brief references in texts depicted the orthodox position. James A. Tinsley reintroduced the topic in a 1956 article that noted the problematical nature of the evidence. "Considerable evidence pointed to the guilt of the Negro battalion," he wrote, "but such evidence was far from conclusive." He extended equal credibility to the soldiers' testimony and suggested their continued silence was "weighty evidence that [no conspiracy] . . . existed." In his focus on Roosevelt's motivations, Tinsley anticipated research for the next fourteen years. He believed Roosevelt denied the men "long-established Anglo-American concepts of law and justice" to counter criticism of his celebrated

White House dinner with Booker T. Washington and because of his layman's distrust of the law.[53]

Curiously, after lengthy neglect of the Brownsville affair, followed by a spate of articles from the mid-1950s, two book-length treatments appeared almost simultaneously in the early 1970s. Ann J. Lane carefully examined the background of the attack and documented the black reaction. She lamented the headstrong attitude of Roosevelt and the politicization of the issue by the president and Foraker. Less generous than some of her predecessors, Lane described Roosevelt as "narrow-minded and self-righteous," embodying the least attractive of Victorian characteristics. Washington, who "could be ruthless with those he identified as his enemy," defended the man in the White House partly to maintain his own political influence and partly because his stance of nonconfrontation coincided with his philosophy on race. Foraker's crusade, though mixed with opportunism, at least suggested "an honest attempt to establish a reputation as champion of the oppressed." Sympathetic to the "unfortunate men," she viewed the soldiers as relegated to the margins of the conflict on the political stage.[54]

Her sympathy toward the troops stopped short of proclaiming their innocence:

> It is possible that some of the black soldiers of the Twenty-fifth Infantry were guilty of the attack. . . . It is possible they [were] not. . . . What was decisive in the handling of the entire episode was the unwillingness of the Government investigators to examine the evidence judiciously and to ignore preconceived notions in an effort to treat the troops as men with the right to be heard and respected.[55]

The previous year, 1970, John D. Weaver presented the most energetic defense of the soldiers since Foraker's unsuccessful effort more than six decades earlier. In a scathing rebuttal of the official opinion, Weaver endorsed the minority report and strongly suggested a civilian plot.

> On the opposite side of the garrison wall, white Southerners had spent the summer day rehashing the story of an attack on a white woman by a black soldier. The angry, hard-drinking, pistol-packing Southerners had a motive for violence; the soldiers had none.[56]

Weaver succeeded where Foraker had failed; he vindicated the soldiers. The readers of his persuasive tract included U.S. Rep. Augustus

Hawkins (D-California), who in 1972 introduced legislation to grant honorable discharges to the unredeemed 153 men of the 1st Battalion never allowed to reenlist. The Nixon administration, in a departure from its "benign neglect" racial policy, responded affirmatively while avoiding criticism of the Republican Roosevelt or targeting blame for the raid. The congressional authorization of a $25,000 pension, without back pay or allowances, benefited only one man, ex-Pvt. Dorsey Willis, then eighty-six years old. Almost a lifetime earlier, the young soldier had testified after the shooting, "I was in bed sir; in quarters in garrison; Company D quarters." Ignored and reduced to a life of menial tasks, the new subject of attention confirmed his testimony sixty-six years later: "None of us said anything because we didn't have anything to say. It was a frameup through and through."[57]

Research since mid-century has emphasized the arbitrary treatment of the soldiers in an age permeated with racial prejudice. The reams of documents amply illustrate the frailty of evidence that precluded even a single indictment from a highly partisan grand jury or one court-martial of an enlisted man. Indeed, Foraker's insistence on legal process assumed that the government could not make its case. The administration's refusal to grant the soldiers their day in court overwhelms every aspect of the controversy.[58]

The question of guilt or innocence is of tougher substance. While the evidence arguably lacks the "reasonable doubt" required for conviction, it does not relieve the garrison of all suspicion. One may dismiss the eyewitnesses as excited and biased, and the conveniently discovered shells as planted by perpetrators or overly zealous believers. Yet Roosevelt plausibly questioned that a town would attack itself merely to eject unwanted troops. Considering the lack of harmony in any community, the fact that no one ever stepped forward with information to settle a score or draw public attention is as striking as the soldiers' sustained silence. A raid planned from outside might be expected to carry the same burden of uncooperative witnesses and conspirators. The government correctly pointed out the complete lack of evidence supporting a local or outside attack.[59]

Much of the evidence is contradictory. On the one hand, the town witnesses included reputable, tax paying citizens and community leaders with no record of the deceit and malevolence requisite to plan or conceal an act that terrorized their neighbors and families. On the other hand, the 1st Battalion contained its share of heroes, men with long and honorable service records. Some of them had exhibited personal generosity to the people of the town they allegedly attacked.

To dismiss the testimony of the entire body of either community is difficult in the extreme. The testimony of Tamayo, the post scavenger, is perhaps the most interesting and significant of all. A civilian of Hispanic origin with family still in Mexico, he had no reason to protect black soldiers, whom he had known only a short time.[60]

Surprisingly, the townspeople and soldiers agreed on one point of dubious nature. Each insisted they harbored no ill will against the other before the attack. This argument bolstered each side's contention of innocence by removing vengeance as a motive. Every civilian witness under questioning denied prejudice against the black troops, a claim absurd on its face. Equally improbable, the soldiers denied resentment against the recorded abuses and other indignities. Other disciplined units had reacted angrily to physical actions or threats from the time they returned to the United States in 1898. The fact that each community voiced a unity of sentiment that collided with experience invites skepticism toward both sides.[61]

While the passage of time and absence of new evidence make clarification unlikely, a lesser-known continuation of the affair offers another insight into the drama. Several months after Captain Macklin arrived with his battalion at Fort Reno, Oklahoma, he fell victim to a gunshot wound from which he never completely recovered. On the evening of December 21, 1906, while dining with his wife and young son, he heard someone attempt to enter their quarters through a locked door. When the officer called out, a voice responded, "I have a message for you." Macklin went to the door and admitted a tall man, dressed in military clothing, a hat pulled down low over his bandana-covered face. The individual exposed a pistol and demanded the money from "upstairs," an apparent reference to the post exchange funds, which the captain kept at his residence. Before Macklin could respond, however, the man shot him in the left temple, the bullet lodging in the opposite jaw. A brief struggle ensued, in which Macklin received another bullet in his left side. The intruder then fled, leaving his head covering behind.[62]

The moment passed so quickly that none of the witnesses could identify or accurately describe the assailant. Macklin, while recovering, could not recall if the clothing had been khaki or brown. The maid thought it brown. Mrs. Macklin had rushed upstairs to locate a gun, therefore seeing little of the man. No one could decipher his race or color, though Macklin and the servant believed his hands were either dark or gloved. There was no consensus even to the number of shots the assailant fired. Mrs. Macklin, the maid, and a nearby sentry counted two shots, but the victim remembered an intermediate shot that missed him during the scuffle.[63]

Weeks passed with no clue to the gunman's identity. Sensational newspaper stories circulated of officers walking the post armed against a feared garrison mutiny. The most widely held theories on the shooting had the culprit either a current or recently discharged member of the 25th regiment, bent on avenging the cashiered battalion. The confused accounts of his military clothing and apparent knowledge of on-hand post funds strengthened that supposition. Yet, an immediate roll call, instigated by Major Penrose, revealed no men missing or showing signs of struggle. In the only good news of the first days, post surgeon Benjamin J. Edger removed two .38 caliber balls from Macklin and predicted recovery.[64]

The first break in the case occurred on January 5, when fourteen-year-old Jesse Fuqua and his older brother, Charles, found a khaki army jacket partially submerged in a creek near the target range. With the buttons and insignia removed, the top curiously bore a bullet-sized hole in the left sleeve, five .38 cartridges in a pocket, what appeared a blood stain, and the initials E. L. K. The young men excitedly reported their discovery to a soldier at El Reno, who contacted his superiors.[65]

The trail led to Company A and the arrest of twenty-nine-year old Cpl. Edward L. Knowles, a second-term enlistee from Memphis, Tennessee. Ominously, Knowles acknowledged ownership of the jacket and admitted not having reported it stolen. A physical examination revealed an abrasion on his left forearm, corresponding to the hole in the jacket. This raised expectations as the second shot recalled by Macklin. The army believed it had a strong case against Knowles, notwithstanding his denial of guilt, presence at roll call with no visible injury, and an explanation of having injured his arm on a nail in a bathroom door. He was arraigned on two charges and specifications of intent to kill and to commit robbery in violation of the 62nd Article of War. Corporal Knowles, refusing to testify either at the preliminary hearing or the court-martial, pleaded not guilty to all counts.[66]

The court-martial convened on May 6, 1907, at Fort Sill, Oklahoma, in the wake of Macklin's acquittal on the Fort Brown charges. The court consisted of twelve officers from the 1st, 8th, and 13th Cavalry and the 9th and 26th Infantry regiments, all white units. First Lt. William F. Herringshaw, 13th Cavalry, filled the role of judge advocate. Unfortunately for the defendant, neither of his two attorneys, a second lieutenant and a civilian, had ever argued a case at a court-martial.[67]

Captain Macklin, who had questioned the evidence against the 1st Battalion at his and Penrose's trials, found himself the prosecution's first witness. His testimony disappointed those expecting a clear cut accusation of Knowles. In his reiteration of the brief encounter and struggle, he acknowledged that the discovery at Target Creek had influenced his memory of the khaki clothing worn by the intruder. His inability to identify Knowles and his lack of previous association with him further weakened the prosecution's argument.[68]

Much of the army's case revolved around Macklin's testimony of an intermediate shot and the condition of Knowles's arm. Proof that the undiscovered bullet had lodged in the corporal would resolve all mystery and seal the case against the defendant. Regrettably for that premise, no one else within audible range had heard more than two shots, both of which had struck Macklin. Knowles's abrasion after weeks of healing appeared too shallow for a bullet wound, even if, as the prosecution contended, he had worn additional layers of clothing. The defense demonstrated the unlikely angle at which the bullet would have pierced Knowles. The prosecution countered by pointing to a similarly improbable stance that would have been necessary for the accused to have punctured his arm on a door nail.[69]

The question of whether Knowles could have committed the crime unseen and returned to formation within the elapsed time recalled the controversy at Brownsville. The army's scenario prompted considerable exchange about the exact distance involved, the specific route, the time of the shooting and the muster, and the culprit's avoidance of detection. The acting adjutant marked the distance at 1,143 yards. By the prosecution's calculations, the accused enjoyed up to one and a half hours to complete the rounds. The Company A commander, for his part, estimated a period as brief as thirty minutes, presenting a considerably more difficult task.[70]

The government's most compelling evidence consisted of the abandoned clothing. The jacket bore the initials of the accused, fit him properly, and revealed traces of struggle. Indeed, Knowles had immediately admitted ownership. Still, the apparel established no undeniable guilt. An earlier search near the site had failed to discover it. While supposedly submerged for two weeks, the jacket had retained undissolved blood stains. For the culprit to have concealed his face and employed an unidentifiable nonissue weapon, while neglecting to remove the initials from the jacket defied logic. Cross-examination of the boy Jesse Fuqua elicited the damning information that he had conjectured aloud that the clothing belonged to Knowles before the authorities had charged the soldier or even known his identity. The prosecution declined to place in evidence the retrieved campaign hat, which, according to the defense, was smaller than Knowles's head size.[71]

The army skirted the issue of motivation by charging Knowles with both intention of murder and robbery. Initial reactions conjured a member of the discharged units shooting his superior for revenge. The accused, however, had served at Fort Washakie, Washington, before coming to Fort Reno in mid-1906. He had never garrisoned Fort Brown. Witnesses reported the intruder had demanded money, which indicated robbery as the motive. Yet, he shot Macklin before the officer could comply and escaped without taking any money from the victim's clothing. If robbery was the motive, virtually everyone associated with the post knew Macklin kept exchange funds in his quarters. Revenge, likewise, could have appealed to a wide range of people sympathetic to the First Battalion or antagonistic to Macklin's legendary stern discipline. The assailant, of course, may have planned robbery and then panicked. Knowles, the only suspect, denied any knowledge of the shooting when arrested and declined to testify.[72]

The defendant's barracks mates served him poorly. Reminiscent of the Kipper trial, the judge advocate reprimanded three of them for altering their testimony favorably toward him. Since Knowles had enjoyed no opportunity to consult with anyone after his arrest, their contradictory testimony presumably stemmed from their own initiatives to aid a friend or assist a perceived victim of circumstances. A bathhouse orderly admitted dressing an arm wound for Knowles, but could not recall the date, the circumstances, or the nature of the wound. The accused never explained why he had sought treatment from an orderly, rather than the post medic.[73]

Civilian witnesses, ironically, offered testimony more favorable to Knowles. A private detective, hired by Macklin's brother, followed a bloodhound, tracing the scent of the culprit's hat, to the Darlington rail station. The wife of the Darlington station master noted a shadowy figure hovering near the depot on the night of the shooting. Caught in the light of an approaching train, he disappeared behind a pile of coal. The investigator believed the assailant escaped on the outbound train.[74]

The problematic nature of the prosecution's case gave little pause to the judges. They found Knowles guilty on each charge and specification, dishonorably discharged him from the service, and sentenced him to fifteen years of hard labor at Fort Leavenworth, Kansas. The term fell only two years short of maximum permissible punishment. Subsequently, the government repeatedly denied the prisoner's petitions based on circumspect circumstantial evidence, stringency of the sentence, and inexperience of counsel.[75]

The death of Macklin in 1911, reportedly from complications arising from the wounds, sealed Knowles's fate. Responding to the prison warden's recommendation for clemency, the judge advocate general stated, "beyond denying his guilt by a formal plea of not guilty submitted by the counsel, he made not the slightest personal efforts to explain his actions or to break the network of circumstantial evidence wove about him." In other words, the accused had jeopardized his case by exercising his constitutional right to silence.[76]

The court-martial of Corporal Knowles coincided in spirit with the government's hasty action in summarily discharging the Fort Brown garrison and met the same public approval. It further instructed that due process did not necessarily inhere in an official judicial proceeding, notwithstanding Foraker's optimism. Convicted on questionable and perhaps contrived evidence, Knowles, perceivably perpetuating a "conspiracy of silence," became the 168th soldier punished for the Brownsville raid. Worse, his nation never conceded him an opportunity for reenlistment or considered a posthumous honorable discharge.[77]

Five

Return to the Pass

The 25th Infantry returned to El Paso in early 1906, as the West Texas city began to realize its long-treasured expansionist dreams. The population stood at forty thousand when the International Water Company sank wells into the mesa near Fort Bliss. The enterprise promised sufficient water to expand the city into the surrounding foothills and valley. A new dam and canal seemed close at hand, and several manufacturers stated intentions of locating at the mountain pass. A crosstown streetcar route approached implementation, and Washington moved closer to its ancient vow to make Fort Bliss a regimental headquarters. In this vein the army announced an immediate expenditure of $39,000 in December, 1905, for improving and enlarging the installation.[1]

The 2nd Battalion moved effortlessly from Fort Reno, Oklahoma, to Fort Bliss early the next year. News reports predicted that white troops would garrison the post upon completion of the construction, a familiar assurance in racially nervous army towns. The anticipated monetary and defense advantages of a large base at least partially eased misgivings against the regiment.[2]

The civil and military sectors strove toward cooperation in all areas. The post commander, Maj. Joseph M. T. Partello, approved a series of band concerts in the downtown plaza, which drew accolades from the press. The officers' wives, appropriately white, scheduled weekly "At Home" days at the fort, at which they welcomed ladies of their hue from the city. The black soldiers organized a baseball team to compete against local nines. El Paso blacks eagerly visited the newly arrived troops, who arranged dances at the post.

A newspaper happily noted that payday passed with "very little drunkenness among the troops" and confided that "No complaint has yet been received . . . in regard to the misconduct of soldiers." It chose not to publish a premature rumor of the departure of the black units.[3]

The military construction and the expansion of the transit system warmed the economy and elevated real estate values; still the army-town accord deteriorated. Our Place, a much frequented saloon on the county road near the fort, sparked first rumblings. A black soldier killed another in an Easter tragedy involving a woman and an argument over usury. Many of his garrison mates resented the assailant so intensely that rumors of vengeance circulated following the man's arrest. A particularly chilling tale had a number of armed soldiers going into town after the prisoner, though assuredly not to free him. Periodically thereafter, El Pasoans read of black soldiers and civilians, local and distant, arrested for various misdeeds.[4]

An ominous report reached El Paso during the summer of 1906. Military authorities, acting on threats from white national guardsmen against black regulars, postponed the participation of the 25th Infantry at the encampment in Austin until after the white militia had departed. The order affected the units at Fort Bliss and black soldiers stationed at various other posts along the border. An officer later acknowledged that the army took the action after Texas guardsmen "had threatened to use ball cartridges in the maneuvers" if the blacks appeared.[5]

In mid August, the much-publicized Brownsville raid, allegedly involving the 1st Battalion of the 25th Infantry, sent racial shock-waves through the nation, which boded ill for the black troops at the pass. As accusations against the soldiers mounted, El Pasoans read of 150 armed and angry civilians blocking the post road to Brownsville and vowing to kill any soldier who left the military reservation. White Texans seemed to cry in unison for expelling black troops from the state. The Department of Texas, reeling from the mass demand, recommended to Washington the withdrawal of African-American units from all points along the Mexican border.[6]

The Fort Bliss contingent of the maligned regiment experienced the tremors from the Brownsville quake. Within several days of the incident, a former El Paso newsman residing in Fort Worth reminded readers that members of the same unit had stormed the El Paso jail and killed Officer Newton Stewart. An El Paso janitor, who as a hospital corpsman had testified against Sergeant Kipper, commented: "I believe it was the same bunch of fellows who caused the Brownsville trouble that caused the trouble here." The man, Henry Freeman, recalled that he had served in the battalion earlier at Custer, Montana, which included an element of "trouble makers."[7]

The Kipper murder trial received renewed attention from Congress and the War Department. The latter prepared information on the matter for a congressional investigation of the Brownsville affray. The research revealed to El Pasoans that the regiment allegedly had also shot up Fort Sturgis in the Dakota Territory in 1885.[8]

El Paso newspapers now supplied fascinated readers a heady diet of racial incidents at home and abroad. A local baggage master fired his black foreman and swore never again to hire blacks after his men protested the dismissal by quitting. Georgia troops shot down blacks in an Atlanta race riot. The notorious Our Place was the site of more shooting deaths, including that of the proprietor. Jealous of attention paid to his girlfriend, a Fort Bliss corporal shot away part of the lip of a Pullman porter in a crowded chop suey parlor. A black recruit almost precipitated a riot in a Houston train station when he struck a white man for calling him a nigger. Following the murder of a deputy sheriff, Big Spring residents ordered all propertyless blacks out of town and gave the propertied fifteen days to depart with their lives.[9]

The civilian-military détente collapsed at El Paso when Mayor Charles Davis struck a Fort Bliss sergeant. The incident reportedly sprang from the mayor and three other city officials overhearing a drunken private aboard a streetcar threaten to "shoot up the town," while brandishing a revolver. The soldier's nervous comrades attempted to remove the man from the car, but Davis summoned a policeman. An army sergeant who had run to the scene suffered blows from the cane-wielding town father, who considered the noncommissioned officer interfering. The soldier who instigated the affair, W. J. Rogers, worked out a fifteen-dollar fine on the city chain gang before the army discharged him "for the good of the service."[10]

The Democratic newspaper, the *Times,* in contrast to its editorial policy following the Stewart murder, hammered away at the presence of black troops in the state:

> It is given out that all the negro troops are to be stationed in some Southern town. Why not at some Northern town where it is presumed there is no racial prejudice. Or, better still, why not place them permanently in the Philippines? . . .
>
> Senator Bailey says his effort will be to have all negro troops removed from Texas. He might truthfully allege in support of his proposition that Texas climate henceforth will probably be too hot for them. . . .
>
> Every negro has an uncontrollable contempt for the white man that accepts him as their equal. . . .

> The Twenty-fifth Infantry, no doubt, has many good soldiers,
> but there are a lot of disgraced uniforms in the regiment and
> the quicker the companies are purged the better for the nation.[11]

A new wrinkle in race relations appeared in early 1907 when a new housing division, Bassett's Addition, opened to much fanfare. A product of the housing boom created by the expansion of Fort Bliss, the development displayed prominent ads asserting property restrictions. None of the enlisted men then at the military reservation could racially qualify to buy, rent, or lease within the tract.[12]

The army maintained official silence while planning the withdrawal of the 2nd Battalion. A retired commander of the former Department of the Southwest defended the men: "It is hardly possible to commend any one organization above the other, but if there is any choice in the infantry it is in the battalion . . . now stationed at Fort Bliss." No chorus of assent emanated from Washington, which in early 1907 ordered all stateside black regulars to prepare for transfer to the Philippines.[13]

The garrison remained favorites of El Paso blacks until their departure in June, 1907. "The enlisted men of the post gave a hop last night," stated a news report in March, "and it was attended by a large number of negro society folk from El Paso." At their embarkation, an item noted, "the station had been crowded for hours with many dusky maidens who had come to bid their soldier friends farewell, and when the train finally pulled out there was a demonstration on the part of the colored sweethearts left behind."[14]

Curiously, in light of the controversy that had attended the presence of black troops, a Herald report read simply: "The negroes have been stationed here for over a year and have made a good record."[15]

The reactions of El Paso to the 25th Infantry on the two occasions of 1900 and 1906 stand in ironic contrast. In the first instance, the city remained outwardly composed, save for the emotional outbursts in the immediate aftermath of Stewart's death. Neither the tensions of the tortured judicial proceedings nor the extended delay in the transfer of Company A created a general outcry against the unit. Conversely, the 2nd Battalion, guilty of no significant breach of decorum during a seventeen-month tour of duty, became a vitriolic target for much of the white community, including particularly the Democratic press.

The unwarranted hostility of the latter period stemmed from remembrances of the Stewart murder, the tightening racism that strangled the state and nation during the intervening years, and the self-assertion of a community strengthened by the certain expansion of Fort Bliss. But it also sprang from fear of a recurrence of the Brownsville raid as understood by the white population of El Paso. To that unworthy chapter of American history must be added the further indictment of damaging race relations in distant West Texas.

Antipathy failed to succumb to violence because of the city's long-standing dependence on the army, the time-honored cooperation between civilian and military sectors, and especially the risk of jeopardizing an expanded fort. Accordingly, El Paso persevered in continuing formally correct relations with the army. In the end the policy paid and the Pass of the North attained the best possible Fort Bliss: a regimental headquarters, blanched to respectability.

Six

Something Inspiring to Behold

The 9th Cavalry, withdrawn from Texas following the raucous events at Rio Grande City in 1899, returned to the state a dozen years later as part of the Manuever Division assembled at San Antonio to protect the border from escalating revolution in Mexico.[1]

In the interim the unit had served thousands of miles from the state that had applauded its transfer above the Red River. In early 1900 Troop D vacated Fort Ringgold for Fort Grant, Arizona Territory, Troop M left Fort Clark for the same destination, and Troop I, entrained at Fort Brown for Fort Wingate, New Mexico. They subsequently proceeded to San Francisco for passage to the Orient in company with Troops A through H. The contingents disembarked at Nagasaki, Japan, with intention of joining the international relief force in China. Since the intervening armies essentially had stabilized conditions at Peking by that time, the command implemented the secondary plan of dispatching the troops at Manila.[2]

The Philippine Islands, scene of recurrent insurgency since American annexation, became the regiment's center of activity for the next two years. When Troops I, K, L, and M reached Manila in mid-1901, the entire regiment faced grueling duty. Search-and-destroy missions punctuated the daily tedium. On one occasion a combined force of four columns under Capt. M. W. Day found itself "in almost continual combat" en route from Camilig to Jovellar, a rebel stronghold. Accomplishing its mission, the detail encountered determined resistance on its return, costing three American and thirty-five Filipino lives. The commander optimistically assessed the matter: "The destruction by our troops of the insurgents' cuartels and supplies resulted in practically clearing the Province of organized bands." But the fighting continued.[3]

The last year of the Philippine tour witnessed fewer heroics from the 9th Cavalry as native resistance slackened. In February Troop D explored an overland cavalry route from Nueva Caceres to Tayabas Province, a distance of 165 miles. The difficult terrain proved impracticable for large bodies of mounted troops, causing an abandonment of the path. On a later sweltering march, a detachment from Troop C lost two men to Asiatic cholera. The men no doubt exhaled a collective sigh of relief when they read orders in September, 1902, for rotation to the United States.[4]

Stateside duty involved five relatively tranquil years in the West and heartland. Reaching the Golden Gate without incident, the troops took stations along the West Coast at San Francisco, Monterey, and Walla Walla. The 2nd Squadron spent the first half of 1903 without mounts and the remainder of the year breaking and training their new steeds. The 3rd Squadron passed its first summer at home next to nature in California national parks, seeking out "sheepherders and other predators." In the fall of 1904, the War Department transferred the unit to Kansas and Missouri. Four troops drew the honor of parading in President Roosevelt's inaugural ceremony. A like number settled for marching down the main street of Atchison, Kansas, and escorted the secretary of war at Kansas City.[5]

The 9th Cavalry ended its mainland service in May, 1907, and returned to the seething Philippines. Transport carrier *Logan* touched at Honolulu and Guam amid unusually pleasant weather and calm seas, jolted by the sudden death of a Troop L private. After settling into the new routine, the regiment fielded a talented team to compete in a departmental athletic meet at the end of the year. Defeating all competition, the team won a silver cup, while Pvt. William Caldwell, Troop H, gained the gold medal as best all-around athlete in the shot put and 220-yard run.[6]

By 1910 the regiment again garrisoned a stateside post, at Fort Russell, Wyoming. Near the end of the year, the 9th Cavalry suffered attrition with the expiration of enlistments made for the Philippine campaign. Comparatively few reenlisted. The situation improved the next year, raising operational strength near maximum. It appeared that every man would prove necessary when an upheaval a thousand miles to the arid South suddenly changed the station of the 9th Cavalry and numerous other units. On March 7 the War Department ordered the horsemen back to Texas, each man equipped for the field and carrying two hundred rounds of ball ammunition.[7]

A decaying dictatorship, rather than an invading army, drew the Ninth Cavalry and other regiments to San Antonio in 1911. Octogenarian Porfirio Díaz had ruled Mexico with the proverbial iron fist for thirty years, but his grip was deteriorating rapidly. The previous year Díaz had jailed his reformist presidential opponent Francisco Madero and prepared a lavish celebration of the Mexican centennial. The old tyrant, however, took only brief pleasure from the festivities, for Madero escaped to San Antonio, Texas, and urged a national uprising. The overwhelming response, particularly in the northern state of Chihuahua, stretched the once-vaunted Porfirian *federales* to the limit. In the desert borderlands revolutionary heroes Abraham Gonzalez, Pascual Orozco, and Pancho Villa flocked to the banner of Madero, who crossed back to his homeland. Rebel activity along the Rio Grande endangered towns from El Paso to Brownsville.[8]

President William Howard Taft selected a long-standing military site for massing the largest fighting force since the Spanish-American War. San Antonio, founded by missionaries and soldiers in 1718, arose from the presidio as well as the chapel. It served as military headquarters of Texas throughout the Spanish and Mexican periods. The martyrs of the Alamo indelibly linked the town to the defense of liberty in the Anglo mind. The military tradition carried into American statehood as the United States Army established a quartermaster depot at the Alamo in 1845 and designated the city as headquarters of the Eighth Military District four years later. Maj. Gen. David Twiggs surrendered all army installations in the state from his office at San Antonio in 1861.[9]

Fort Sam Houston, destined to be one of the major posts in the nation, entered the planning stage in 1870, when city fathers donated to the federal government forty acres of land at Government Hill. Parsimonious Congresses withheld implementation funds for six years but eventually authorized construction on the Quadrangle. The city continually increased the acreage while the work progressed. Finally, General Order 99, September 11, 1890, attached a venerable name to the installation:

> By direction of the President the military post at San Antonio Texas will hereafter be known and designated as "Fort Sam Houston" in honor of General Sam Houston, commander-in-chief of the Army of the Republic of Texas—the first [*sic*] President of the Republic of Texas—the first [*sic*] Governor of the State of Texas.[10]

The post quickly attained status to match its name, the War Department establishing it as Headquarters of the Department of Texas. Numerous regiments and branches exchanged garrisons before the end of the decade, including the 24th and 25th Infantries. At the beginning of the Spanish campaign, the post quartermaster supplied the flamboyant Rough Riders of Col. Leonard Wood and Lt. Col. Theodore Roosevelt. Training downtown, they attracted the most public attention since the captive Geronimo arrived by special train twelve years earlier.[11]

The fort enjoyed accelerated expansion between 1898 and 1911. The Department of Texas, briefly abolished the previous year, was restored in 1899 with headquarters on the Quadrangle. The federal government purchased additional property to the north in 1903, enabling completion of cavalry and artillery facilities. By the end of the period, infantry, artillery, and cavalry posts crowded the reservation to witness President Taft's dedication of the first chapel. The troop concentration in 1911 summoned the 10th, 17th, 28th, 11th, 15th, 13th, and 18th Infantries; 3rd and 4th Field Artilleries; Signal Corps and Engineer components; and the 9th Cavalry, the only black unit in the mobilization of twenty-five thousand men. The huge numbers necessitated the acquisition of terrain north and east of the fort for the provisional division commanded by Maj. Gen. W. H. Carter.[12]

To enterprising San Antonians the recognition, attention, and profitability accompanying the military influx presented a logical culmination of historical forces. A provincial seat of government in both Spanish and Mexican Texas, San Antonio continued to prosper from its strategic location, productive farm land, attractive setting, and sunny climate throughout the subsequent period. In 1870 the town was one of only two Texas urban centers containing more than ten thousand inhabitants, while by 1900 its 53,321 residents had surpassed Galveston as the state's leading city. The mission city had developed from a trail drivers' port of call into a cattle and produce shipping point. The 1910 census showed the city still leading the state with 96,614 people, an 81.2 percent increase in ten years. Mexican natives comprised the largest portion of the foreign-born. The 10,716 blacks equaled 11.1 percent of the population, down from 14.1 percent in 1900.[13]

Various factors portended relative community acceptance of the incoming black regiment. A thriving cosmopolitan center embracing the state's largest foreign-born population, San Antonio appeared comfortable with diversity. Residents had grown accustomed to the sight of soldiers on the streets, and blacks had garrisoned the area frequently in the late nineteenth and early twentieth centuries. Indeed, much of the citizenry consisted of retired servicemen, giving rise to the description of the Alamo City as "the mother-in-law of the army." The business establishment appreciated the financial impact of an expanded garrison and the need to support military policy as well as any El Paso merchant.[14]

Still the city suffered tensions capable of creating racial incidents. The highest illiteracy rate in the state indicated the marginal existence of numerous Hispanics. Dallas and Houston, rapidly gaining in population, challenged San Antonio for new industry and immigration. Elements of the local press, especially the *Texas Republic,* demonstrated an appetite for the controversial. Racial segregation applied as stringently as in other parts of the South, and problems endemic in accommodating a military force unprecedented in size could direct anger toward blacks. Unlike the exposed border towns, San Antonio felt no danger from invasion. Conversely, virtually all its citizens remembered the Brownsville affray, enhancing collective uneasiness about the return of black troops to the military reservation.[15]

San Antonians read of the troop movement within hours of the issuance of orders. Even so, they received the report after Mexico, the most interested party. President Díaz and his finance minister, José Ives Limantour, criticized the action from their vantage points at Mexico City and New York City, respectively. The elderly dictator saw no reason for the United States to "butt in" on Mexican affairs by mobilizing near the border and dispatching coast artillery to Galveston. Limantour, freshly returned from Paris where he had marketed a reported $50 million in government bonds, scoffed at the suggestion that Mexico could not handle the insurgents or protect foreign property: "It is to laugh, this talk of Mexico requiring the aid of a foreign power to do this."[16]

Although the report dominated the front pages of local newspapers on March 8, the news hardly came unexpectedly. Ominous stirrings in Mexico had become daily fare, official Mexican denials notwithstanding. The announcement ended several days of speculation over increased government purchases of local supplies, an item of great interest to the business community. Sensing no direct danger from the rebellion more than a hundred miles distant, many people interpreted the concentration of soldiers strictly in economic terms. The initial coverage of the story contained upbeat commercial analysis: "The presence of 20,000 additional troops in San Antonio will mean a boom for business for San Antonio merchants. The urgency with which they have ordered leaves little choice other than to buy the greater part of subsistence and other supplies in this city." The writer judged the timing highly propitious, "coming at the end of the tourist season." He believed the mobilization would attract visitors to the area "into the summer and maybe longer." Clearly, a long and harmonious relationship with the troops would benefit everyone.[17]

Since a racial incident could jeopardize the projected windfall by provoking a public outcry against the army, the 9th Cavalry posed a considerable potential problem. As if by arrangement, the press concealed the color of the charges until after their arrival. Military orders required the departure of the regiment from its Wyoming station at 3 P.M. on March 11. With the troops still en route to San Antonio, a news report circulated that the 9th would join the 11th Cavalry on border patrol virtually upon arrival. In the meantime U.S. Rep. James Slayden of San Antonio optimistically told reporters that the War Department was seriously considering the city as headquarters of a permanent division. In that spirit an editorial beamed: "San Antonioans are becoming so used to the Division Post that she doesn't feel that she will ever be able to get along without it."[18]

The press turned attention toward the 9th Cavalry as the unit completed its long journey south. Only the day before the troops' entry, a news story devoted a single sentence in a lengthy account to them: "The Ninth is expected to arrive tomorrow. . . . lack of transportation is blamed for all the delay in the movement of troops." The appearance of the black regiment dashed any hope of further concealing its racial composition. News items on March 16, announcing the cavalry's presence, carried headlines and text. One edition referred to "The Black and Tan Regiment," another to "the only negro regiment" within the division. The coverage suggested a desire to place the readers at ease. A segment exuded a tone of good cheer: "A noisy half hour of hoofs thundering over ramps saw all the horses leave the cars." Another reassured the wary that white officers commanded the troops and noted the unit's assignment to the southeastern corner of the reservation, "isolated as far as possible from the other regiments of the division." The military report, addressing a less impressionable audience, stated simply that the soldiers "arrived in San Antonio, Texas at 7:00 A.M., March 15 and immediately went into camp."[19]

The San Antonio press maintained a circumspect attitude toward the black troops in their first weeks of training. In an obvious attempt to forestall criticism of the 9th Cavalry that could jeopardize the city's relationship with the army, the newspapers declined to report an incident that eventually reached the public and provoked a furor at distant Washington, D.C. Although the time, place, and exact descrip-tion of the confrontation remained obscure, scattered references and innuendoes over a period of weeks sketched its general dimensions. Evidently, shortly after the arrival of the 9th Cavalry, some members of that unit refused to heed the Jim Crow seating arrangements on a local trolley. During a verbal exchange with the conductor, one of the troopers apparently pushed or struck the transit employee. Despite immediate press silence, the fleeting encounter ballooned to alarming proportions. By contrast, the shooting of a San Antonio woman by a white soldier and the burning of a Galveston brothel by angry white recruits within two weeks of the incident elicited no such excitement. A local newspaper, in fact, printed an editorial praising the "Anglo Saxon" soldier.[20]

The *Texas Republic,* a weekly organ customarily the most provoca-tive of the San Antonio newspapers, issued the earliest disclosure of the trolley fracas on March 25. Beneath the headline "Get Rid of Negro Troops," an editorial by Maj. Mose Harris stated, "A couple of weeks ago, members of the Ninth Cavalry brutally assaulted a con-ductor of the railroad train because he sought to do his duty and obey a law these same Negroes are sworn to uphold." The editor paired this brief statement with a lengthy reprint from the Quanah *Tribune-Chief* of an alleged black military riot at Wichita Falls. "We are told," began the hearsay account, "the Negroes that passed through Tuesday made themselves very obnoxious . . . swagger[ing] around, elbowing citi-zens out of the way and displaying a readiness to pull their guns that set bad blood immediately." Only the brevity of their stay prevented violence: "Before leaving some of the bunch broke a show case in one of the stores near the depot." When the commanding officer forced the soldier to pay the damages, the latter returned angrily to the train and "knocked the white brakeman down, without any provocation, whatever." His comrades then joined in the spirit, wrecking a saloon and "help[ing] themselves to all the whiskey they could hold."[21]

The San Antonio weekly echoed the sentiments of the North Texas paper. The Quanah periodical assailed black troops as "swaggering semi-savages" whom the War Department should retain in the North. The big city journal employed less flamboyant language to urge a more drastic course, calling for their elimination from the military. "Why should the blacks be enlisted as private soldiers," it asked, "but never be commissioned as officers? If they are good enough to be soldiers, they are good enough to be officers." To this rational assess-ment, the editor appended a damning judgment: "There is no need of making soldiers out of the blacks until they have reached a higher state of refinement and cultivation." The editor reserved the salvos for the conclusion: "It is the conduct of such savages as the men of the Ninth Cavalry and Twenty-fifth Infantry which brings disgrace upon the whole African race. Therefore, remove the cause." The reference to the 25th Infantry revived the specter of the Brownsville raid.[22]

A visiting correspondent, one of many who descended upon the garrison city with the call for mobilization, reported in a national magazine racial attitudes of the citizenry akin to that of the most zealous Texas newspapers. Arthur Ruhl, staff writer for the widely read *Collier's,* commended the discipline of the army regulars for limited surface disturbances, adding:

> Of all the ten thousand the Ninth Cavalry were the only ones not universally welcomed, and the little happening of the other day deserves to be thoroughly understood. Since the Brownsville episode this part of Texas has been extremely sensitive, in the matter of negro soldiers, and it might have been more tactful not to have sent the Ninth to San Antonio at all. . . . it is not pleasant to hear men say that they'd like to see any negro sentry tell them where to go, to have a regiment juggled here and there, and to have well-behaved negroes assumed to be troublemakers.[23]

The writer's observation on juggling regiments referred to the War Department's countermanding of its own decision to transfer the 9th Cavalry out of San Antonio. Public sentiment for removing the unit increased after the disclosure of the transit incident. The San Antonio *Express,* previously a model of decorum in its treatment of the unit, reflected the deteriorating situation in an editorial on April 1, "Soldiers Are Temperate." The essay responded to a jibe from the Denison *Herald* that Alamo City breweries would "have plenty to be thankful for by the time November comes around." Instead of defending American soldiers as a group against the charge of intemperance, the editorial insisted that "white enlisted men" no longer conformed to the military stereotype fashioned by earlier foreign-born enlistees. "Rowdyism and blackguardism upon the part of the negro troops should not be laid to the door of the white soldiers . . . [who] have astonished even the old army men by their splendid demeanor," it pontificated. "They are as good a body of men as can be found anywhere." In the absence of other recent racial incidents, the editorial obviously referenced the trolley car encounter. As such it enabled the newspaper to express a conviction about blacks that conformed to the opinion of much of the citizenry while defending the majority of the troops so vital to the prosperity of the community and the growth of the army post.[24]

Washington appeared unaware of any difficulties at San Antonio until Rep. John Nance Garner of Uvalde interjected the matter into a foreign policy discussion with President Taft on April 3. Garner, a fifth-term congressman from the Fifteenth District, which did not include San Antonio, curiously raised the issue in the absence of influential Representative Slayden, a San Antonian. Whether acting from personal prejudice, bitter memories of the Brownsville raid, which had occurred in his district, or public complaints addressed to him, the South Texan recounted the story and his concerns to a receptive chief executive. Taft, as secretary of war, had concurred in Roosevelt's decision to cashier the garrison at Fort Brown. Sensitive to expressed fears of black soldiers at Texas's largest city, he sought cordial relations with the new Democratic majority in the House of Representatives. At the close of the discussion, Garner publicly announced his intention to introduce a bill disbanding the black unit, citing demands from the states of Washington, Vermont, and Texas.[25]

The Garner-Taft story contained the first direct mention in a local daily of the streetcar incident. An opening paragraph explained, "This is the outgrowth of friction which has been caused by negro troopers refusing to observe the 'Jim Crow' laws respecting streetcars in San Antonio." In a second reference several paragraphs below, Garner "informed the President of the incident of a few weeks ago when negro troopers refused to sit in the negro compartment of a streetcar and attacked the conductor." The wording of the article indicated that the gathering protest against the 9th Cavalry had stemmed from the single action in the first days of the regiment's presence. The situation had finally reached the boiling point when Garner attended a cattlemen's convention in San Antonio, where delegates apprised him of the occurrence. "As Brownsville is in his district," the reporter concluded, "he has not forgotten the shooting up of that town by the negroes of the Twenty-fifth infantry." The writer, speculating that the War Department would remove the troops not only from the city but beyond the Department of Texas, damned the unit with faint praise for its role in the Cuban campaign: "This regiment has been given some credit for the capture of Santiago in the Spanish-American War."[26]

The publicized meeting between the Texas congressman and the president quickly moved the War Department to action. That same day the adjutant general wired General Carter about conditions at the post and city. The division commander responded tersely, "With reference to your telegram of 3d, no difficulty between men of Ninth Regiment U.S. Cavalry and civil authorities at San Antonio." Nevertheless, on the following day the department transferred the "Ninth Cavalry from San Antonio and from Independent cavalry brigade to replace the Third Cavalry on the Rio Grande." The order specifically excluded Brownsville from the unit's assignment, although the regiment would operate in Garner's district. A company of the white 23rd Infantry at Laredo was readied for additional duty at Brownsville, should the necessity arise. The 3rd Cavalry, in turn, would rotate to San Antonio to join the cavalry brigade.[27]

If the War Department had hoped to stem the controversy over black troops in Texas by merely moving them out of the state's largest city, it suffered disappointment. Although government spokesmen stiffly described the order as "routine," few knowledgeable individuals could have doubted the connection with the trolley incident. Representative Garner fumed over Carter's contention of "no difficulty" between the black troops and the city, offering to produce evidence from peace officers and representatives of the transit company to substantiate his version of the story. Inwardly, he undoubtedly seethed from the realization that he had unwittingly introduced the blacks into his own constituency. Congressman Slayden, who like Garner had demanded the ouster of black troops from the state after Brownsville, walked a thin line. As a longtime advocate of expanding Fort Sam Houston, the fourth-term representative from the Fourteenth District constantly nurtured harmonious relations with the War Department. On the very day of the transfer order, Taft publicly endorsed Slayden's proposal to designate the base a permanent division post and to augment the military reservation by seventeen thousand acres. While a permanent division post would almost surely attract black garrisons at some future point, Garner's bill to scuttle the black regiments might create havoc in the War Department, which understood the importance of every enlisted man. Upon his return to Washington, Slayden issued "no statement" on Garner's proposed legislation, though he could hardly avoid resenting the neighboring congressman's intrusion into his bailiwick.[28]

In contrast to the politicians and elements of the press, a number of individuals stepped forward to defend the beleaguered 9th Cavalry. Responding to rumors of the impending transfer, various commissioned officers pronounced the move as "drastic and unnecessary." Col. John F. Guilfoyle, 9th Cavalry commander with twenty-two years of experience in the unit, attributed the attacks to "Southern prejudice." A news report described regimental officers "from the Colonel down to the youngest Second Lieutenant" as "indignant that such action should even be contemplated." They claimed to have investigated every complaint brought to their attention and repeatedly found the men victims of mistreatment.[29]

Area newspapers felt compelled to inject editorial commentary into the news items defending the black troops. The Dallas *Morning News* challenged the officers' remarks in its own story by adding: "Despite this there is no question that the negro troopers have been violating the Jim Crow law . . . and that *frequent* [italics added] clashes between them and white passengers and conductors on the cars have occurred." When Gen. Leonard Wood, army chief of staff, told the president that "not a whimper of complaint regarding the negro soldiers had come from San Antonio," the San Antonio *Light* retorted: "San Antonio never whimpers, General."[30]

Interestingly, voices in support of the 9th Cavalry swelled beyond regimental boundaries. A Missouri Grand Army of the Republic post commander, vacationing in San Antonio to improve his health, called for "fair play" directly to President Taft:

> I have been on the streets every day since the arrival of the troops at this station. I have seen members of the 22nd Infty., 10th Infty., in fact every regiment here including some of the batteries, under the influence of liquor, and yet I have not seen one negro soldier drunk, and because these men were drunk it is not right to condemn the entire regiment and so it is with the negro soldiers. . . . I do not believe this regiment ought to be disciplined . . . at the request of a lone Congressman from this state.[31]

Two officials close to the scene deflected the recent outpouring against the regiment. W. H. Tuttle, president and general manager of the San Antonio Traction Company, owner of the car where the altercation took place, advised: "We have had only one case of serious trouble between negro soldiers and a conductor, some infraction of [the] Jim Crow law reported during [the] first few days. . . . For the past week negro soldiers have complied . . . without hesitation and have been orderly in their deportment on streetcars." A telegram from San Antonio Mayor Bryan Callaghan to the War Department confirmed, "Police Department has made but few arrests and all for trivial offenses." Somewhat less yielding, Bexar County Sheriff John W. Tobin acknowledged receiving no official information on misdeeds of the 9th Cavalry, "but had heard of two or three fights with them."[32]

Border communities shared with supporters of the 9th Cavalry their disapproval of transferring the unit from San Antonio, albeit for quite different reasons. Opposition to the presence of black garrisons rolled from South Texas like thunder. A hastily assembled citizens committee at Eagle Pass beseeched Secretary of War J. M. Dickenson to reconsider "transferring colored troops to this point." Laredo Mayor Robert McComb implored Garner to intervene, asserting that black troops had "shot up" the town "several times." Del Rio businessmen voiced opposition to the impending move, and the mayor of Brownsville, a city not affected by the decision, joined in the chorus:

> We do not know whether it is contemplated sending them here, but under circumstances of which you are fully aware and in view of the sentiment of our people to do so would be exceedingly dangerous and would almost inevitably result in trouble. On behalf of my people I respectfully and earnestly request that no negro troops be stationed at or near Brownsville.[33]

Plainly on the defensive from a barrage of criticism leveled against the 9th Cavalry, the War Department, which had not set a date for the regimental transfer, vacillated. A general officer expounded on the difficulties of sending the unit into the torrid reaches of the Rio Grande in the heavy clothing issued at Fort Russell, Wyoming. He cited to a skeptical press the problems of patrolling the extensive boundary from Fort Hancock to Sam Fordyce, a distance of over six hundred miles. In a rather curious addition, considering the public criticism of the 9th Cavalry while off duty, he noted that the cavalry brigade had just been paid and deserved the respite. A San Antonio daily captioned a speculative report "Negro Matter Is Drifting."[34]

A beleaguered John Nance Garner used the brief delay to schedule a second meeting with President Taft. Ironically, the mild statements from local officials that he had solicited earlier in the hope of facilitating the transfer of the cavalry now strengthened his plea that the troops remain at San Antonio. Sensing that Garner had committed a political error and recognizing the Texan's importance as a member of the House Committee on Foreign Relations, the president immediately acted in the congressman's behalf. That same day, April 6, Taft instructed the secretary of war to rush telegrams to the commanders of the Department of Texas and the Maneuver Division: "Suspend movement of Ninth Cavalry to relieve Third and retain. Officers and men of the Third are thoroughly familiar with their duties." In his haste to rectify the sensitive situation, Taft embarrassed the representative by instantly disclosing his decision to the press, when Garner had believed the conference confidential.[35]

More embarrassment awaited the Uvalde legislator, for even though Washington perpetuated the fiction that both orders had derived from military considerations, San Antonio newspapers exploited the opportunity to chide a neighboring congressman. The *Express* wrung amusement from the story describing Garner's anguished conference, featuring headlines "Uneasy Day for Garner" and "Congressman Busy Doing Diplomatic Acrobatics." It tittered that before the revocation, the War Department "had lifted the Hon. John N. Garner off the pan and dropped him carefully in the fire." "The Ninth was sent to the border," stated the writer, "and an hour later was returned to the maneuver camp—all on paper. Both moves were prompted by Mr. Garner." The daily had previously described the border towns' clamor as "Rapid-Fire Telegrams" and "A Kick to Garner's Gun."[36]

Editorial writers enjoyed themselves at Garner's expense. The *Light* described the representative as "jumping out of the frying pan into the fire," and teased his district as "Cactus Valley" and "Chaparral Thicket." The daily reserved a mild rebuke for the War Department's sudden reversal of orders: "If the Ninth Cavalry should march as far 'cross country as it does on paper the official speedometer would show a trifle less than 500 miles this week. The Ninth . . . went to Laredo this morning and returned in time for lunch." The *Texas Republic* switched metaphors, viewing Garner in "a nice kettle of fish." Tongue firmly in cheek, the editor praised Garner, who "in the kindness of his heart undertook to represent [Slayden's] . . . District."[37]

The source of the controversy, the 9th Cavalry, earned mixed reviews from local editors. The *Texas Republic* persisted in its vindictive denunciations, taunting in one editorial: "The Chocolate Soldier of the Ninth Infantry [*sic*] don't appear to be as popular in San Antonio as the Chocolate Soldier of the stage." Several days later the newspaper commented. "The white soldiers do not sympathize with the Negro soldiers (Ninth Cavalry) in their recent conduct on the 'Jim Crow' law. In fact, the sentiment of the camp is against the Negroes." Without elaboration, the editor exclaimed on April 15: "Will those Ninth Cavalry Negroes never learn to obey the civil laws of Texas?"

Although no newspaper, including the *Texas Republic,* had reported a new racial incident involving the unit, Harris volunteered, "Their officers should impress upon them the fact that martial law has not yet been declared."[38]

The more favorable commentaries on the 9th Cavalry by the major dailies contrasted sharply with the stance of the provocative weekly. When reporting that the unit would remain at San Antonio the *Express* stated, "The organization showed itself master of public manners by refusing to show it was conscious of the rumpus in Washington." It noted, "No lines were thrown around the regimental camp; San Antonio people visited and were entertained by drills and music." Subsequent news stories praised the regimental discipline and skill. Actress Sarah Bernhardt joined the ten to fifteen thousand visitors at the maneuver camp on a public occasion in which she viewed the guard mount of the 9th Cavalry and listened as the regimental band played "Marseillaise." A reporter commended the band as "one of the finest in the army" while describing a benefit concert for the St. James M. E. Church, at which management reserved five hundred seats for white patrons.[39]

The moderate tone reflected San Antonio's commitment to a military relationship and sentiments from a portion of the community that viewed the black troops as victims of circumstance. In a letter to the editor of the *Light,* a musician from the 3rd Artillery band queried: "Please tell me . . . why the [9th Cavalry band was] . . . never permitted to parade or take part in any public demonstration in your city? . . . they are the best musical outfit in the service today, possibly excepting the 24th colored band. . . . Why not be fair-minded?" State Rep. Otto Wahrmund of San Antonio volunteered unexpected support in a telegram to the War Department: "Exception of street car incident . . . have not heard of misconduct or drunkenness on part of large number of soldiers stationed here. Best health prevails." Although primarily a defense of the white majority of troops and clearly designed to ingratiate his district to the army, Wahrmund's testimonial minimized the alleged misdeeds of the 9th Cavalry. Significantly, he transmitted the message through Congressman Slayden, a devoted adherent of Fort Sam Houston expansion.[40]

The *Express* carried two editorials within an eight-day period in April that defended the 9th Cavalry while inadvertently revealing the frailty of that support. On April 7, immediately after Taft halted the regimental relocation, the daily asked justice for the well-behaved majority of black soldiers: "The instant a few of them sought to set some of the local civil laws at defiance there was an aroused prejudice that did the body of the regiment injustice." The writer described the conduct of most members "as exemplary as that of any other soldiers at any other time" and exhorted: "The Ninth Cavalry should suffer no reproach until it has deserved it, and only then as the same sort of reproach would apply to the white soldiers."[41]

This remarkable defense of black soldiers in a southern city, however, suffered from racial preconceptions that diluted its own arguments. The writer began the essay with an incriminating summary of the Brownsville raid: "They committed a great offense against law and order and against the discipline of the army. . . ." President Roosevelt "did the proper thing in disbanding the entire battalion," while Senator Foraker, who criticized the executive action, "attempted to make political capital out of it for himself." Black leaders compounded Foraker's frivolity, "trying to excuse the outrage instead of joining in condemnation of it." The writer raised the spurious charge that the soldiers' alleged attack on Brownsville "aroused a prejudice against the negro soldier that had not previously existed." The editorial burdened its plea for fairness with a condescending racial assessment: "We should rather make some allowance for his less developed intellect and the training which he must undergo—still maintaining that he shall keep his place and preserve his good behavior." In the spirit of the piece, the 9th Cavalry constituted a cross that the community must bear to remain the recipient of federal largess.[42]

The subsequent *Express* editorial of April 15, entitled "A Tempest In A Teapot," drew this perceived bargain more closely. Citing "Considerable excitement . . . at Washington over the sending of negro soldiers to San Antonio," the writer reassured the readership, which included officials at Washington, of the actual tranquil conditions in the garrison city. "One little outbreak on a street car occasioned some comment," understated the author, "but aside from that few arrests have been made, even for very trivial offenses." Indeed, the 9th Cavalrymen had "deported themselves as well as have other troops, which means a well as could be expected."[43]

The remaining majority of the essay centered on the perennial good relations between the city and the army and the mutual benefit of the arrangement. "[B]usinessmen of San Antonio have uniformly shown themselves appreciative of the action of the Government in establishing a post here," insisted the writer, "and have realized the financial value to the city of such an institution." The army in turn profited from the "climate and location" of San Antonio, which afforded ideal training conditions and proximity to Mexico, the Panama Canal, and South America. The editorialist omitted reference to the extreme heat, which extracted "barrels of perspiration" from the soldiers, according to another source, and the continuing heavy rains, which created "the deepest and stickiest" mud "of the century." The writer certainly hit the mark with his acknowledgment of the financial value of the post, however, as the War Department pumped an estimated $400,000 monthly into the local economy.[44]

The newspaper argued not for a retention of the military status quo, subject to change dependent upon conditions in Mexico, but for an expansion of the permanent post at Fort Sam Houston. "All of these considerations taken together," it concluded, "Point inevitably to the establishment in San Antonio of the greatest army post in America." Here the writer tied together the two themes of the editorial. "Hence the cooperation of the citizens with the efforts of the Government and of the army . . . is highly important, both to the Government and to the city. . . . Fairmindedness and impartial justice should mark speech and actions in all matters pertaining to the army." To the influential daily, a temporary black garrison for an expanded permanent post made a fair trade.[45]

The tacit bargain with the War Department and the restrained conduct of the 9th Cavalry assuaged the political and business establishment of San Antonio. Confidence that Washington would withdraw the regiment at first opportunity also encouraged patience. Before the arrival of the unit, the press speculated that the 9th Cavalry would immediately join the border patrol. After the army hastily recalled the order to send the troops into Garner's district, newspapers aired an unfounded report that the War Department planned to return the regiment to Wyoming within two weeks. Even the acid-tongued *Texas Republic* mellowed somewhat in its coverage of Emancipation Day ceremonies, in which the 9th Cavalry band participated. The weekly organ termed the program "a most creditable exhibition," noting that "white folks" cheered a motor procession of former slaves, "still rever[ing] the memories of the faithful slaves of the South." When the War Department stated its intention in July to withdraw half of the Maneuver Division from San Antonio, as the border momentarily quieted, the press prominently displayed the inclusion of the 9th Cavalry.[46]

While awaiting the departure of the Ninth Cavalry, San Antonio received several mild aftershocks of the April quake. The Bexar

County grand jury returned twenty-three indictments against Pvt. Samuel Lacue for forging the name of Capt. H. A. Sievert to checks drawn on a Cheyenne bank. Representative Garner produced a letter from a San Antonio attorney applauding his stand against the black troops. General Carter turned over to local authorities an H Troop private, John F. Sands, charged with the stabbing death of white Pvt. Robert C. Johnston, 11th Cavalry, during a dice game. A direct reminder of Brownsville jolted San Antonians as they read of the death of Capt. Edgar A. Macklin, who had served as officer of the day at Fort Brown on the evening of the attack.[47]

Meanwhile, the frenzy in Mexico that had prompted the organization of the Maneuver Division wound down. In May insurrectionists seized Ciudad Juarez, Chihuahua, mortally wounding the Díaz regime. On July 9 the 9th Cavalry, bound for Fort D. A. Russell, Wyoming, led the troop movement from San Antonio. The *Light* broke its editorial silence by praising the departing regiments without excepting the maligned black unit:

> San Antonio, it goes without saying, regrets to see them depart. . . . It is doubtful if any large body of soldiers encamped in the vicinity of any large city ever deported themselves so well. . . . The disorders that have arisen have been unimportant and none of them have been worth discussion. . . . San Antonio will be glad at any time in the future to welcome them back [as soldiers and men].[48]

As at El Paso in 1900, enlightened self interest at San Antonio triumphed over raw emotion, enabling the city and the black troops to escape the direct confrontations acted out at less sophisticated garrison communities. Both military cities succeeded in divesting themselves of their black garrisons as soon as possible and granted less patience to subsequent black units. When the 8th Illinois Infantry garrisoned San Antonio in 1916, as part of another troop concentration along the Mexican border, some members violated the Jim Crow laws. Public and press reaction strongly condemned the men, several of whom were shot by white provost guards. While the 8th Infantrymen appeared more assertive than the 9th Cavalry five years earlier, San Antonians demonstrated considerably less restraint than in 1911. The local reaction in the two episodes was reminiscent of the El Paso situation in 1900 and 1907. The civilians' perseverance paid off. Precisely as Fort Bliss continued to expand, Fort Sam Houston attained ever-greater rewards. In sequence the $3 million installation graduated to headquarters of the Southern Department, VIII Corps Area, and the Fourth United States Army.[49]

The much-desired expansion of the reservation at San Antonio's northeast section was, in the words of a military historian, "something inspiring to behold."[50]

Unidentified infantryman
at Camp Logan,
Harris County, Texas.
Courtesy Metropolitan Research
Center, Houston Public Library,
Houston, Texas.

Members of the Ninth Cavalry Band.

Courtesy National Archives, Washington, D.C.

Officers of the Twenty-fifth Infantry.
Top photo: Col. A. S. Burt (*middle row, second from left*),
Maj. Chambers McKibbin (*middle row, third from left*).
Bottom photo: Capt. H. R. H. Loughborough
(*front row, far right*).
Courtesy National Archives, Washington, D.C.

Erubian Holland Rubottom.

Courtesy National Archives,
Washington, D.C.

Members of the Tenth Regiment
taken prisoner in Mexico, June 21, 1916.
Courtesy Fort Bliss Museum,
DPTMS, Fort Bliss, Texas.

Twenty-fourth Infantry Regiment, black troop band.

Courtesy Institute of Texan Cultures, San Antonio.

Source: U.S. Signal Corps.

Court-martial trial of members of the 24th Infantry at Fort Sam Houston.

Courtesy Mike Kaliski, Camp Logan World War I drama production,
San Antonio, Texas.

In this plot of Ground
are buried 18 members
of the 24th U.S. Infantry
Hanged near this site for mutiny
at Houston Texas Aug. 23rd 1917

Original burial site at Fort Sam Houston
of members of the 24th Infantry found guilty of mutiny.
Courtesy Mike Kaliski, Camp Logan World War I drama production,
San Antonio, Texas.

Seven

A Hero's Welcome

At barely eight o'clock on the morning of June 29, 1916, the El Paso sun already throbbed unrelentingly on the expectant assemblage at the international bridge to revolutionary Mexico. Unmindful of either the seasonal heat or the long days of anticipation and disappointment, the multitude peered anxiously toward the dusty streets of Ciudad Juarez for the first glimpse of the familiar uniforms and faces. Movie cameramen jostled global correspondents to capture for posterity and a waiting audience the celluloid images of the twenty-three returning troopers of the 10th Cavalry and Mormon scout Lem Spillsbury.[1]

The occasion marked the release by President Venustiano Carranza of the recent captives of Carrizal. Their courageous loss to superior numbers, accompanied by the death of a commanding officer and ten regulars in the Chihuahuan desert, had moved the neighboring countries to the precipice of war. These members of Gen. John J. Pershing's expeditionary force in pursuit of Pancho Villa had drawn the assignment of scouting Villa Ahumada to evaluate a military contingent possibly threatening the American line of communication to the border. The soldiers, commanded by Capt. Charles Boyd, had failed to reach the location due to a confrontation with a Mexican unit outside Carrizal. In a confusing encounter marked by attempted negotiation, possible deception, and Boyd's determination to push through the opposition, the sides exchanged deadly fire.[2]

The Americans had performed gallantly in the losing effort. According to an officer, "For forty-five minutes the men fought, joking among themselves all the while, even though they realized we had been trapped and had little chance of getting out alive." Striving to stem outraged public opinion without expanding military intervention, President Woodrow Wilson demanded the immediate release of the prisoners.[3]

Now, eight days after the battle, the soldiers disembarked from the train carrying them to the border. A series of cheers went up from the left bank as a military escort provided by Gen. George Bell, Jr., accompanied the men from the international boundary. Despite appearing "worn and drawn from their experience," the black heroes marched smartly in pairs. One member, unidentified by the press, undoubtedly spoke for the group when he smiled broadly to reporters, "We are glad to be back."[4]

The warm reception, augmented by the solemn funeral of seven cavalrymen at El Paso, belied the tension-ridden relationship between white Texas communities and black garrisons. Only two months prior to the homage paid the blacks at the Pass of the North, a dismally familiar racial incident had shaken Del Rio, four hundred miles down the Rio Grande. Ironically, the ensuing controversy had hastened the transfer of the 24th Infantry to the combat zone in northern Mexico, where it joined forces with the heralded 10th Cavalry, whose martyrs evoked a national outpouring of grief.[5]

The brief appearance of the 24th Infantry in Texas during 1916 signaled the unit's first presence in the state in thirty-six years. The regiment initially arrived in 1869 and garrisoned virtually every Texas military post before its departure in 1880. Perhaps sharing in less acclaim than its cavalry counterparts, it nevertheless participated in the climactic campaigns that chased the durable Apache renegade Victorio into Mexico and won the Red River War. Components of the 24th witnessed considerable action in the Del Rio area in the 1870s, where raids and rustling constantly disrupted the peace. On one occasion Lt. John L. Bullis and troops from Fort Clark overtook a band of Indians at Dolan Falls on the Devil River, killing several and driving the remainder into the surrounding hills and canyons. Like the other black regiments, the 24th migrated to the Far West after pacifying the Plains Indians in the grueling Texas campaigns.[6]

Belated recognition of regimental valor came in full measure during the Spanish-American War. A supporting unit in the advance up San Juan Hill, the African-American infantrymen filled gaps in the line and charged the block house with three other regiments, contributing significantly to the American victory. Sustaining the loss of two officers and ten enlisted men and the wounding of six officers and sixty-seven enlisted men, the 24th exchanged gunfire the rest of the day and sent a detachment of sharpshooters to bolster an artillery offensive. The American commander awarded the regiment the honor of occupying Fort San Juan after the surrender of the Spanish forces.[7]

It earned additional accolades in the aftermath of the fighting. Attached to the Medical Department, the soldiers comforted the ill at Siboney and volunteered for service at a yellow fever pesthouse. The disease ravaged the staff and attendants, grimly disproving the theory of black immunity to the plague. An officer expressed his admiration for their labor: "In the forty days not even a murmur was heard from a soldier of the Twenty-fourth Infantry. . . . they bore all bravely and patiently, faithfully doing what they could, showing in these colored soldiers unexpected qualities of the highest order."[8]

Unfortunately, not even their departure from Cuba ended the soldiers' trials. Outwardly healthy officers and men, evidently harboring the illness in their systems, sickened at Montauk Point, New York, with "several dying" at the sanitized and modern facility. After a welcome respite in Montana, the regiment joined the fray against the Filipino rebels. In the first three years of duty that stretched intermittently into 1915, the unit suffered 11 combat deaths, 22 casualties, 4 missing in action, 16 captured, and 109 deaths from diseases.[9]

Often the men challenged unfavorable odds in the tropical setting. Near Santa Ana four hundred insurgents attacked K Company, which repelled them "with heavy loss . . . until it was too dark to see to shoot." In another instance villagers displaying a neutral flag suddenly opened fire on an expedition, forcing the soldiers to swim across a river to safety. Although most reached the sanctuary of the opposite bank, they lost all their weapons to the swift current, which also claimed an H Company corporal. He drowned "not asking help lest it should prevent the crossing of the rest."[10]

The years of jungle warfare finally passed with relocation of the regiment to Fort D. A. Russell, Wyoming, in early 1916. But the machinations of another insurgency shattered the prospect of routine duty and propelled the unit into another revolutionary environment. On March 9 Mexican rebel Pancho Villa, chafing at his deteriorating fortunes and a perceived bias of President Wilson, assaulted Columbus, New Mexico. The raiders took eighteen American lives and burned the town beyond recognition. The following day the president ordered General Pershing and six thousand regulars across the international boundary to punish Villa. This dramatic action placed the 10th Cavalry in a chain of circumstances that produced the tragedy at Carrizal and positioned components of the 24th Infantry along the Texas-Mexican border.[11]

The War Department separated the 24th Infantry into two groups, directing them to New Mexico and Texas in late March. Headquarters of the 2nd and 3rd Battalions, Machine Gun and Supply Companies, and Companies E, F, G, H, I, K, L, and M, with detachments of Sanitary troops and Quartermaster Corps, reached Camp Furlong, New Mexico, on March 26. Most of the components rendezvoused with the Pershing expedition on subsequent days. Meanwhile, head-quarters of the 1st Battalion and Companies A, B, C, and D, with detachments of Sanitary troops and Quartermaster Corps, proceeded by rail to the Southern Department at San Antonio. From that point Company A detrained at Marfa, March 26; Company D reached Fabens on March 25; and headquarters and Companies B and C arrived at Del Rio, 8 A.M., March 26.[12]

Del Rio, destination of the largest contingent of the Texas-bound unit, considered itself a city on the move. Of more recent origin than the border towns on the Escandon tract, the area remained neglected until late in the colonial era. Reportedly, missionaries erected a short-lived outpost at San Felipe Creek in 1808, and two Americans estab-lished an ill-fated settlement in 1834. Fifteen years later, a U.S. military road from San Antonio penetrated the region, facilitating immigration. Still, growth remained slow despite the natural advantages of a pure water supply and terrain conducive to sheep, goat, and cattle ranch-ing. The 1880 census counted only fifty souls at the location on the Rio Grande.[13]

As elsewhere, the iron horse brought permanency and prosperity to the struggling village. The Southern Pacific completed its survey through the area in 1881 en route to meeting the Texas & Pacific at Sierra Blanca, linking Del Rio with rail centers of the state and na-tion. Its bridge spanning the Pecos River reputedly was the fourth highest in the world. The town's first newspaper started its presses in time to proclaim the selection of Del Rio as the seat of newly orga-nized Val Verde County in 1885. Irrigation canals carried water from the springs to the valley below, and the population leaped to nearly two thousand by the end of the decade.[14]

By 1910, the date of the most recent census before the return of the 24th Infantry, Del Rio saw itself as a young giant. The county population stood at 8,613, with Del Rio providing about half the count. Males outnumbered females by a thousand, Hispanics greatly outnumbered Anglos, and both ethnic groups dwarfed the county's 153 blacks. Numbers had increased substantially over the slightly more than five thousand residents enumerated in 1910. Negroes marked the exception, maintaining a virtually constant population that reduced their percentage from 3 to 1.8 in the ten-year interim.

Val Verde County, comprising over three thousand square miles of rolling plains and broken surface, ranked third largest in the state geographically.[15]

Del Rio's business sector lauded "the progressive spirit," which it claimed had transformed the city. The secretary of the recently founded Commercial Club proclaimed Val Verde "the banner sheep county of Texas" and only second in mohair production. The river town acted as the division point on the Southern Pacific system between San Antonio and El Paso "and by far the most important city between these cities." As evidence, the monthly railroad payroll approached $40,000. Customs and immigration officials, a district court, and a weather bureau emphasized governmental interest in the location and assured ongoing federal expenditures. A recent congressional appropriation of $90,000 cleared the way for construction of a new government complex. Fine schools, churches, fraternal organizations, and "a bountiful and inexhaustible" labor supply of Mexicans "at wages that are not prohibitive" promised further business development. Accelerated residential construction and expanded passenger and freight traffic fueled optimism.[16]

The Commercial Club publicity overlooked or understated the darker side of the picture. Del Rio housed little or no manufacturing, and nonirrigated expanses held little prospect for commercial agriculture. The presence of a Mexican consulate, which "fostered and advanced the relations of the two neighboring countries," failed to eradicate ancient concerns over property claims, banditry, and insurrections. The overthrow of Porfirio Díaz exacerbated conditions. The "exceptionally gratifying" wages actually identified a massive underclass, replete with frustration and resentment. Acknowledging the Hispanics' "own communities [and] own amusements" euphemized their social and economic isolation from the Anglo minority. An intended reassuring note, "The town has very few negroes," scarcely trumpeted a welcome to incoming black troops.[17]

By 1916 the Mexican Revolution had provoked a feeling of chaos at Del Rio and other border points. The state had augmented the Ranger force at the border in 1911; the War Department shipped the white 14th Cavalry to the old camp ground outside Del Rio in 1913. Villa's attack on Columbus escalated fear of raids all along the left bank. When shots rang out at the Southern Pacific Pecos High Bridge, alarmed residents summoned the military reinforcement from Del Rio, nearly fifty miles downriver. An investigation disclosed that a sentry had fired without effect on four Mexicans who disobeyed his order to halt. Reassured only marginally, the populace pressed Washington for more protection.[18]

A complex set of factors weighed on Del Rio's reaction to the arrival of the 24th Infantry. Instinct for community survival suggested appreciation for the defenders, regardless of color. The existence of a federal contingency of customs and immigration officers had familiarized the citizenry with an arm of government and introduced civil servants theoretically less wary of the military and blacks. The railroad accelerated the intrusion of the outside world and demonstrated advantages in altering the status quo. The small but energetic business sector appeared amenable to changing fortunes and aware of the pecuniary benefits of garrisons. Finally, although Del Rio had until recent years separated from its earlier military tradition, many residents could remember that symbiotic relationship.[19]

Less favorable conditions paralleled those at Laredo and Rio Grande City. Hispanics suffered persecution along with discrimination, while often experiencing racial pride in the Revolution. Some directed this fear, anger, and envy against the uniformed black. Anglos nurtured southern customs, prized their leadership role, and feared a recurrence of the Brownsville affray. Texas Rangers, now posted at Del Rio, continued to eye black soldiers critically. After years of proving their mettle in Philippine combat, the 24th infantrymen could muster little patience for the racial barriers that confronted them in the Southwest Texas town.[20]

The companies of the 1st Battalion assumed occupation of Camp Del Rio unobtrusively. The regimental commander described their first days as "perform[ing] the usual field duties. . . ." The units "remained on border duty at Del Rio, Texas" until mid-April, when "pursuant to telegraphic instructions" they "proceeded, by rail, to Fort Bliss, Texas."[21]

Racial exclusion, a contributing influence on every civilian-black military conflict in the state, sparked a fatal shooting at Del Rio on April 8. The series of events paralleled those of Texarkana, but with grimmer results. Some Saturday night revelers attempted to enter the Greentop, a house of prostitution. Denied entrance, the soldiers left but returned to assault the building with missiles or bullets. The commotion and the plea of a fleeing prostitute summoned the local constabulary and two Texas Rangers. In a confusing sequence, Ranger W. L. Barler shot and killed Pvt. John Wade of Company C, allegedly resisting arrest.[22]

Wire services, with minor variations in description, rushed the story to the front pages. Due to the prominence of the military during the Mexican crisis, even the distant *New York Times* devoted coverage. Dailies accorded the incident compelling headlines. The *Houston Post* introduced the article: "Negro Infantrymen Rioted—One Killed"; the *San Antonio Express:* "Negro Soldier Dead At Ranger's Hand in Race Riot At Del Rio"; the *Dallas Morning* News: "Negro Soldiers And Texas Officers Clash"; the *El Paso Herald:* "Soldiers Shot To Show Wrath"; the *El Paso Times:* "Negro Troops In Riot At Del Rio"; and less provocatively, the *New York Times:* "Soldier Shot Dead In Row Over Arrest." In racially haunted Texas, captions depicting black race riots, particularly after Brownsville, packed powerful emotional content.[23]

The reports, based on nonmilitary testimony, generally substantiated the substance of the headlines, minus the stark tone. In a rather measured narrative, the Associated Press referred to a "disturbance in a house in the restricted district," rather than a riot. By its account sixteen black soldiers were turned away from every establishment in the red light district. About 9 P.M. the management of one house refused the protesting band and telephoned authorities. By the time Sheriff John Almond and Rangers Barler and Delbert Timberlake responded, the frustrated soldiers had abandoned the vicinity. About two hours later they returned armed, hurling rocks and firing rounds at the brothels. As the frightened prostitutes took refuge in the courthouse, the lawmen rushed back to the scene and arrested three men. Reportedly, while the officers escorted the prisoners to camp, Wade seized Barler from behind. In the struggle the Ranger fired "a chance shot over his shoulder," striking the soldier mortally in the neck.[24]

In the confused aftermath, some soldiers fled and others fired indiscriminately as many as a hundred rounds without result. Peace officers hauled a number of the men to Camp Del Rio pending investigation, at which time several renegades encountered and disarmed Deputy Sheriff Japinto Vann. Deciding not to harm the Hispanic lawman, the soldiers released him and hurried away.[25]

The community placed the blame for Private Wade's death squarely on the victim and the actions of his comrades. A coroner's jury ruled that Ranger Barler "act[ed] in self defense and in the discharge of his duty." Townsmen insisted that the soldiers had fired all the shots heard during the fracas, since residents owned fewer than a dozen Springfield rifles and all were accounted for. Residents seethed with "extreme indignation" toward the infantrymen as local officials barraged the War Department with demands to remove the black troops.[26]

When even the army refused to defend the soldiers, indicating a harsher attitude since Brownsville, curious inconsistencies in the press reports escaped examination. The Associated Press offered two versions of Wade's death in the same story. In one account "Wade attacked Ranger Barler from behind and as *both went to the ground* [italics added] the ranger drew his pistol, taking a chance shot over his shoulder . . . killing him almost instantly." In another segment "Wade jumped on Ranger Barler, *pressing him to the ground and clubbing him on the head with the butt of his revolver* [italics added]. Lying on his back, Barler drew his pistol and fired over his shoulder, killing him instantly." Neither version quoted a source, explained how the private suddenly acquired a gun, or described Sheriff Almond's actions during the fight.[27]

Other press reports divided on or modified the accounts. The International News Service employed the instant reaction description. A special telegram to the San Antonio *Express* concurred. The *New York Times,* however, recounted Wade beating Barler with "a revolver," not necessarily his own. An unidentified correspondent for the *El Paso Herald* had Barler on his face while receiving the pummeling that ended with a fortuitous shot.[28]

Reports also differed on the verbal exchange between the soldiers who accosted Deputy Sheriff Vann. The Associated Press and *New York Times* described the exchange. "Shall we kill him?" "No, we are only after the white folks." The International News Service presented a sharper response to the query: "No, but we'll get all the whites." The special telegram to the *San Antonio Express* carried additional dialogue: "We will get every white man in this town before we get through." Only one account quoted Vann as personally observing soldiers shooting.[29]

While extensive, the coverage lacked balance. None of the reports indicated an attempt to interview any of the prisoners or to give the soldiers' version. No article mentioned racial barriers imposed by the community or cited the unit's combat record in Cuba and the Philippines. One incorrectly identified the regiment with the Brownsville raid.[30]

Unreported, a review of the events for the commanding officer of Camp Del Rio presented certain particulars in quite different terms. First Lt. Alexander W. Chilton, a twenty-nine-year-old Minnesotan and graduate of the state university, initially heard of the fracas between 10:30 and 10:45 P.M., April 8. Maj. William Newman awakened him with the news that a soldier had been shot near or in the Greentop. The commander directed Chilton to proceed immediately to the site with an armed company guard. While the lieutenant awaited the forming of the guard, Privates Farreira and Wilson ran into the post exclaiming that Private Wade had been shot to death. Wilson appeared in "a state of hysteria" and Farreira had an abrasion on his arm, which the private described as a bullet wound but which Chilton attributed to an accidental self-injury. The junior officer placed sentinels around the camp and accompanied a lieutenant of the 19th Infantry and an eight-man detail to the brothel.[31]

Reaching the restricted district within minutes by automobile, Chilton positioned a guard at each corner of the Greentop to prevent anyone from leaving. He then heard ten to twelve indistinct shots from a westerly direction, but could not judge their caliber or location. Medical Corps Capt. J. A. Wilson joined him shortly and the two men examined the body, still lying in the street. Blood-stained clothing prevented scrutiny of the lesions, but Chilton later observed Wade at the morgue and counted an array of wounds: "One in the right groin, one in the left side of the belly below the line of the navel, one between the shoulder blades and one in the left arm near the elbow." The officer failed to note any neck wound, the supposed cause of death.[32]

A second volley of shots summoned Chilton from the street to the Greentop. The fusillade apparently emanated either from the ravine in front of the house or the high ground at the rear. The lieutenant recorded about fifteen shots around 11:15 P.M. which he identified as projectiles from a Springfield service rifle. All passed high, incurring no damage. At this point Sheriff Almond appeared, evacuated the women, and left requesting Chilton to retain a guard at the site. The latter telephoned the officer of the day to check weapons at the camp. Examining the rifles of his own patrol, Chilton satisfied himself that no member of the detail had participated in the firing. Only a few minutes later a third round of shots broke the stillness, this burst containing about five reports. Chilton retired to the post after an ambulance removed the body and reached camp at midnight. He again inspected the weapons of the guardsmen, finding the rifles still unfired.[33]

Some of the mystery surrounding the rifle fire unraveled when post guards brought in two enlisted men about 12:30 A.M., weapons and belts in tow. Privates Gay and Wilson acknowledged going into town with Wade and first learning of his death. The men rushed back to camp, armed themselves, and left independently of Chilton's detail.

They claimed to believe that the lieutenant had turned out the entire company. When near the Greentop, they heard shots, possibly from an earlier patrol, which they thought were directed at them. The soldiers returned twenty-four rounds, according to a check of expended ammunition. They further admitted confronting "a Mexican with a gun," evidently Vann, who had shot at them. They reported losing his confiscated revolver but handed over twenty-five bullets to Chilton.[34]

Lieutenant Chilton calculated that six men had been in Wade's party. All returned to the post after the shooting and remained there, except for Gay and Wilson. Six others missed the midnight inspection, two absent with passes, three on an unauthorized auto trip to Brackettville, and one absent with a friend from a cavalry detachment, without permission. All the men guilty of breaking regulations received company punishment. For their more serious transgressions, Privates Gay and Wilson faced a general court-martial, although Chilton sympathized with the extreme mental anxiety of the men at the time. "Neither made any attempt to conceal any of the facts concerned with their absences from camp," the officer commented, "and neither had any idea of the enormity of his offense."[35]

Chilton's report to the post commander indirectly clarified some of the issues, but raised other questions. The confessions of Gay and Wilson resolved the identity of the soldiers who disarmed Deputy Sheriff Vann and accounted for most of the shots heard by Chilton outside the Greentop. The several weapons checks ruled out significant participation in the firing by other soldiers. Considering the news reports of a hundred rounds of ammunition expended, a cautious observer might question either that number or the denial of citizen involvement. The alleged fusillade against the brothel, which turned out the peace officers, remains unexplained. Without the urgency that moved Ranger Barler to employ the most drastic form of restraint on his prisoner, the circumstances surrounding Wade's death take on more puzzling dimensions.[36]

The condition of Wade's body when examined by Lieutenant Chilton contradicted the official verdict that Ranger Barler felled the attacking soldier with a fortuitous shot to the neck. The officer discovered four wounds, two in the midsection, one near the elbow, and one in the back, but none in the neck. A scenario more consistent with the bullet wounds would suggest that Barler fired several shots point-blank at Wade and shot him from behind when the wounded soldier staggered away.[37]

Indeed, similar stories involving dubious activities of Texas Rangers circulated in South Texas at the time. The almost mythical organization continued to enjoy a favorable image with much of the white population; the coroner's jury "completely exonerated" Barler, and the press described him as a five-year veteran with a good record. However, a rising chorus condemned "gunpowder justice." Following the Brownsville affray, Capt. Bill McDonald had issued disparaging remarks about the black troops and only reluctantly allowed federal officials to handle the matter. Hispanics alleged that lawbreakers in the custody of Rangers often did not live to face the courts. The year following Wade's shooting, Rangers rounded up twenty-five Mexicans supposedly involved in a raid on Presidio and executed them on the spot.[38]

After a series of complaints from Hispanics, Texas Rep. José Tomás Canales, of Brownsville, persuaded the Texas Legislature to investigate charges in 1919. Accusations of Ranger irregularities included the discharging of pistols in San Diego streets, intimidation of residents, threatening the life of a constable, torturing and brutally beating a prisoner, and demonstrating political favoritism. While the legislative joint committee threw out some of the complaints, it substantiated enough of them to release a stinging pronouncement:

> That as to the charges made for misconduct . . . unwarranted disregard of the rights of citizenship . . . the unnecessary taking of life . . . the entering of private residences, and the taking and confiscating of arms . . . without warrant of law, the improper arrest of parties . . . the confining of them in jail without taking them before a magistrate . . . and the taking of life of prisoners by some members of the force, we find that many of these charges have been established by sufficient and competent evidence.[39]

Pursuant to the committee recommendations, the adjutant general reorganized and reduced the Ranger force. As part of the reform, the state disbanded Company E, commanded at that time by Capt. W. L. Barler.[40]

Incredibly, the army declined to press the issue of Private Wade's death, despite the dubious official explanations. There is no record that Chilton even queried the apparent witnesses about it. The War Department, which had established a penchant for removing black troops when pressured by irate garrison towns, again demonstrated its vulnerability to public demands.[41]

The demands arose immediately and loudly. A group of local officials wired U.S. Rep. John Nance Garner at 3:33 the following morning:

> As a culmination of trouble caused by Negro soldiers threatening and mistreating civilians for about two weeks or since they have been stationed here[,] Ranger killed Negro soldier about two hours ago[.] Negro soldiers surrounded house and fired three broadsides into it[.] No civilians killed yet[.] Very much fear repetition of Brownsville incident and request early urgent action to have Negro soldiers removed.[42]

The receptive Garner, who had insisted on the removal of black garrisons on numerous occasions, asked for the earliest possible appointment with Secretary of War Newton Baker. U.S. Sen. Morris Sheppard joined in the clamor "to prevent a second Brownsville affair." Gen. Frederick Funston, commanding the Southern Department, received the indignant telegram from Del Rioans after newsmen had informed him of the story. A reporter described him as "much concern[ed]" as he contacted Del Rio. "While he would make no statement," according to the correspondent, "his manner indicated that the Negro soldiers would be withdrawn, probably from all points along the Texas border and white soldiers placed on patrol duty there."[43]

The army fulfilled the journalistic prophecy within hours. News releases dated April 10 announced Funston's order to remove the two companies of the 24th from Del Rio, leaving the three companies of the white 19th Infantry in place. Newspapers matched their headlines with their editorial predilections. The *Houston Post,* remote from the scene of violence, stated simply, "Negro Troops At Del Rio Will Be Sent To Mexico," while the *El Paso Herald,* whose audience reacted keenly to military-civilian conflicts, trumpeted: "Del Rio Loses Rioting Negroes." On April 16 Headquarters, First Battalion, and Companies B and C entrained for Fort Bliss, covering the 451 miles in less than a day. On April 20 and 21 the contingents departed for Columbus, New Mexico and Mexican border duty.[44]

The 24th's evacuation of Camp Del Rio signaled the dispatch of the entire regiment to the Mexican boundary or beyond. With the 2nd and 3rd Battalions already assigned to border duty or the Punitive Expedition, Company A departed Marfa and Shafter for Columbus on April 21, while Company D left Fabens for the same destination on the same day. The former Del Rio companies spent the remainder of the year in and around Camp Dublan, Mexico, performing routine duty and protecting the line of communication for Pershing's invading army. Lieutenant Chilton received promotion to captain, en route to an eventual colonelcy, in November. There were no reported racial incidents.[45]

The unchallenged shooting of Pvt. John Wade at Del Rio in 1916 added a deeper element of tragedy to a dismally repetitive situation in early twentieth-century Texas. In times of crisis communities demanded military protection, but remained intransigent on the color line. When black soldiers railed against southern mores, even access to the crudest institutions, the public applauded the harshest punishments against them and insisted on their removal. The transgressors found no solace from any level of public officials or even from the military command, particularly following the Brownsville debacle. With supreme irony Texans could bestow honors on the returning warrior "glad to be back" at El Paso but muster no remorse or compassion for his fallen comrade at Del Rio, already home.

Eight

The Very Best Type of Manhood

As the Great War of 1914 approached American shores, many black leaders hoped that African-American participation in yet another military campaign would insure the social contract so long denied. This aspiration vied with the trepidation at the race-conscious Southern Democratic administration at Washington, heightened white resistance to equal rights, and the failure of the military to protect black soldiers from public abuse. The pessimistic view again prevailed; Congress limited enlistments to the capacities of the four regular regiments and eight guard units open to blacks and sealed off most opportunities for combat.[1]

The War Department's decision to train National Guardsmen at sixteen carefully selected sites across the nation indirectly returned the 24th Infantry to Texas only a year after Ranger Barler's shooting of Private Wade at Del Rio. Immediately receptive to the financial rewards of securing a cantonment with attendant government contracts and payrolls, cities and towns throughout the United States lobbied Washington. Their public relations pitches extolled actual or desired advantages of location, climate, water supply, availability of requisite acreage, and unmatched patriotism.[2]

Waco, Texas, no less than sister cities everywhere, aggressively courted the federal largess. An aspiring municipality of thirty-three thousand residents, 77 percent white, it appeared to satisfy all government mandates. Dubbing itself "the Heart of Texas," the county seat of McLennan County claimed blessed proximity to the geographical and demographic center of the state and boasted topsoil superior to the Nile, Euphrates, and Ganges Valleys. Situated alongside six rail lines and the Brazos River, the city rested on an agricultural and expanding commercial base. Politically, Waco sported a reformist commission-type government as a badge of Progressivism and counted three former governors among its contributors to public service. Of considerable interest to the moralistic secretary of war, Newton D. Baker, the community embraced a vigorous Bible-oriented population and hosted Baylor University, the region's foremost Baptist institution.[3]

An effective Chamber of Commerce, headed by James Marr Penland, carefully orchestrated the city's nomination for a training campsite. The first director of the Waco organization, founded in 1916, Penland originally hailed from North Carolina, moving with his parents to Dallas at age twelve. Penland relocated to Waco in 1908 at thirty years of age and subsequently formed the Waco Drug Company. A pillar of the community and a Baylor trustee, he sensed the business needs of his adopted city and how a military cantonment would contribute. Penland coordinated the securing of enormous tracts of land by enterprising Wacoans when the War Department undertook inspections of viable locations.[4]

Waco, however, possessed a sinister side not advanced by city fathers. Perhaps owing to its frontier legacy, the town early acquired a reputation for lawlessness that earned it the title Six-Shooter Junction. While civic leaders managed to remove some of the tarnished image by the second decade of the century, vestiges of its violent origins remained in the acceptance of brutal lynchings. In a state that ranked third in informal capital punishment, Waco had contributed signally to the shocking statistics. An angry mob in 1905 hanged Seth Majors, a black accused of assaulting a white woman. Even more horrendous, white Wacoans in 1916 hanged, burned, and mutilated the body of black convicted murderer Jesse Washington, a deed that attracted national attention as "the Waco Horror." Even five years later, Curly Hackney, a white man who allegedly molested an eight-year-old girl, would succumb to citizens' vengeance in a morbid example of racial equality.[5]

Although only a small minority of the residents participated in the foul actions and a segment of the community voiced opposition, the culprits enjoyed widespread active or passive support. Reportedly, businessmen and even local officials pressed to the city hall lawn or stood at windows to view the desecration of Washington. The ribald throng included high school students taking advantage of their lunch break and well-attired women, one of whom cheerfully applauded the writhing figure.[6]

Blacks, the principal target of lynchings, remained silent or conciliatory while the press pontificated on the necessary evil of mob justice. After the death of Majors the *Times-Herald* editorialized, "the negro's best friend is the Southern white man," who only punished him with cause. It called on the black to "cry out against" the crimes committed by his race and to "unite with his white fellow citizens" in apprehending the offenders. The newspaper later assessed the East St. Louis riot as impossible of duplication in the South due to the "harmonious relationship between the two races." While demanding the eventual return of African Americans to Africa, the paper observed, "The whites control the government and expect to do so forever." The *Morning News* regretted the lynching of Washington, but expressed greater indignation toward distant press attacks on Waco and the South.[7]

Local judges had not compiled an enviable record of protecting the rights of blacks. Judge Carmack fined a black, Sam Foster, the sum of $100 for criticizing the murder of Majors. Judge Munroe refused to draw his pistol to spare Washington from a courtroom kidnapping and "spill innocent blood for a nigger." Likewise, most church pulpits continued preoccupied with less worldly matters.[8]

Other issues occupied the minds of most Wacoans, however, when army officers visited prospective cantonment locations during the Mexican Revolution. Gen. George Bell called at Waco as early as 1914, airing reservations initially. Believing their political influence inferior to that of competing communities, local businessmen, supported by U.S. Rep. Tom Connally, promised authorities ample terrain and a plentiful water supply and sewage disposal system. After an agonizing delay, news filtered to the Brazos that only Colorado Springs had impressed the War Department more favorably. Finally, on June 11, 1917, the welcome news arrived beneath a seven-column headline. Waco, along with Houston and Fort Worth, had secured the coveted Texas training camps, eliminating competitors Dallas and El Paso.[9]

The banishment of Lucifer scarcely could have occasioned more joy in Waco than the news of the award. Practically every factory whistle sounded, and bedlam reigned. "Staid businessmen of Waco almost embraced one another on the streets," exclaimed a reporter. The object of the jubilation was the governmental leasing of eight thousand acres, later ten thousand, in the northwestern section of the municipality as a mobilization point for as many as three anticipated divisions en route to France or returning from the Mexican border.[10]

The monetary implications of constructing and provisioning an encampment for upwards of twenty-seven thousand men never escaped the business sector. The first news account hinted broadly of "something never dreamed of by the people of Waco." One eager property owner abandoned plans to repair a structure near the site and replaced it at twice the cost of renovation. Lest anyone fail to comprehend the situation, an army captain at San Antonio attested, "I do not know what you have had to do in order to secure this camp, but can say to you that no matter what it was, you were justified. . . . Remember what I say—you have secured a really big thing."[11]

Busily counting up profits, the municipal leaders also urged patriotism and civic responsibility on the beneficiaries. "It is up to every citizen to cooperate to the fullest extent with the Chamber of Commerce and the Young Men's Business League," asserted an editor, "in meeting every demand for a successful army camp." Penland cautioned rental property owners against advancing rates during the impending housing shortage and asked merchants to restrain profit margins. The leadership viewed the cantonment as a harbinger of numerous governmental and commercial relocations, if handled to the satisfaction of the War Department. It correctly read Secretary Baker's impatience with civilian exploiters and resolved to erase any doubts at Washington about the selection of the central Texas city.[12]

Although the quantity and identity of the forthcoming troops eluded Wacoans, the work proceeded smoothly. The War Department designated the cantonment Camp MacArthur, in honor of Gen. Arthur MacArthur. It named Maj. Matthew Hansen as construction quartermaster and Fred A. Jones of Dallas as contractor. Hansen arrived from El Paso, where he had supervised National Guard units along the border. Jones trekked the shorter distance from his North Texas-based operation, which had also drawn the Houston contract for Camp Logan. Envisioned essentially as a tent city, Camp MacArthur nevertheless required permanent and more costly structures for officers' quarters, depots, a post office, and a hospital.[13]

As construction forged ahead, transportation demands imposed additional difficulties. Troop and supply movements necessitated extension of a spur from the nearest rail head, five miles distant. The Cotton Belt line delayed work elsewhere to complete the connection, at a cost of more than $100,000. Expansion of trolley service constituted another hurdle. The Texas Railway Company of Dallas hesitated to augment the system in the face of material shortages, although the Waco franchise reputedly earned higher profits than any other in the network. Amid public discussion of authorizing jitneys to supplement the inadequate streetcars that passed some blocks from the camp, the company's president relented. Eventually, two trolley lines connected the reservation to the city.[14]

Wacoans soon discovered that Washington's demands exceeded mere training facilities. President Woodrow Wilson's crusade for international democracy melded with Secretary Baker's war on vice. The War Department encircled military installations with a sheltered zone to screen out the twin evils of alcohol and prostitution. The regulations forced Waco to forego its long-standing toleration or lose the dearly won prize. At the behest of Gen. James Parker, commanding the Southern Department, Police Chief Guy McNamara ordered all unsavory residents of the "restricted district" to leave town by August 11 or face arrest.[15]

The decree brought a mixed response expected of a community ground in conflicting traditions of religion and license. Many citizens applauded the arrival of Elizabeth M. Speer, an officer of the Women's Anti-Vice Commission. Requested by Baker's department "to see that the men are not subject to crude forms of temptation," she pledged the support of all women's organizations in the state to assure "that the men in camps . . . are well cared for." Like-minded residents introduced a petition to the city council asking that two women be added to the police force to assist in the campaign. The board approved the request one week later. While those opposed to the suppression of the unhallowed tradition seldom publicized their sentiments, an editorial writer expressed some compassion for the uprooted women, stating that most were ill-equipped to lead productive lives. He suggested that a sympathetic civic organization donate a modest sum to facilitate the rehabilitation of the more adaptable females.[16]

Waco proved equal to every task. Within twenty-five days, at a cost of $700,000, Camp MacArthur stood in pristine readiness for guardsmen from Michigan and Wisconsin. The latter state posed a temporary problem when the governor, alarmed at unfounded reports of malaria in the region, attempted to block the movement of his units to Waco. After receiving assurances from both the military and Wacoans of the salubrity of the station, the state executive withdrew his objections. Even money was no object: civic leaders raised over $90,000 for land and improvements in a matter of days. The investment turned a nice profit as the government added an airdrome, dispatched thirty-five thousand military consumers, and pumped almost $2.5 million into the local economy before the end of the war.[17]

The successes belied the fact that the triumphs and relative tranquility of wartime Waco hung in the balance during the tense summer of 1917. Controversy swirled around the unexpected arrival in July of the 1st Battalion of the 24th Infantry to guard the construction site. The regiment carried an enviable record to the Brazos. Uninvolved in the Texas clashes that preceded the Mexican Revolution, various components had earned a good-conduct commendation in New York, a loving cup from Manila, and endorsements for their conduct from San Francisco and Columbus, New Mexico. But the recent public outcry over Del Rio doubtless burdened the thoughts of the citizenry and the military.[18]

The disclosure that the War Department had assigned the regiment to guard construction sites at Waco, Houston, and Deming, New Mexico, reached the Brazos city in a terse wire from General Parker only six days before the battalion arrived from El Paso. The officer followed the missive with a polite but pointed telegram to Chamber President Penland: "As these men are United States soldiers, it may be relied upon that they will be law abiding and it is earnestly hoped that they will be received with a patriotic spirit. . . . It is believed that they will be so received at Waco." The Southern Department commander noted that the tour of duty probably would not exceed six weeks.[19]

The town fathers nervously eyed the dilemma. A racial conflict, which might arise from the mere presence of the black troops, could jeopardize the retention of Camp MacArthur and quash any possibility of a permanent installation. On the other hand, refusal to accept the battalion would surely produce the dreaded result. Accordingly, Penrose wired General Parker the following day that the men would be "received in a patriotic spirit and accorded every consideration."[20]

As a prominent part of the establishment and major opinion-maker, the Waco press played a crucial role in this delicate issue. The two dailies shared the ambivalence of much of the leadership in favoring a white garrison but understanding the necessity of accommodating the military. George C. Robinson, copublisher and editor of the *Times-Herald,* was born in 1857 at Huntsville, Texas. With Chauncey J. Glover he managed a Belton newspaper until 1899, when the two relocated at Waco to take over the evening newspaper. Ephraim S. Fentress, born in 1876 near Parsons, Kansas, compiled extensive journalistic experience before purchasing the *Morning News* with editor Charles E. Marsh in February, 1917. Although neither a native southerner nor a long-time Wacoan, Fentress apparently adapted easily to southern mores, judging from the paper's editorial stance on race. He may have been influenced by the spillover from the Brownsville raid at Fort Reno when he operated the *Oklahoma City News* in 1906. Fentress would later expand his print universe by purchasing Marsh's interest in the *News* and buying the *Times-Herald.*[21]

The local news media deemphasized the military racial issue in its first reports. The organs announced the impending arrival of the six hundred black soldiers without editorial comment or racial identification on July 23. The sparse news competed with the more voluminous coverage of a heated Texas League pennant race, in which the local club seriously contended, continuing accounts of Gov. James E. Ferguson's mounting problems, and customary graphic depiction of racial disturbances around the nation. Several days later, the newspapers posted Penland's assurances of "courteous treatment" of the soldiers. Still omitting references to color, the story included the businessman's plea for "every citizen [to] feel it is his duty to see that Waco's promises to the government are fulfilled." The battalion, it noted, would return to Fort Sam Houston immediately upon completion of the camp.[22]

Not even a reticent press could conceal the pigmentation of the troops indefinitely. On the day of their expected arrival, July 28, a *Times-Herald* headline proclaimed, "Negro Soldiers Assigned to Waco and Houston." The article reiterated the dialogue between Parker and Penland and expressed optimism "that no trouble is anticipated as long as they comport themselves as soldiers should."[23]

Precautionary measures made this belated announcement a bit premature. The troop train from San Antonio reached the station about midnight but retained the warm and weary occupants until past six o'clock the following morning. The delay evidently arose from a conference between Capt. Charles F. Andrews, the battalion commander, Penland, and local law officers, who, despite the lateness of the hour, awaited the battalion at the depot. Andrews drew approval from McNamara for the provost guard to patrol the city nightly and deliver to the commanding officer for punishment any soldier arrested for disturbing the peace.[24]

Aboard the train the soldiers reflected on the orders of conduct repeatedly given them. Before departing Columbus and again en route to Waco, the company commanders instructed:

> It is desired to impress on all of the members of this command, particularly the young soldiers who have but recently joined, the necessity for a prompt, orderly, and cheerful obedience to all municipal laws or ordinances of the City of Waco, Texas. . . . Men must remember constantly that they are soldiers of the Army of the United States and strive constantly to win and hold the confidence and respect of the city . . . to

which they are now entitled so that upon departure for other parts, the citizens may justly say—"they are fine soldiers and a credit to their government and country."[25]

All military personnel reported to camp by noon, those in the loading section remaining last at the depot. Captain Andrews dispatched six provost guards to the Waco police station, as arranged, at 7:00 P.M. He again cited the orders of conduct at retreat, limited passes to 50 percent of those eligible, announced an 11:00 P.M. curfew, which enabled the men to return by midnight, and posted the customary three sentinels. Having completed a long and tiring day, the officer retired to his quarters. He would not rest long.[26]

The ordeal began suddenly. At 11:15 a corporal of Company D awakened Andrews after having sighted a platoon of men armed with rifles moving toward town. Hastily reacting to a clear violation of the curfew and safety regulations, Andrews aroused Lt. Eugene W. Fales, battalion adjutant and a twenty-nine-year-old native New Yorker, with orders to telephone Chief McNamara. Andrews then called every soldier in camp to formation, ordered an arms inspection, and placed guards in every company street to accost anyone entering or leaving the base. At that moment two other army officers, having visited their wives in the city, returned to camp by automobile. Andrews assigned six guards to one of them, Capt. James A. Higgins, who impressed the vehicle and raced to intercept the armed soldiers.[27]

A series of incidents had preceded the soldiers' fateful decision. Earlier that evening numerous pleasure-seeking enlisted men had gravitated to the "colored quarter" of the city, an area replete with red-light district, movie theater, and a disreputable drinking establishment called the Waco Club. As the soldiers filled the sidewalk, passing whites accused them of blocking their path, some uttering disparaging racial remarks. Some infantrymen took umbrage at the segregation laws, as earlier at San Antonio, insisting on service at a drug store that refused blacks and tearing down "White" and "Colored" signs at a restaurant with admonishments not to replace them. City police cleared the Waco Club amid conflicting reports of possible rowdy behavior by the servicemen. The law officers forcibly removed soldiers from the sidewalk in front of the saloon, a policeman breaking a finger while striking Pvt. Willie Jones on the head. Curiously, neither the police nor the provost guards reported the incidents to Captain Andrews. In the face of a gathering white crowd, a few of Jones' comrades whisked him to safety and promised an armed return to the scene.[28]

Company C Commander Higgins, a forty-two-year-old Pennsylvanian with an infantry and signal corps background, failed to spot the wanted men on the road. He proceeded to police headquarters for supplemental information. Told of the recent disturbance at the Waco Club, Higgins formed a security force from police and provost guards and headed in that direction. After a policeman sighted a soldier in an alley, the captain asked that only his military detachment approach the opening. Within ten feet of the passage, the detail drew fire from the far end of the alley. Warning his men to take cover, Higgins eased within a few feet of the aperture and stared into the darkness. A volley erupted from the back of the alley, mercifully wide of the target. As Higgins and his men reassembled on a side street, the shooters escaped into the night. Scouring the area by car with police and additional military personnel, Higgins found no trace of the wanted men.[29]

Meanwhile, other policemen discovered and detained Jones, whose injury had prompted the attempt at retaliation. Although armed himself, Jones at first denied knowledge of the action. Under questioning from Higgins, he submitted names of participants, a smaller number than those who had left camp. The private stated that a policeman had struck him after he protested "having his toes stepped on." Following the incident, several friends decided to "go back and get our rifles." The missing men eventually returned to the base during the early morning hours, with Andrews placing them in custody pending an official inquiry.[30]

The Waco press ended its reserved portrayal of the 24th Infantry by showcasing the events of the previous night in banner headlines. The *Morning News* treated the story in a particularly sensational style and, perhaps because of the early deadline, presented a number of inaccuracies. It depicted the firing from the alley as a shootout between police and twenty-nine rioting soldiers, in which Night Chief Charlie James led the attack against the shooters and Jones took a bullet in the head. The account warned of blacks possibly hiding out in Cameron Park. The evening daily, the *Times-Herald*, adopted a less strident tone by crediting Higgins as the organizer of the search. It also recalled the regiment's fine service record, though the organ felt compelled to display the lead story in multiple headlines and estimated the number of rifle shots at twice the number deduced by the military.[31]

The difference in the reportage may have stemmed from the response of the business community to the morning account. Captain Andrews had appeared at a Rotary Club luncheon later that day to clarify the situation and ask continued public support. He stated that only about a dozen soldiers had failed to report to camp on time and that not more than half that number had participated in the shooting. All were now accounted for and awaiting trial. There had been no organized plan, only a spontaneous action emanating from the crowded condition of the streets, undue haste by some police in clearing the area, and "hotheadedness" on the part of a few soldiers. The battalion commander promised to prevent recurrences by monitoring passes and securing weapons.[32]

The audience not only applauded the remarks of Andrews, but criticized the reporting of the *Morning News*. C. F. Link introduced a resolution "deploring the sensational and in some respects untrue account." Edgar E. Witt considered the motion "not nearly strong enough," urging condemnation of the newspaper. Following an exchange of comments, the group opted to appoint a committee to discuss with the management a more cautious policy of reporting military news. Although editor Marsh defended the coverage to the organization and later in an editorial, the criticism clearly troubled him. He prefaced the editorial with praise for the soldiers' previous record, which "proved them efficient . . . easily amenable to the discipline of their officers."[33]

After a conference with Andrews and McNamara, Penland added his support for public restraint:

> It is not right to hold the entire regiment responsible for what twelve men do. It would be just as improper to hold the people of Waco responsible for what twelve of their citizens do. I would ask that no slurring remarks be made about negro soldiers so long as they conduct themselves in an orderly and peaceful way.[34]

With the community leadership still behind the military, the army opened its investigation. General Parker relayed the known facts to Washington as soon as he learned of the incident. He then dispatched Col. G. O. Cress, inspector-general of the Southern Department, to Waco. The latter arrived at Camp MacArthur on July 30 and met with Captain Andrews, members of his command, and the military committee of the Chamber of Commerce. He completed his labors in two days and filed a report with the Southern Department on August 1.[35]

In contrast to the emotional news releases of the first day, Cress presented a passionless factual account of four typed pages. He described events largely as they appeared in the evening newspaper, noting the clashes on the sidewalk, in commercial establishments, and in the alley. The officer observed that neither the police nor the guards had considered any of the incidents sufficiently important to notify Andrews. Refusing to list police brutality, cited by the enlisted men, as provocation, Cress acknowledged, "Waco has its contingent of disreputable white characters whose actions cannot always be controlled, and if any future trouble occurs it will be in result of an act on their part." Recruits of only a few months service participated in the shooting, the older men "not in the least in sympathy" with their conduct. Agreeing with Andrew that no conspiracy lay behind the incident, the inspector general emphasized the absence of casualties.[36]

The departmental report commended the actions of the civilian and military authorities. The civic leaders had "made a conscious effort, which they are still continuing, to see to it that the colored soldiers are treated with all the consideration, kindness, and courtesy that is due them." The police cooperated with the army in apprehending the wanted men, the chief providing an automobile to Higgins for transportation back to camp. Addressing criticism that Andrews had neglected assigning an army officer to supervise the soldiers on pass, Cress judged sufficient his installation of a telephone line to police headquarters, his agreement with the police chief, and the detailing of provost guards to town. He praised the battalion commander for securing the arrest and identification of the wanted men within hours. The inspector attributed the apparent passivity of the military police in allowing soldiers to obstruct the sidewalk to their absence of weapons and identifying insignia.[37]

The colonel concluded that all sides had taken reasonable precautions, that no recurrence should be expected, and that no further action beyond the impending trial of the suspects was necessary. By declining to question the obvious lack of communication between the police and the camp, despite the professed accord between McNamara and Andrews, Cress's report demonstrated the army's resolve to smooth over the racial issue until the completion of the 24th's assignment.[38]

While awaiting the conclusion of the courts-martial, not published until September, the city and the military sought to maintain tranquility in the battalion's last days. General Parker ordered company commanders to sign passes of all men absent from camp, to conduct three roll calls daily, and to familiarize themselves with municipal regulations. The commander of the Southern Department also prohibited more than three soldiers from gathering on city streets. The city, in turn, moved against white malcontents who threatened to incite a racial crisis. Within a week of the shooting incident, police arrested a man for disturbing the peace and insulting a black infantryman. Assistant Chief James declared the slur a serious offense in light of the potential for injury. Now clearly determined to cooperate with the military, he reminded Wacoans that soldiers carried strict orders to report any transgressions against them to the police, who pledged to arrest the instigators. Subsequently, police detained an individual who threatened a detachment of black soldiers guarding the payroll at a local bank.[39]

The strengthened accord contributed to a tighter rein on the military off post. A policeman and provost guardsmen arrested two soldiers who interfered with the civil detention of a black woman. The guards returned the men to the base, where the company commander dispensed punishment. When three servicemen missed the departing troop train in late August, lawmen puzzled over whether to place them in the charge of the new company commander or deliver them to departmental headquarters.[40]

Meanwhile, formal public appearances of the 1st Battalion improved its tarnished image. With Wacoans lining the field on all sides, the unit staged an evening parade as the New Hope Sunday School Band performed. Prominent local blacks honored the regiment with a banquet under the auspices of St. Paul A.M.E. Church. Guests included Mayor John Dollins, a native Kentuckian and former Waco police chief. The Waco Navigators reserved a section of the bleachers, where for twenty-five cents admission the men could follow the pennant chase, ultimately a losing effort. Other business enterprises also sought to share in the $25,000 payday at Camp MacArthur.[41]

Beyond public view the military continued its judicial deliberations. Captain Andrews named a three-man board, finally consisting of captains Higgins, Joseph E. Barzynski, and recently promoted Fales, to investigate the shooting fray. The panel took testimony from July 31 through August 6, announcing its findings the following day: Considering themselves "mistreated by civilians and police in Waco," twelve soldiers had returned to camp, obtained their rifles and ammunition belts, and "went to town." The rebellious soldiers, identified by testimony and arrests were: Pvts. James Williams, Medical Department; Willie J. Jones, Company C; Walter Lusk, Company C; Howard Hood, Company A; James H. Johnson, Company A; Willie Lewis, Company C; Luther Briggs, Company D; James B. Lindsey, Company D; James E. Mitchell, Company D; Robert Davis, Company

C; Willie Fletcher, Company B; and Henry Mays, Company B. When they arrived at a point about three hundred yards from camp, five of the men—Williams, Fletcher, Lindsey, Davis, and Mays—decided to return to quarters. The remaining seven, minus Jones, who struck out on his own and wound up in police custody, continued their march. The board cited Briggs, Hood, Johnson, Lewis, Lusk, and Mitchell as the armed men in the alley who fired "about twenty-five rounds" at Captain Higgins and his detail. Although evidently "not aware . . . that they were firing on members of the 24th infantry," the accused men faced trial by general court-martial.[42]

The six defendants shared similar backgrounds. In common with the larger number who planned an attack on Waco police and civilians, all were recent recruits and most hailed from the South. Military investigators had emphasized these factors in their first reports, insisting that only inexperienced, insufficiently trained soldiers participated in the rebellion. This observation, of course, placed the long-term regulars in a better light. The southern origins assumed a familiarity with segregation such as existed at Waco; youth and inexperience supposedly deluded them into thinking that such restrictions would not apply to uniformed fighting men.[43]

Other similarities existed, among them limited education and occasional civilian scrapes with the law, traits not uncommon in army recruits. An exception to the southern majority, Mitchell was born in Pennsylvania in 1895. He quit school in the tenth grade and worked in a grocery store and laundry. Reportedly a beer drinker "from early childhood," the youth won acquittal on a charge of obtaining money under false pretenses. He joined the army in April, 1917, only three months before the Waco incident. Lewis, born in Kentucky in 1900, never attended school. He entered the work force at age nine as a house servant. Employers praised his trustworthiness and capabilities, but also noted an "ungovernable temper when aroused." He had no arrest record from civilian life and described himself as a total abstainer.[44]

Most attention focused on Private Briggs, the only defendant to plead not guilty at trial and the man some witnesses identified as the rebel leader. Born in Virginia in 1893, he dropped out of school in the eighth grade. Having worked as a clerk, cook, and molder, Briggs earned a good work record and evidently drank only moderately. He was arrested on one occasion for stealing a ring and on another for gambling before volunteering for the army in April, 1917.[45]

By command of General Parker the court-martial convened at

Camp MacArthur on August 21 with Capt. Edward H. Andres as president and Captain Fales as judge advocate. Capts. Sanford W. French, Higgins, Barzynski, and Alex E. Harrison and 2nd Lts. Alexander J. Levie, Oliver Graves, and Paul J. Dowling constituted the court detail. Higgins and Barzynski received exemption from service on the grounds they had formed an opinion as members of the board of inquiry. The army jointly arraigned the accused:

> CHARGE: Violation of the 93d Article of War.
> SPECIFICATION: In that [all defendants named] . . . jointly and in pursuance of a common intent, did at Waco, Texas, on or about the 29th day of July 1917 with intent to commit a felony, viz: murder, feloniously assault Captain James A. Higgins and detachment 24th infantry, by shooting at them with service rifles.
> C. F. Andrews
> Captain 24th Infantry[46]

Of the accused, Johnson, Hood, Lusk, Lewis, and Mitchell pleaded guilty to the specification and the charge. Briggs alone pleaded not guilty to each. The president explained the gravity of the pleas of guilty to the five defendants: "You are hereby advised that the punishment that the court may adjudge each of you for the offense . . . is within the discretion of the court, there being no limit in time of war." They allowed their pleas to stand, leaving the judgment on Private Briggs the major issue before the tribunal.[47]

Testimony of witnesses and apparent opportunity congealed into a formidable case against Briggs despite his denial and the presentation of a defense witness. Three of the accused, Hood, Mitchell, and Lewis, placed him at the scene during the shooting. Hood had identified Briggs during the investigation as the leader: "Private Briggs gave the command for firing, and was in charge. . . . [He] said on the way back to town that he knew where the people were who had mistreated the soldiers and would lead the way to them." Mitchell testified that Briggs had threatened Hood "for telling about the men who did the firing" and suggested shooting two soldiers who turned back from the march. Lewis stated that he was "positive that Briggs was there." Various witnesses at the inquiry, however, either could remember none of the men who went to town or failed to recall Briggs's presence. Private Lindsey had considered the unarraigned Williams the leader but identified Briggs as a participant and issuer of threats against "anyone who might tell on him about the shooting." At the trial Lindsey's vacillating testimony earned him a rebuke from the court for risking perjury.[48]

Briggs, testifying in his behalf, categorically denied any complicity in the plan or the shooting. He swore that he had left camp after retreat, between 6:30 and 7:30 P.M., and attended a movie in town. He then met a Miss Ural Blair, whom he invited to church. Following the service, Briggs visited her house until about 11:15. When he started for camp some whites, including a policeman, began taunting him with racial remarks. One of them grabbed at Briggs, who struck him and fled. Wandering aimlessly after evading his pursuers, the accused returned to camp hours later. The woman corroborated his story until the time that Briggs left for camp, but Captain Fales testified to finding a rifle and ammunition belt outside the base where Hood said Briggs had left them before returning to the post. A check indicated that the equipment belonged to a private who had remained in quarters that evening.[49]

The prosecution and defense lawyers submitted only brief closing arguments. The latter termed Briggs's account "entirely probable and possible" and emphasized Miss Blair's corroboration. The prosecution reminded the judges that five of the men had acknowledged their guilt and that four witnesses, counting the ambivalent Lindsey, had placed Briggs in the alley at the time of the shooting.[50]

Following short personal appeals for leniency, the five admitted perpetrators received identical sentences. Each received dishonorable discharges, forfeiture of all pay and allowances during incarceration, and a sentence of five years at hard labor. Briggs, judged guilty, received the same penalty with the exception of a ten-year term at hard labor. Briggs's portion of the trial subsequently underwent scrutiny and adjustment, with the War Department reducing his term to five years as the Judge Advocate General concluded that Briggs's attorney "did nothing for his client." Still, authorities declined to recommend transfer of any of the prisoners from Fort Leavenworth, Kansas, to a less harsh environment. A report on Briggs noted, "Has a bad record in U.S. Penitentiary."[51]

Only two days later, news of an alleged mutiny of the 24th Infantry at Houston burst like a shell over Waco. The night of violence, August 23, 1917, sprang from a set of circumstances frighteningly similar to that at Waco, but left at least twenty persons dead or dying in the streets. The Camp Logan story and the departure of the 1st Battalion combined to arouse the previously reserved *Times-Herald*. On August 25, the date of the unit's withdrawal from the Brazos, the newspaper opined in its customary restrained tone, "the government . . . [should] take steps to prevent a recurrence of the happenings in that city and this. In each case only a few of the negroes were concerned in the rioting, but innocent people suffered." The following day, with the black soldiers safely away and white National Guardsmen occupying the completed Camp MacArthur, the organ's tenor changed. It now suggested the removal of all black troops to the North, "where they are nearer social equality than here." The editorialist observed the "same spirit" of vengeance wreaking havoc at Brownsville, Waco, and Houston against racial separation. Only the closer proximity of the Waco camp to town and the prompter response of military officers to complaints from the police department saved their community from the fate at Houston.[52]

Other factors than those cited by the writer spared "the Brazos community." Indeed, there was no police communication to Captain Andrews on the evening of the clash. "The closer proximity" failed to prevent the rebellious soldiers from eluding provost guards until they had reached the alley way, where only bad marksmanship prevented shooting deaths. The fragile accord between the police and the camp, which nearly unraveled during the sidewalk confrontations and the clearing of the Waco Club, ultimately saved the day. Chief McNamara's acceptance of Andrews's request to enter the alleyway with only military personnel precluded a shootout between police and soldiers that could have wrought the direst consequences. The unilateral police actions prior to the shooting incident and the passivity of the provost guards remained enigmatic throughout the judicial proceedings. Critical civilians accused the guards of overly sympathizing with the soldiers. Enlisted men thought the police too responsive. The guardsmen's deference to civil authority offers a plausible explanation. The police chief assigned the guards to specific beats and directed their movements. The mere presence of white armed officers in a southern town arguably intimidated the disciplined military police. The local lawmen demonstrated no desire to share their traditional peacekeeping function with black guardsmen, regardless of any understanding with the base commander. McNamara showed more faith than his men in the accord by allowing Andrews his rein at the crucial moment.[53]

The near catastrophe buttressed the determination of the civilian and military communities to cooperate for the duration of the battalion's tenure at Waco. The remaining weeks witnessed the degree of mutual restraint desired by civilian and military leaders from the outset. In the end, the dream of Waco's business community materialized handsomely, if not permanently. The Brazos city survived the month-long ordeal of garrisoning the 1st Battalion to greet the keenly awaited new residents of Camp MacArthur. Extolling the virtues of the white Michigan and Wisconsin guardsmen, entering on a seemingly endless round of banquets, dances, and church socials en route to the Marne, a proud citizen exclaimed. "the[se] men are the very best type of manhood."[54]

Nine

Hell Has Broken Loose

Houston, the nation's forty-fifth largest city, reacted no less enthusiastically than its smaller rival Waco to the award of a National Guard cantonment. A community on the make since its establishment by sibling land speculators in 1836, the town had steadily grown despite an uninviting location, the loss of the capital to Austin, and the competition from a true deep-water port, Galveston. A rapid succession of events at the turn of the century placed it firmly in the fast lane: a storm that knocked Galveston from its pilings; an unprecedented gusher at Beaumont that moved oil companies down the railroad tracks to Houston; and the opening of a twenty-five foot ship channel at Buffalo Bayou, finally confirming the Allen Brothers' fantasies of international commerce.[1]

The most recent official census, 1910, counted 78,800 souls at the Bayou City, a dramatic increase of over 75 percent from 1900, on the way to a population of 138,276 by 1920. In the words of a local businessman: "The discovery of oil, the opening of the ship channel, and the expansion of markets for gasoline and lubricants combined to give Houston an economic momentum that continued to accelerate."[2]

The gleam in the eyes of the business community glowed from the federal lease of seventy-six hundred acres of woodlands as one of sixteen training sites for preparing American combatants for duty in the Great War. Designated Camp Logan for Mexican and Civil War veteran Maj. John A. Logan, the area lay about five miles west of the city in rural Harris County. Built at a cost of $1,962,000, the camp eventually housed fifteen hundred buildings for the 33rd Division, nestled between uncut oak trees, which permitted maximum protection from the summer sun and winter winds.[3]

The three daily newspapers, in accepted booster fashion, treated their readership to a heady diet of lucrative facts and figures on the progress of construction throughout the summer of 1917. The largest, the evening *Chronicle,* reported in July a force of 179 men with 116 mules "making the dirt fly," improving the city road to the camp. The following day saw two hundred men awaiting 5 million feet of lumber and four carloads of wire on order. The *Morning Post* assured the War Department that the local Chamber of Commerce would "fully redeem the pledge" to treat the anticipated Illinois unit with utmost fairness in their purchases. The evening *Press,* the smallest, youngest, and most unconventional journal, showed unaccustomed racial restraint in this instance. On July 23 it stated simply, "The troopers ordered here to serve as guards are negroes, from the 24th U.S. Infantry, now stationed at Columbus, New Mexico." The terse comment introduced the 3rd Battalion, which like the 1st at Waco drew the assignment of protecting the construction site until late August.[4]

The battalion would augment the state's largest African-American community. Numbering in excess of fifty-four thousand in the 1910 census, blacks comprised 30.4 percent of the population, some residing near the cantonment site. Outwardly, they appeared to enjoy a rare status among southern counterparts. Houston, having recorded no lynchings, enjoyed a perhaps unexamined reputation for racial tolerance. But it also sported the southern label of "the Magnolia City" and adhered to strict racial segregation. Indeed, the vibrant economic and social life of the minority community functioned within clearly established boundaries. In response to their exclusion from white community events, blacks organized baseball teams, drill squads, goat races, and an annual celebration named No-Tsu-Oh, paralleling a week-long white festival. Separatist legislation mandated distinct YMCAs, Carnegie Libraries, streetcar seating, and even specific streets from which to view parades. A black activist noted that "more colored citizens are acquiring homes in Houston than in any other purely Southern city," but also observed rental houses in the black section with outdoor toilets and ponds of stagnant water.[5]

Houston African Americans reserved their deepest grievances for the police, whom they considered particularly abusive. No shortage of examples bolstered this belief. Superintendent Ben S. Davison recommended in 1915 that the city acquire, "a pack of bloodhounds" to exert "a moral effect . . . especially among the negro race." A white Houstonian defended the police to a visiting reporter two years later with the assertion, "Our policemen have to beat the niggers when they are insolent" and insisted "only . . . the colored people" spoke ill of them. The department had employed a few black officers since the 1870s to patrol predominantly black neighborhoods, but they could arrest white offenders only with the assistance of a white colleague and faced instant dismissal if criticized by the citizenry. In 1917 the Houston force of more than 150 officers contained only two blacks. Even in later decades they lacked promotional opportunities and were excluded from motorized patrols. Still, their uniformed presence offered African Americans a modest role model, though exacerbating the suspicions of the bigoted.[6]

Historically not a garrison town, Houston had avoided much contact and friction with black troops. A local news reporter had written favorably of the 10th Cavalry as the unit passed through the city in 1899, even after the scrape at Texarkana. Still, someone had fired on the troop train just beyond the city limits. The favorable image of black combatants in the Spanish-American War had steadily diminished as Houstonians read of incidents involving the troops in Texas communities, particularly at Brownsville and San Antonio. The recent East St. Louis race riot, which left 125 African Americans dead and twenty whites imprisoned, had set the population on edge. While the business establishment considered the cantonment a net monetary gain, many white Houstonians, facing conscription and other sacrifices and unnerved by rumors of espionage, saw the introduction of black soldiers as another unsettling influence in their lives. Because of this apprehension, the city fathers walked a razor's edge. Disregard of white sentiment would risk necessary community support for the war effort, the city's prosperity, and, perhaps, the officeholders' political careers. Failure to accept the black battalion would, in turn, jeopardize the federal largess and perhaps accelerate the debilitating exodus of Houston blacks to northern labor markets at a costly loss to local employers.[7]

The community leaders, abetted by a cooperative press, placed the best face on the situation. They emphasized the troops' discipline and past glories and the short duration of their assignment. The *Press,* ordinarily the most provocative of the dailies, assured its readers, "The officers, of course, are white." The *Post* quoted a transportation officer's assessment, "Discipline among the negro regiments is almost perfect." The *Chronicle* ran a lengthy feature story under the patriotic headline, "Men Who Were With Pershing Now On Duty At Camp Logan." Praising their efficiency in settling into their routine, the reporter lauded the soldiers' service in Mexico, the borderlands, Hawaii, and the Philippines. He recorded their avowed pleasure at viewing the verdant countryside after years of "sand, rocks, and sagebrush." The readers received comforting assurance that strict regulations governed passes to town, prohibited weapons on the streets, and commanded 11 P.M. curfews. "Well disciplined" and "full of regimental pride," the soldiers, in any case, were expected to complete their service within six weeks.[8]

Companies I, K, L, and M, consisting of 645 enlisted men and seven officers under command of Col. William Newman, moved into temporary quarters at the western city limits, one-half mile east of Camp Logan, on July 28. About 150 feet south of the location lay Washington Avenue, which ran eastward to downtown, some three and one-half to four miles, and westward, as Washington Road, to the cantonment. A scattering of houses occupied by blacks adjoined the site on the north and west. Extending eight blocks to the east, Brunner Addition comprised a rather isolated working-class neighborhood, while a few more whites resided to the south of the camp. The two routes into the city from the battalion's quarters emanated from Washington, one crossing the bayou two miles to the south, connecting with a streetcar line, and the other running southward along Brunner Avenue to San Felipe. The second route led through a black section of the city.[9]

Both the municipal and military leadership demonstrated their best behavior at the outset. Maj. James Parker, Southern Department commander, promised the Chamber of Commerce a law-abiding battalion. Indicating the tenseness of the relationship, he added his expectation, as at Waco, "that they will be received with a patriotic spirit." James George, chamber secretary, responded in like manner, "The people of Houston are not negrophobes . . . [the] negro soldiers . . . will be properly received and . . . their comfort will be given due consideration." George's amicable statement, however, contained a potential disclaimer: "You need anticipate no trouble as long as they comport themselves as soldiers should."[10]

Despite the proclamations of accommodation, the strained accord rested on the bases of segregation and deference. The city provided amusements in the form of picnics and recreational programs, with displays of the troops' musical and athletic abilities for Houston audiences. Colonel Newman sought to placate his men and limit their visits to town by allowing black Houstonians ready access to the camp. Contrarily, only the most highly disciplined soldiers earned the privilege of routine passes. The commander diminished the whites' fears of armed blacks by denying even the military police their weapons while in the city. The MPs, nevertheless, regularly patrolled the sections most frequented by the garrison.[11]

The conciliatory measures proved inadequate. Tempers increasingly flared between the guards at Camp Logan and the white workmen. Racial slurs from the laborers prompted pointed responses from the soldiers, who particularly railed at the epithet *nigger*. Racially labeled drinking water containers so upset the guards that Newman designated a tank simply bearing the sign "Guards." The Jim Crow restrictions off base posed even more onerous problems. As at San Antonio in 1911 and at Waco on the first night of leave, the soldiers resisted segregation ordinances on streetcars and in businesses. Some enlisted men refused to sit behind the screens racially partitioning the trolleys, on occasion tossing the dividers from the car.[12]

The simultaneous defiance of Jim Crowism in Houston and the 1st Battalion's march on Waco at the start of its tours of duty sorely tried the favorable Bayou City press. The *Chronicle*, in a brief item, blamed the incidents on excitable recruits and carried the calming statement, "It is expected that . . . necessary orders will be given to prevent any like occurrences hereafter." The *Post* reacted to Waco's near disaster by asking restraint of "some unruly spirits" among the black soldiers and "that element of whites that is prone to aggressive and strife-breeding conduct." It followed its balanced editorial by attributing the alleged high failure rate of African Americans on physical induction exams to conditions of poverty. When the *Press* reported later infractions by the 3rd Battalion, the two larger dailies maintained their upbeat coverage. All three kept silent on the troubles at the camp construction site until a citizen's committee investigation brought them to light.[13]

The flurry over Waco produced repeated statements guaranteeing security at Houston. The newspapers announced that soldiers could not congregate on city streets in groups of more than three. An enlisted man was arrested for remaining in town after midnight. "Military Police Get Good Results," a headline confirmed. The police chief lauded the troops' discipline as "the best of existing order everywhere." Houstonians approved the news that a white minister was preaching to a gathering of blacks.[14]

Prominent news articles clarified the reason for media restraint. A downtown merchant "detected an acceleration in retail trade currents by reason of the army camp." Construction workers received $17,000 on their first pay day in early August. Daily stories tracked the pace of construction, attendant expenses, and the magnitude of the task. "The camp will be larger than most of the cities of Texas," marveled a scribe, encompassing "a population twice as large as the Houston

Heights and about a third as large as Houston." References to the rapidly approaching completion date praised the project while signaling the imminent departure of the black battalion.[15]

Nevertheless, a condition of unease clouded the bright economic picture. The *Press* played to this sentiment with harsher reporting than its competitors. It headlined the Waco incident, "Negro Troops Start Trouble . . . And Street Battle Ensues." All three newspapers noted the arrest of a 3rd Battalion soldier who drew a knife on a deputy sheriff after refusing to relinquish his streetcar seat to a white. Unlike the problems at the camp site, such public conflicts would not bear concealment. A reporter declared the prosecution of the knife-wielding soldier "the first time a case of this kind has been tried before a Harris County court, though the negro population is large."[16]

An approaching referendum on prohibition kept the race issue before the public. Predicting the arrival of three thousand black troops of the Illinois National Guard after the completion of the cantonment, a proponent urged passage of the measure to control their behavior. Advocates reinforced the specter of the Brownsville raid in the absence of any evidence that alcohol had contributed to the shooting. The federal enforcement of prohibition in areas adjacent to military camps sparked occasionally publicized arrests, with a demand for closer surveillance.[17]

Lynchings, a staple of the newspapers, continued to stir racial emotions. In early August, Houstonians read of an Arkansas mob taking a lawman's black prisoner accused of murdering a white. "Doubtless," the reporter concluded, "the negro has been lynched."[18]

The reports of local arrests only hinted at the combustible relationship between police and the soldiers. Unlike the situation at Waco, the Houston department made no accord giving the military control over its arrests. Houston policemen ignored any role for MPs, giving rise to soldiers' complaints of degrading statements and physical abuse at the hands of the department. Further, lawmen essentially recognized no distinction between military police and other servicemen. In defiance of orders supposedly issued by the chief, they demonstrated the same lack of courtesy to their military counterparts as to other black soldiers and civilians.[19]

Unsurprisingly, a police incident, reminiscent of earlier conflicts at Laredo, El Paso, and Waco, triggered violence at Houston. On the morning of August 23, two police officers, Lee Sparks and Rufus Daniels, broke up a dice game involving black youngsters near the battalion camp. As the boys fled, Sparks, already under investigation for abusing a suspect, shot at them and burst into an adjoining house, seeking their whereabouts. Sara Travers, the resident, apparently exchanged words with Sparks, who arrested and forced her into the street in her bathrobe. When Pvt. Alonzo Edwards, Company L, happened by and questioned the procedure, the officer pistol-whipped and arrested him.[20]

Accounts of the incident varied widely, with Sparks accusing the woman of belligerence and the soldier of drunken conduct. Mrs. Travers, a mother of five children, stated she was ironing clothes when the officer entered, searched her house, and cursed her: "You all God damn nigger bitches. Since these God damn sons of bitches nigger soldiers come here you are trying to take the town. . . . Don't you ask an officer what he want in your house. I'm from Fort Ben[d] and we don't allow niggers to talk back to us. We generally whip them down there."[21]

The woman's version, corroborated by several eyewitnesses, fit the black community's perception of police conduct. White colleagues acknowledged that Sparks often spoke of beating blacks. Only days later he was charged with shooting and killing a black man engaged in a dice game. The contention that the presence of black troops encouraged local African Americans to question their subordination hearkened back to the criticism of free blacks in the pre–Civil War South.[22]

A more serious confrontation followed this violent, if common, action. Later that afternoon, Cpl. Charles Baltimore, a military policeman from Company I, approached Sparks and Daniels near the scene of the arrests and inquired about Private Edwards. Although Baltimore acted within the line of duty and, according to Daniels, posed no physical threat to Sparks, the latter clubbed the unarmed soldier with his pistol butt and fired several shots at the fleeing figure. The officers pursued the corporal into a residence, dragged him out, and placed him in custody. Sparks later claimed that he attacked Baltimore in response to the man's abusive language and that he fired the shots into the ground. Witnesses refuted the statements. A resident of the neighborhood insisted that the officer "shot right at him . . . into a street full of women and children."[23]

Rumors that police had killed Baltimore spread back to camp. The battalion adjutant found the men "excited and talking to one another." When the report reached Maj. Kneeland S. Snow, former Company I commander and recent replacement of the transferred Newman, he sent Capt. Haig Shekerjian to the police station to investigate the matter. The officer returned an hour or so later with the bruised but living Baltimore. Snow learned that Police Chief Clarence Brock had suspended Sparks without pay and planned to visit the camp the next day to discuss the situation. Realizing Baltimore's importance to the troops, Snow assembled his first sergeants to inform them of developments and presented the beleaguered corporal to authenticate his statements. The major instructed the noncommissioned officers to relay the information to their men and canceled passes for the night. The commander's order, intended to ward off potential trouble in town, postponed a watermelon party scheduled for Emancipation Park that evening. He assigned three additional camp guards to secure the post, raising the total to six.[24]

After taking measures in the afternoon to curb possible outbreaks, Snow lapsed into an unaccountable lethargy. Despite his observation "that the men were uneasy and very much incensed," the major prepared to leave the post in the evening. Shortly before eight o'clock, Sgt. Vida Henry, Company I, approached Snow with the comment, "Major, I think we are going to have trouble tonight." Snow, subsequently accused of "gross neglect and inefficiency in not interpreting conditions within his command," proceeded to the company street. He saw a number of men raiding ammunition from a supply tent. Snow quickly assembled the troops for roll call and weapons check. When no loose ammunition turned up, he walked to the rear of the company area and confronted a threatening crowd of about thirty armed soldiers. According to the commander, his order to disarm ignited a heated discussion from the men on whether to shoot him. At that point a cry sounded: "They are coming! The mob is coming to camp." The shout, allegedly from Pvt. Frank Johnson, set off a stampede of soldiers to the ordnance tent for their rifles. Amid random firing, a large part of Company I and a representation from other units rushed from the camp, supposedly directed by Henry. Other soldiers formed a defensive line inside the camp to protect themselves from perceived invaders.[25]

Despite the confusion, a majority of the garrison obeyed orders to remain in camp. Capt. Bartlett James, officer of the day, kept Company L "under excellent control," according to the military review. By the largest estimate of the mutineers, 20 to 25 percent of the troops left the post, and various members began returning within a few minutes. Doubtless, some revolted from fear of attack, either by invaders or angry noncommissioned officers or comrades who had demanded they join the rebellion. The greater number remained in battle-ready condition at the military reservation. According to the army and most researchers, a small number of men plotted the raid to settle grievances against the police and other whites.[26]

The march of perhaps upwards of one hundred soldiers wreaked ghastly results. The column divided into several groups, proceeding easterly and northerly through Brunner Addition toward downtown Houston. "These rioters appear to have fired indiscriminately at whites," concluded an inspecting officer. "From among the civil population there were fifteen killed and twenty-one wounded; of the killed, four were policemen. Of the fifteen killed, seven were more or less mutilated by bayonets." The next morning the bodies of Sergeant Henry and Pvt. Brant Watson were found along the route; two wounded soldiers, one shot in camp and another on the streets, later died. Firing from the camp killed E. A. Thompson, who was driving west on Washington with his wife, sister-in-law, and a friend. A. R. Carstens had just stepped off a trolley car with a companion when someone in the column shot him to death. Charles Wright, visiting his parents on Wood Street, stepped outside the house to view what he thought was a sham battle and received mortal wounds in his arms, chest, and abdomen. Teenager Fred Winkler met his death by turning on a porch light and walking out to investigate night noises. His young friend William Drucks took a bullet in the arm, which necessitated amputation. Fifteen-year-old Alma Reichert, assisting in her father's grocery store, survived a serious gunshot in her abdomen. Less fortunate, Manuel Gerardo received a fatal bullet while he slept.[27]

In an episode that prompted a separate court-martial, guards at Camp Logan abandoned their posts in an apparent effort to join the march from the 24th Infantry camp. Accompanied by John Wilson, corporal of the guard, they moved with loaded rifles toward Houston after hearing shots from the battalion area. Two of their number immediately left ranks and returned to the post, later appearing as prosecution witnesses, while fifteen others kept to the pace. They approached a group of white people in front of a neighborhood restaurant, reportedly threatening them, and shortly afterward fired into an approaching jitney that refused to stop at their command. The burst killed the driver, E. M. Jones.[28]

Meanwhile, a column from the 24th Infantry camp fired into a car occupied by four guardsmen and a policeman speeding to the scene. Bullets cut down Capt. Joseph Mattes, of the 2nd Illinois Field Artillery, and Officer E. G. Meinecke, while wounding several others. Prosecution witnesses drawn from the ranks testified that the soldiers then paused to discuss their plans, with most recognizing the futility of continuing their mission. Sergeant Henry, the once-reluctant leader, refused to accompany the men back to camp, insisting that someone shoot him. As dejected soldiers turned back, denying him his wish, Henry supposedly took his own life.[29]

Elsewhere, Major Snow continued to flail about for control over his men. He freely acknowledged they "paid no attention to me whatsoever. . . . A considerable amount of the firing seemed directed at me." As soon as his officers had reasonably quieted the garrison, Snow rushed off to obtain help. Unable to contact Camp Logan, he telephoned former police chief Davison in a highly agitated condition. "Mr. Davison, hell has broken loose in my camp," the respondent quoted him, "and I can do nothing with the men." The blurted plea ended abruptly, through a loss of the line, prompting Davison to call police headquarters. Snow sped down the thoroughfare in search of a functioning telephone. Druggist F. B. Dyer recalled the major rushing into his pharmacy, several miles from the camp, about 9:30 P.M., in a state requiring aromatic spirits of ammonia. Snow later ordered sentries to block off the camp and visited newspaper and city offices to gather and deliver information on the crisis. By 5:00 A.M. his nervousness had not subsided. "I remember distinctly Major Snow's inability to direct his thought with clearness," asserted a Texas guardsman who recorded the commander's comments. "At any rate," he still believed some years later, "he was weak and a rotten disciplinarian . . . when he needed firmness."[30]

Local officers, for that matter, matched Snow's unintelligible behavior. Chief Brock, a former parks superintendent, and Sheriff Frank Hammond made no special preparations for security despite purportedly receiving various alarms of soldiers threatening trouble during the afternoon. Numerous citizens called in between 8:30 and 9:00 P.M. with sightings of armed soldiers on the streets, yet Hammond left town and Brock retired early. An army investigator considered Brock "absolutely helpless," having no knowledge of the number or whereabouts of his officers that evening. An orderly at the 24th Infantry camp helped save the situation by sprinting to Camp Logan at the first sound of gunfire to inform Capt. L. A. Tuggle of the 5th Illinois National Guard. The commander dispatched his officers and eight hundred men to the 24th Infantry camp, "rendering valuable assistance, in keeping armed citizens away from the camp and in arresting the rioters along San Felipe Street," according to a later report.[31]

Gov. James E. Ferguson proclaimed martial law at first notification, rendering support to Tuggle and local lawmen. In one of his last actions before suffering removal by impeachment, the executive imposed the emergency decree in the early morning hours of August 24. The Southern Department ordered Brig. Gen. John A. Hulen, Texas National Guard, to restore order. Hulen moved three companies of the Coast Guard Artillery Corps from Galveston and a battalion of the 19th Infantry from San Antonio into the city. Sheriff Hammond organized a posse of 250 citizen deputies to complement the military forces. Together they staved off a potential mob of irate whites, who broke into hardware stores, grabbed weapons and ammunition, and exhorted revenge on the black soldiers. By dawn the city lay sullenly pacified, with recriminations in full swing.[32]

Houston newspapers devoted their largest print and most expressive rhetoric to their lead story. The *Post* and the *Chronicle* provided the most extensive coverage, combining local reports, wire service items, and harrowing eyewitness accounts. Based on interviews of residents, peace officers, and military personnel, the articles emphasized casualties with little analysis of motivation other than the bestial nature of the black soldiers and their lack of supervision. They sought a balance between graphic descriptions of the horrors and proclamations of civil self-righteousness on the one hand and efforts to calm the public on the other. The *Chronicle* employed headlines such as "Murderous Riot Replaces Negro Watermelon Party" and "Eye Witnesses Tell Version of Mob Riots" alongside "Plans Are Forming For Speedy Courtmartial" and "Negro Rioters Are Indicted." In only a mildly reassuring note, the organ noted that downed telephone lines at the camp, initially thought to be deliberately cut, actually resulted from random gunfire. Beneath a six-column banner, "Martial Law Declared," the *Post* assured its readership of returning tranquility. The *Press* ran an emotional and inaccurate headline, "The Negroes Terrorized The City All Night."[33]

Accusations abounded on the morning after. Chief Brock received a considerable share, even as critics praised his officers, such as Daniels, who died on duty. His suspension of Sparks created a spate of denunciations from that officer's supporters and a debate over whether the chief had instructed the force to cooperate with the military police. A former police inspector confirmed the order, but Sparks denied receiving it. Examinations of the riot demonstrated the tenuous control that Brock held over his subordinates, with many still looking to Davison for leadership. Some Houstonians ridiculed Brock's order that patrolmen refer to blacks as "colored" instead of "negro." In truth the African Americans objected to the utterance "nigger." A citizens' committee censured the police chief's ineptitude during the crisis.[34]

The newspapers and public leveled their biggest guns against military mismanagement. The *Chronicle* sounded the theme: "This dreadful situation which has fallen upon the city is one of purely military character." This position served the dual purposes of eliminating racial abuse as a provocation and removing the stigma of a black garrison, thereby allowing its retention. The approach enjoyed only partial success: the first part of the proposition met with widespread support, while the second irritated Houstonians who, with the Texas congressional delegation, wanted to banish all black soldiers from the state. "The notion that negro troops can not be quartered in the South, if they are properly officered and controlled, is nonsense," the editorialist insisted. "But," he added as a nod to a large segment of opinion, "the negro temperament is such as to require absolutism on the part of those who command." The newspaper represented the more enlightened business view that recognized the present and potential economic value of federal installations and the necessity of accommodating governmental policy.[35]

The other newspapers joined the attack on lax military discipline as the cause of the mutiny, but opposed stationing black troops in the South under any conditions. "Keep Negro Troops Out Of The South," began a *Post* editorial. Predicting future turmoil if they remained, the writer asserted, "The Southern cities are not going to change their laws to suit the demands of negro soldiers." The *Press* concurred: "Houston wants no more negro troopers brought here. This city has not sufficient confidence in the ability of the army officers to control them, regardless of their own confidence in their ability." In a subsequent editorial, the paper assailed the *Chronicle*'s position.

> There is an element in Houston—a small minority—money grubbers—who are favorable to the bringing of more negro troops here to be trained. . . . They are itching for the money these negroes would spend in Houston, and this coin looks bigger to them than the lives and safety of Houston's people. In Brownsville, San Antonio, Waco, and Houston negro troops have revolted and run amok. . . . There is plenty of room in the North for them.[36]

Although local and regional sentiment ran strongly against the military's mismanagement, the disposition of the troops became a divisive issue. At first word of the shootings, Sen. Morris Sheppard cornered Secretary of War Newton Baker, who consented to withdraw all black troops from the state. In his stance, Sheppard echoed the convictions of the entire Texas delegation. Baker insisted, however, on locating black guardsmen in southern training camps, which meant dispatching a black Illinois regiment to Camp Logan. Houston Chamber of Commerce President J. S. Cullinan refused to contest the secretary on this point, but the chamber board of directors disagreed. They telegraphed Cullinan at Washington, "the intense feeling against negroes in uniform caused by the outrageous murders . . . will take years to blot . . . out. . . . It would be better not to have the camp at all than to be subjected to race riots such as we have had." While Baker remained adamant, the division within the business establishment reflected the newspaper war.[37]

Conversely, many of the people anxious to rid Houston of black troops wanted to retain the forty indicted battalion members for trial, charged largely for missing roll calls or being found off base the night of the riot. The men became enveloped in a spirited civilian-military controversy similar to, but briefer than, the Kipper affair at El Paso seventeen years earlier. Initially favoring state prosecution, some locals reconciled themselves to military trial after General Bell clarified the army's position: "Their [the soldiers] disposition is in the hands of the military. . . . The justice meted out by army authorities will be much quicker obtained than it could be by civil procedure." The Southern Department commander reminded the public that the regiment had not participated in the Brownsville affray and had comported itself well at its last station.[38]

Still, the abrupt departure of the indicted men for Columbus, New Mexico, stirred emotions at Houston. Sheriff Hammond turned the wanted soldiers over to General Hulen without consulting with the district attorney or the magistrate who had issued the blanket murder warrant for the death of Officer Ira Raney. Justice Leon Lusk termed the release unlawful in lieu of his court's permission. District Attorney John H. Crooker agreed, and the Harris County grand jury vowed to probe the incident. Hammond argued that he considered the prisoners as detainees for the army. In any case, the soldiers were gone, and the jurisdiction battle moved to the location of the court-martial. Strident Houstonians demanded holding the military trial in Houston to guarantee swift justice; the army demurred in naming a venue.[39]

The ensuing debate on the court-martial indirectly involved more than the army suspects. A popular view stated that a Houston trial would exert a salutary effect on the local black population, while the results of a distant prosecution might go unnoticed. The argument underscored the often-unpublicized fear that the presence of black troops, with relative freedom and authority, caused African-American civilians to question their own subjugation. Local punishment, swift and severe, would demonstrate that not even black role models were immune from community mores. Indeed, police abuse, which sparked the revolt, made the same point. The press contributed to the silent campaign to separate the natural allies by vigorously reporting white citizens' complaints of the licentious nature of black Houstonians who had visited the camp. In other words, respectable blacks had distanced themselves from the soldiers, a premise at odds with the facts and the attitude of the black community.[40]

The media, cognizant of the debilitating migration of blacks northward and the fear of reprisals in minority neighborhoods, sought to extend the dichotomy of good and bad African Americans. All three newspapers assured peaceful blacks of their safety, taking the opportunity to congratulate whites on their restraint since the mutiny. The assurances, while self-serving, actually filled a need, as many blacks had fled to the countryside in the wake of the shootings, and others stayed quietly in their homes. Black leaders accepted the statements as an extended hand. The Houston District Colored Conference met at a local church to "condemn in unmeasured terms the unwarranted killing of innocent citizens." Third Ward residents issued regrets over the riot and recommended against stationing other black troops in the South, "since conditions here do not warrant such a course." A group of teachers concurred in both statements, while still acknowledging "a certain pride in off-duty actions of some" soldiers who engaged in charitable work. Black opinion of a more critical nature went unreported in the establishment press.[41]

Recurring rumors of an impending racial clash strained the tenuous tie between whites and blacks in the Bayou City. The media's praise for white restraint, designed to place the city in the most favorable light, also attempted to perpetuate the calm. Unfortunately, stories persisted that one or the other race planned an attack. Some rumors evidently arose from a general unease stemming from recent events in Houston, East St. Louis, and elsewhere, while others sprang from malevolence. A news item described a white man who spread alarm in both communities. Racial fears opened another rift in the newspapers' once-solid front. At a time when the two larger publications discounted such stories, the *Press* headlined an alleged black plot overheard by one of its newsboys. This fresh provocation incurred the wrath of city and military officials, who denounced the coverage. The unrepentant daily countered that suppression of facts had facilitated the riot and that "talk" could incite black civilians. After defending its seventeen-year-old source as a respectable Methodist and Boy Scout, the paper quietly allowed the story to die.[42]

Civilian and military investigations followed closely on the heels of the mutiny, generating much duplication of information with discernible differences over causation. Mayor Dan Moody appointed a seven-member panel, which an official labeled "determined, courageous, and efficient," ostensibly because the army findings would be unavailable to the citizenry. As a practical matter, it also afforded the city an opportunity to place its own version of the facts before the nation. Unsurprisingly, after several days of testimony, the board of inquiry placed most of the guilt on the army. It censured Chief Brock's ineptitude and Officer Sparks's misconduct in striking Baltimore, but concluded that the riot would have occurred in any event. The mutiny emanated from "the absolute lack of discipline and immoral conditions" in the camp, with regulations flaunted "as to vice and liquor." The report divided black Houstonians into "the lowest class," who gathered at the camp, and "the higher class," who disdained to mingle. The march represented "much more than revenge on the police," who gave "no cause for hostility," as soldiers fired indiscriminately at whites. The board judged the action "murder, murder in the first degree under the laws of civilization, and each of the participants should receive the punishment provided by law for such crime." Yet, in ironic contrast to the later military judgment, the board dismissed Baltimore as a culprit.[43]

The report, lacking any judicial application, earned the praise of the Houston establishment. In a representative editorial, the *Chronicle* deemed it a "splendid document" in accord with national sentiment, which "has already acquitted Houston of all responsibilities." Clearly, the other local newspapers had acquitted their city. A *Post* editorial began, "There Was No Provocation," inasmuch as a wronged soldier could have filed a complaint. The *Press* adhered to the spirit by favorably quoting General Bell's condemnation of poor discipline, which appeared in the report, though it defended Brock "from his enemies."[44]

The assessments found less support among African Americans. A Houstonian declined to discuss the riot with an investigator from the National Association for the Advancement of Colored People. "It's like this[,] lady," he apologized. "I could talk all right, but I'm afraid." The questioner, Martha Gruening, reported widespread fear among the city's blacks and surmised, "Police brutality and bad discipline led up to the riot." The organization's journal, *The Crisis*, asked "no mitigation of punishment" for the soldiers, but noted, "Contrary to all military precedent the Negro provost guard had been disarmed and was at the mercy of citizen police who insulted them until blood ran." Locally and nationally, blacks emphasized the abusive treatment of the soldiers, even as they acknowledged the gravity of their deeds.[45]

Col. G. O. Cress, Southern Department inspector, conducted a series of inquiries, which led to a somewhat broader view of the Houston riot. A veteran of many similar investigations of lesser import, Cress took two days of testimony in Houston and traveled to El Paso and Columbus, seeking out 156 prisoners and other regimental members. He discerned an absence of serious complaints against the soldiers prior to August 23 and discounted allegations of excessive drinking as contrary to experience. Cress reserved judgment on the charges of immorality at the camp until further inquiry. As in previous investigations of Texas military conflicts, the officer cited evidence of racism among police and the general population: "The attitude . . . is . . . in substance, that a nigger is a nigger, and that his status is not effected by the uniform he wears."[46]

In Cress's view the conflict "was inherently racial" and proceeded from a series of contributing and direct causes. In the former category he listed the influence of the East St. Louis riot on blacks; the white treatment of black Houstonians and their resentment; the incompatibility between the civil authorities' attitude toward the black and the military's inculcation of self-respect and justice; and the "incompetency and inefficiency of the city administration of Houston," especially the police department. In the cluster of immediate causes he placed the "brutal, unwarranted, and unjustified assault" on Corporal Baltimore by Officer Sparks; the defiance of Sergeant Henry and other men of the 3rd Battalion toward their officers; the panic that seized the soldiers who remained in camp after hearing the alarm, "They are coming!"; a prearranged plan for revenge, probably conceived in Company I with the assistance of a few men from other companies, that included the alarm; the lack of discipline enforced by Colonel Newman, which warranted a special investigation; "gross neglect and inefficiency" of Major Snow in improperly interpreting conditions and failing to enact effective remedies; "the tendency of the Negro soldier . . . to become arrogant, overbearing, and abusive, and a menace to the community in which he happens to be stationed"; and the soldiers' "spirit of insubordination and lack of proper discipline" in refusing to observe the segregation laws. Except for the inclusion of white racism and abuse, the colonel's analysis markedly resembled white Houston's perception, even to the supposed negative tendencies of the black soldier. Despite the increasing turmoil between the communities and the military, the army appeared moving closer to the civilian view.[47]

The inspector proposed stringent measures to forestall a reenactment of the tragedy, which he believed otherwise likely. He recommended prosecuting guilty individuals "for mutiny, murder, and riot"; court-martialing Major Snow and a subordinate officer on grounds of neglect and inefficiency after the trials of the enlisted men; commending certain officers and enlisted men for their efforts to control the soldiers; commending the prompt action of the Illinois National Guard in dispersing crowds and arresting rioters; adding a full complement of field officers and captains to the 24th Infantry; and, following the trials, assembling the regiment "at some Northern station or camp for training with view to early service abroad."[48]

Cress's investigation and the ensuing preparations for the largest court-martial in American history filtered back to Houstonians. They read that three officers of the regiment had formed a board of inquiry to travel to El Paso, where the suspects were confined. One reporter described them as "sullen" while awaiting trial; another thought them "enjoying their respite from duty." The army, meanwhile, held its cards close to the vest, commenting minimally with emphasis on the certainty of justice. Locals learned that Gen. John Ruckman had reviewed the findings of the 1st Battalion court-martial but declined to publicize the verdict. No specifics on the time or place of the impending trial reached the newspapers until mid-September, and some of that proved inaccurate.[49]

While Houstonians maintained their press vigil, military-related events moved at a rapid pace. They saw the completion of Camp Logan, watched the arrival of black troops among the Illinois National Guard, read of the transfer of the 24th Infantry to the Philippines, and shuddered at a Chicago race riot. A grand jury indicted Officer Sparks for shooting a local black man, but he escaped conviction. Citizens committees planned a round of recreational activities for the guardsmen, and the camp commander banned women and whisky from the premises. Houstonians received assurances that discipline would reign, on and off post. The perseverance advocated by exponents of the *Chronicle* view prevailed: the city obtained a military air station and learned on December 1 that a court-martial had reached a verdict on sixty-three 3rd Battalion mutineers.[50]

The decision proceeded from the first of three courts-martial held at San Antonio between November, 1917, and March, 1918. The earliest, *U.S. v. Sgt. William C. Nesbit et al.,* tried sixty-three defendants on charges involving mutiny, murder, and felonious assault at and outside the 24th Infantry camp. The second, *U.S. v. Cpl. John Washington et al.,* convened in December to judge fifteen members of the guard who abandoned Camp Logan, resulting in the shooting death of jitney driver E. M. Jones. The third, *U.S. v. Cpl. Robert Tillman et al.,* assembled from later evidence on the main column, which incriminated forty additional battalion members and began February 18. The three tribunals consisted of thirteen, twelve, and thirteen officers, respectively, ranging from lieutenant colonels to brigadier generals, with the first two panels identical, save for two members. Brig. Gen. George K. Hunter served as president of the first two courts-martial; Benjamin A. Poore, holding the same rank, presided over the third. Col. John A. Hull, assisted by Maj. Dudley V. Sutphin, prosecuted the Nesbit and Tillman cases, with Sutphin serving as judge advocate general in the Washington trial. Maj. Harry H. Grier defended the accused in all three cases.[51]

The prosecution and defense agreed on a set of conditions, which "in no wise justified or extenuated the offenses committed, but . . . serve[d] to throw some light upon how the outbreak occurred." Comporting to Colonel Cress's findings, they included the segregation ordinances on and off post; clashes between the city police and soldiers and between soldiers and white workmen; the enlisted men's contempt for the word "nigger, even when this term was used without any intention of casting a slur upon them"; and the mutual distrust between white Houstonians and the battalion.[52]

Rather than arguing collective innocence, as a defense attorney might have done in a Brownsville court-martial, Grier defended the accused as individuals. He acknowledged the culpability of some members of the battalion, while minimizing their numbers, but placed the blame on the police: "If the police authorities . . . had taken the necessary action to co-operate with the military authorities . . . this present trial would never have been necessary." The marchers, a minority of the men, sought vengeance against the police for the beating of Corporal Baltimore, [not] "against the white citizens of the town, except by one or two of the agitators." Most of the marchers acted from a belief "that a mob had come to attack the camp."[53]

In the Nesbit and Tillman cases, Grier named the deceased Sergeant Henry the leader of the deadly march. "Of all the men who left the camp," he asserted, "he alone seems to have realized just exactly what the undertaking meant." Acknowledging the difficulty of linking a plot to the eighteen-year veteran who first alerted Major Snow of impending trouble, the counsel attributed his transformation to "race fanaticism," arising from Henry's support for relieving East St. Louis riot victims. He allegedly misled some of the marchers into believing they were forming a skirmish line and intimidated others into leaving. "He was the organizer, leader, and director of the raid," insisted Grier, "and was obeyed as such by everybody in the column."[54]

A number of the casualties resulted from random firing or mistaken identity, according to the defense. Frenzied shooting from the camp during the alarm accounted for the accidental shooting of four victims. Many men left the post in a confused condition, "so obsessed with the idea of self preservation that they were deaf to all entreaties and acted accordingly. The idea that their act was mutiny or murder never entered their heads." Similarities between the olive drab uniforms of the police and army apparently caused the soldiers to mistake Captain Mattes for a policeman when they shot into his vehicle. Despite stories of atrocities committed on the lifeless Mattes, the undertaker who embalmed the body found no evidence of bayonet wounds. After discovering the extent of their havoc, the avenging soldiers returned to camp, abandoning Henry to suicide.[55]

Finally, the defense faulted the procedure used by the prosecution to identify the accused. Officers, calling the roll under severely limiting conditions, could have inadvertently missed soldiers outside their company areas. Men finding themselves under fire may not have heard their names called in other parts of the camp or recognized potential witnesses near them in the darkness. Grier argued that the prosecution witnesses drawn from the ranks were led by the army officers investigating them or testified from self-preservation or error. Some had testified falsely previously. "A careful reading of their testimony will reveal . . . that it was fear of punishment and not sorrow or regret that caused them to confess." The counsel suggested that black civilian witnesses who reported overhearing damaging statements may have acted from fear of prosecution.[56]

Conversely, the prosecution in the Nesbit and Tillman trials argued the existence of a conspiracy among numerous noncommissioned officers to kill whites indiscriminately. "It is easy to blame all of the trouble that night on . . . [Henry]," stated Sutphin, "but he was not the leader. . . . He was only drawn into it at the very end, and that against his wishes." The assistant advocate cited numerous casualties among nonthreatening civilians, attacking the defense claim of grievances against the police. The plot developed in the aftermath of Baltimore's beating, an infraction that "in no way" excused the soldiers' violence, evidenced by innumerable recorded threats to assault the city and its white inhabitants. The conspirators concocted the idea of a white mob to rally others to their cause and to cover their actions. The soldiers did not fire at random from the camp, but rather to the south and east, directed toward the adjoining white neighborhoods. Genuine fear of an approaching mob would have made them fire to the north, but this would have endangered black residents.[57]

Whether motivated by fear or anger, the accused committed violations even before taking to the streets. "Fear to a soldier," stated the prosecution, "is a crime in itself." Officers testified to insubordination and physical or verbal abuse from the men. The conduct of the soldiers who joined the column contained all the elements of mutiny: willful disobedience of orders; intention to subvert regulations; and open and unlawful resistance to superior military authority. The shootings constituted murder "with malice aforethought," the military definition of the crime, even if unintentional, resulting from "the doing of some reckless and dangerous act." Under the common law, as well as the military code, every participant in the deadly march "was equally guilty with every other member of every offense committed, so long as he did not repent of his conduct and abandon the enterprise."[58]

Because of the concept of equal guilt in conspiracies and the serious portent of the penalty, identification of the participants assumed extreme importance to both sides. The prosecution acknowledged the difficulty at the outset of the trials:

> We are unable to state with mathematical certainty all that took place on that terrible night. . . . The night was a wild one; the amount of men involved was so large; the route of the column was so long; the number of crimes that were committed . . . were [too] numerous.[59]

The army's investigators patched together identifications from concurrent inquiries at Houston, Columbus, and El Paso. "As a rule," the prosecution announced, "the evidence was not accepted as true and presented to this Court unless it was checked from all three sites." The army drew its suspects largely from men who failed to answer various roll calls, those cited by confessed participants in the march, and, in the final court-martial, informants who elicited damning statements from battalion members at El Paso. Hull and Sutphin asserted that the known importance of roll calls would have stimulated every soldier in camp to demonstrate his presence. They justified the indictment of soldiers who had actually answered roll if witnesses sighted them in the column and the timing permitted their participation between checks. On the contested point of crediting confessed participants as prosecution witnesses, they noted the accepted practice of taking the testimony of coconspirators in conspiracy trials and denied promising them leniency.[60]

The Nesbit and Tillman courts-martial convicted ninety-five defendants, imposing twenty-four death sentences, fifty-three life sentences, and eighteen prison terms ranging from two to fifteen years. The courts acquitted seven on insufficient evidence and released one from arraignment due to insanity. Corporal Baltimore, whose beating allegedly sparked the riot, was among those receiving the ultimate punishment, though the Houston civilian board thought him innocent. The army immediately carried out the thirteen executions in the Nesbit court-martial with mass hangings at San Antonio less than two weeks after the sentencing. The abruptness of the disposition, permitting President Wilson no time to review the verdicts, provoked concern and outrage from civil libertarians. The chief executive commuted ten of eleven death sentences mandated in the Tillman case the following year.[61]

The Washington trial, held between the Nesbit and Tillman courts-martial, commenced December 17, 1917. It tried fifteen members of the guard detail at Camp Logan accused of deserting their post, conspiring to join the marchers from the 24th Infantry camp, and firing into an automobile, killing the driver. Defense counsel Grier acknowledged the commission of the crime, but assailed the nature of the testimony, which he deemed vague, contradictory, and biased. "As to the actual number who left," he stated, "and as to any agreements, and as to whether or not the men did leave together, there is considerable confusion." Corporal of the guard Washington reacted prudently when he assembled the guards with loaded rifles after hearing firing from the battalion camp. They left their posts intending to repel invaders and protect comrades. Eyewitnesses disagreed on the number of soldiers in the column and who actually fired into the vehicle. Grier emphasized that the column had not harmed a group of civilians standing on a curb and insisted that at most an advance group of six had participated in the shooting. In effect sacrificing some of his clients to save the remainder, he pleaded, "I merely ask that the court give the benefit of the doubt to any man that it is convinced did not engage in that shooting, or did not countenance it, or did not know that it was going to occur that night."[62]

The prosecution countered with its argument of collective responsibility. This doctrine owed to the necessity of preventing riotous combinations "from committing murder with impunity, and recognizes the impracticability . . . of establishing the identity of the particular individual actually guilty of the homicide." It proposed to prohibit conspirators from selecting one of their number to commit an unlawful deed and escaping punishment because of the state's inability to identify that person. While not specifically charging mutiny, the prosecution described the accused's actions of threatening desertion and violence and leaving their posts without permission as "certainly guilty of mutinous conduct of the most pronounced character." Numerous witnesses reported overhearing threats from guards on the afternoon in question, with a watchman repeating a particularly graphic pronouncement: "The God damned sons-of-bitches of police had beat up one of their men and they were not going to stand for it." Such statements demonstrated proof of intent to the prosecution.[63]

Sutphin rebutted the defense argument of minimal participation in the shooting. He presented testimony in which witnesses described the first rank of soldiers kneeling to fire at the approaching vehicle, permitting those behind to close ranks and fire over their shoulders. "They paid no attention to the groans and cries of the injured and dying, but scattered in all directions," Major Sutphin observed. In a stirring denunciation he concluded:

> These men in Lower "A" Guard heard what was going to happen and deliberately quit their posts, marched down to Washington Avenue and with no pretext or excuse whatsoever fired into an automobile and fatally wounded E. M. Jones and blew the left arm off of Charles Clayton. . . . It was through no fault of theirs that May George and the soldier who sat with her on the rear seat did not also fall victims to their shots; it was through no fault of theirs that Frank Beebe and Joe McCarthy were not blown off the running board on which they were riding, or shot down later as they ran back along the highway. . . . These people were peacefully traveling along a public highway; they had done no harm to any of the colored soldiers.[64]

The prosecution enjoyed a mixed victory. The judges found some five members of the first rank guilty, sentencing them to death by hanging. However, they held the other ten culpable only of leaving their posts, marching in a riotous manner in a public highway, and threatening civilians, assessing sentences of from seven to ten years. President Wilson withstood pleas to spare the lives of the condemned men, although he relented in ten instances in the subsequent Tillman case.[65]

Houstonians who had feared leniency from the army expressed satisfaction at the verdicts, particularly in the Nesbit trial. The *Chronicle*, describing the initial executions as the largest since the condemnation of the St. Patrick's Battalion for desertion during the Mexican War, defended the decision to its more demanding readers: "There will be those to say that the court should have dealt more harshly [with the accused]. . . . But judging by precedent the court seems to have exhibited little weakness." The *Press* headlined the verdict, "It Is Justice," with the military "vindicat[ing] its discipline." Appraising its projected result, the editorialist predicted, "We can live in reasonable security against another such fiendish disturbance."[66]

African Americans assessed the results less enthusiastically. An editorial in *The Crisis*, entitled "Houston and East St. Louis," listed without comment the grim statistics from the two riots:

HOUSTON	EAST ST. LOUIS
17 white persons killed.	125 Negroes killed.
13 colored soldiers hanged.	10 colored men imprisoned for 14 years
41 colored soldiers imprisoned for life.	4 white men imprisoned 14–15 years.
4 colored soldiers imprisoned.	5 white men imprisoned 5 years.
5 colored soldiers under sentenced of death; temporarily reprieved by President.	11 white men imprisoned under one year
40 colored soldiers on trial for life.	18 white men fined.
White policeman who caused the riot not even fined.	1 colored man still on trial for life.
No white army officers tried.	17 white men convicted.

Immediately under the entry, a photograph of a Houston park displayed a sign at its entrance prohibiting hauling, draying, trucking, delivery wagons, and Negroes. The caption simply stated: "A few blocks from this park Policeman Sparks shot Corporal Baltimore and started the riot. Baltimore was hanged."[67]

The mass executions and stringent sentences mollified white opinion of the Houston riot without completely closing the case. A series of appeals followed, heartened by support from civil rights advocates. Wilson's successor, Warren Harding, initiated the clemency process, which freed most prisoners within a decade and the last by 1938. Congress kept the issue alive by providing compensation for the Houston victims and their families. Individuals touched by the tragedy vividly recalled events more than sixty years afterward, and a body of folklore developed in both the white and black communities.[68]

The national collective memory survived essentially on journalistic accounts as the government closed its files. Coinciding with the release of government documents, two masters' theses, an article, and a detailed study appeared in the early 1970s. Although sympathetic to the soldiers' plight, their conclusions substantially confirmed the army's case, thus denying the accused the type of ringing defense that characterized Weaver's assessment of the Brownsville raid during the same decade.[69]

Unlike Brownsville, battalion participation in the Houston riot was never at issue, but questions of motivation and individual culpability persist. Bias in the reports, refusal of the accused, save government witnesses, to acknowledge guilt or other information, and the haste of the military to conclude the cases contributed to the complexity. The Houston citizens committee report denying racism as a factor presented a clearer view of image control than of causation. The army's own caste system included only three black officers, one of whom suffered forced retirement before promotion. The War Department had decided to exclude the four regular army regiments from combat, limiting most black soldiers to menial labor. The machinery that ensnarled over a hundred black enlisted men failed to indict any of the white officers. In truth Washington once again had placed black troops in a threatening situation and left them at the mercy of a hostile society. Secretary Baker's disinclination to "settle the so-called racial issue" by demanding respect for all his soldiers contrasted conspicuously with his relentless campaign to suppress alcohol and vice in garrison towns.[70]

The debate over motivation hinged on the issues of strategy and spontaneity. The question of a white mob divided opinion. Many of the soldiers doubtless believed themselves under attack. Snow described them as "very much incited," even before the first shots. To gain his men's attention a captain grabbed each one, shook him, and shouted in his ear. The prosecution and most historians argued that certain leaders unnerved the troops with rumors of a white mob and used the shout, "They are coming!" as a signal to riot. Colonel Cress expressed the lingering uncertainty over the moment with the statement, "Whether the leaders of those who went out of camp employed this alarm . . . as a means of starting the riot could not be ascertained, but all circumstances point to the fact that the men left back in camp at this time were obsessed with the idea that a mob would attack them."[71]

Retaliation against attack, of course, would suggest the motive of self-defense, raised inconclusively in the Rio Grande City conflict. Some evidence points to the possibility of a degree of civilian involvement. A Houstonian testifying for the prosecution heard "shots from the east" [the direction of Houston], which "sounded like six-shooters" within an hour of the initial rifle fire. A local white policeman thought the first shots he heard "didn't sound like rifles to me." Inspectors located two small holes on the east side of a house in the camp vicinity. Snow obliquely referred to "some wounded by shot gun and not rifle" fire in a parenthetical statement to General Hulen.[72]

Worthy of further study, the references to a mob lack strong corroboration and permit differing interpretations. Widespread fear of a white raid, acknowledged by the prosecution, did not preclude exploitation of that fear. Gunfire from nonmilitary weapons, and possible resultant damage, may have preceded or followed the rifle fire. Even in the former case, little more than sniping is supportable by the record. If numerous army officers testified truthfully, soldiers gathered ammunition and flouted direct orders prior to any sounds of engagement. No manner of evidence demonstrates an assembly of whites fitting the description of an armed mob assaulting the gates. If, as the defense claimed, a majority of the marchers left camp considering themselves in a defensive formation, they surely realized their error once on the empty streets. On its face, the Houston episode more closely resembles the recent Waco march than the murky Rio Grande City shooting of eighteen years earlier.[73]

The mob issue notwithstanding, both the prosecution and the defense posited the existence of a plot within the 24th Infantry camp. Citing leaders complicated the task of the government, which chose not to rely exclusively on the collective responsibility doctrine that it enunciated initially. The army placed heaviest blame on a coterie of noncommissioned officers, although strongly implicated privates shared their punishment. Defense counsel isolated the deceased Sergeant Henry as the central figure, convincing historians more than the judges.[74]

Most versions of the mutiny have placed Henry at the head of the march and a victim of his own hand when he recognized its futility. Yet, this popular view embraces troublesome discrepancies. The native Kentuckian, a thirteen-year veteran of unquestioned loyalty, acting first sergeant, and a strict disciplinarian, first alerted Major Snow to impending rebellion and accompanied him in the search for pilfered ammunition. One military report sidestepped the inconvenient fact by attributing it to another man, a ploy easily deflated. A composite of various testimony at the courts-martial had Henry leading the march and ultimately submitting to protestations of the men to return to camp. Supposedly shot in the left shoulder and right thumb and having received treatment at an unspecified house, he permitted them to leave, though preferring death to surrender. He reputedly asked several people to shoot him, all of whom refused, gave his watch to a soldier, and shook hands all around. Henry apparently shot himself as the men walked away, although not one man saw him do it. According to a chronicler, "Legend has it that Sergeant Henry placed the barrel against the roof of his mouth and, despite a heavily bandaged thumb, pulled the trigger."[75]

The first assertions of Henry's leadership emanated from two privates, Leroy Pickett and James Divins, arrested when returning to the base the next morning. While denying involvement in the shootings, they made no mention of a Henry suicide. The body lying beside the Southern Pacific tracks bore signs of violence but not of the type later acknowledged. All three newspapers described him as a victim of buckshot wounds to the head, the *Press* graphically stating, "His head was shot off with a shotgun." The *Chronicle* noted Henry's rifle missing, though he carried eleven army shells, still in their clips. All accounts assumed that a civilian had shot Henry while the sergeant walked along the rails, perhaps returning to camp. At the time of Henry's unmourned funeral five days later, the mystery remained, although a reporter now suspected the police: "It has never come to light who killed him. It is presumed either Officer Moody or Daniels killed him before they met their deaths."[76]

The Sid Westheimer undertaking company received a call on the morning of August 24 to collect a soldier's body at the corner of San Felipe and the Southern Pacific crossing. "On arriving there," Lincoln Kennerly told justice of the peace and ex-officio coroner J. M. Ray, "we found a negro lying dead about ½ mile south of that point, his head crushed and otherwise injured. He was identified as Sergeant Vida Henry, of the 24th Infantry, by his identification plate, he had been found by a squad of Illinois National Guards."[77]

Several people examined the body at the funeral parlor. Joseph Cooper, who removed the clothes, described the body as dressed in a service uniform, wearing socks, underwear, and an identification plate. The pockets held "a couple handful of cartridges . . . of a caliber used in a Springfield rifle," not in a clip as stated in the news. "Found no gun," the report confirmed. "It evidently had been taken by members of the Illinois National Guard who were stationed at the place where the body was found. Found no cartridge belt." H. D. Goldstein, the embalmer, succinctly and probably unknowingly refuted the suicide-by-gunshot theory. In a sworn statement to Ray, he attested: "His head was badly crushed with a blunt instrument, and he had a knife or bayonet wound about five inches deep ranging from the clavicle to the heart, either wound would have caused death."[78]

Accordingly, Justice Ray entered in the inquest report: "After viewing the body of the above deceased and hearing the foregoing testimony, and in view of the surrounding, I am of the opinion that the said deceased came to death on the 23d day of August A.D. 1917, as a result of having his skull crushed and a knife or bayonet wound at the hands of unknown parties." Interestingly, the body of Pvt. Bryant Watson, collected and examined the same morning as Henry's, indeed bore death-producing gunshot wounds, perhaps the model for the sergeant's supposed suicide.[79]

Major Snow, capping a frantic night, which left him in a nervous and exhausted condition, viewed the remains of Henry and Watson that morning. The latter he accurately diagnosed as "shot through the body," but he unaccountably told a board of officers that Henry's "skull was crushed, *apparently the top of his head has been blown off* [italics added]."[80]

The board of officers met on September 26, at Columbus, New Mexico, to determine whether Henry and three other soldiers had died in the line of duty. The panel, appointed by Major Snow, consisted of Capts. James W. H. Reisinger, Jr., Haig Shekerjian, and Bartlett James, all from the 3rd Battalion. After hearing several witnesses and examining the requested death certificates, the officers concluded that Henry, like the others, "died not in the line of duty and his death was caused by his own misconduct."[81]

Vital information on Henry's death certificate differed dramatically from the inquest report, dated the previous day. Justice of the Peace

Leon Lusk and City Health Officer P. H. Scardino attributed the man's demise to "Gun shot wounds, inflicted by persons unknown," with no mention of number or location and no suggestion of suicide. Information provided by Snow stated simply "Don't know" to questions asking the birthplace of Henry and names and birthplaces of his parents. The certificate listed College Park as place of burial, "number of grave unknown." Identical cryptic wording on Watson's certificate indicated the same haste or carelessness in preparing the documents.[82]

The circumstances surrounding Henry's death never received a reexamination, and the questions remain. The various descriptions of his remains encompass such contradictions as to preclude simple explanation. Newspaper reports, hastily gathered and presenting the city in the best possible light, contained their expected share of factual errors. Major Snow, whose ineffectiveness on the tragic night drew condemnation in both civilian and military circles, may have persuaded local officials to his view of death by gunshot. As with the incorrectly reported wounds of Private Wade at Del Rio a year earlier, who cared how a guilty black soldier met his death? Why question a hypothesis strengthening a suicide theory gaining credibility from pressured testimony of indicted men? Houston, under martial law, was intent on returning to normality, punishing the guilty, and putting the matter behind it. Rapidly moving events pushed Henry out of the news until he reappeared months later in court-martial testimony. By then the suicide theory had firmly taken hold.[83]

Nevertheless, the description of the body at the inquest, minus bullet wounds and bearing marks from blunt and sharp instruments, carried weighty implications. Did Henry meet his fate from frustrated soldiers whom he would not allow to return to camp? Did an abandoned Henry encounter National Guardsmen who wreaked vengeance on him? Was the fallen body a convenient starting point for all manner of concoctions? The answers lie in the stillness of the unmarked and unmourned grave.[84]

Two legacies of Brownsville merged in the Houston crisis. Whereas blacks and white civil libertarians viewed the lack of courts-martial involving the earlier event as an absence of justice, many whites believed the mass discharges permissive. In the end Houston created its own mixed legacy: it laid to rest the ghosts of Brownsville in the white community, while convincing African Americans that swift justice against their own while white violence continued unpunished meant justice denied.[85]

Ten

Last Muster

Civil rights activist Stokely Carmichael in a speech at Jackson, Mississippi, in 1966 referred to black soldiers in Vietnam as mercenaries. His words might have applied to campaigners in Cuba and the Philippines:

> A mercenary is a hired killer and in our ghettos and in our rural areas of the South our only chance is to go into the army, and what this country's said to us is the only way we can have a decent life is to become a hired killer. We've got to stop that. A black mercenary is a man who goes to deliver freedom for someone else when he doesn't have it where he comes from. We're mercenaries. . . . A black mercenary is a man who can get killed in a foreign land and come home and can't get a decent burial in his home town. He's a mercenary.[1]

The conditions that beset black soldiers in southern cities and towns in the late nineteenth and early twentieth centuries were common to the black population at large. Their reactions were not. Determined to exercise constitutional rights historically denied, members of the four African-American regiments acted in advance of their time. As such, these military activists anticipated the later civil rights movement.

Tragically, this same assertiveness sparked physical confrontations that heralded the urban riots of the second decade of the twentieth century and post-World War I period. The clashes at East St. Louis, Chicago, and Detroit stemmed from a shared environment of heightened black consciousness and tightening racial restrictions. These conditions attended the most notorious military racial incidents in Texas, at Brownsville in 1906 and Houston in 1917, though cause and effect remained clouded almost a century later.

Yet these grim events, preceded by injustices and discrimination, were not isolated incidents. They had lesser-known counterparts, spawned under similar circumstances, in the same state. In their totality they paint a tortured picture of the costs of racial prejudice on individuals and society, as mounting tensions led to abandonment of legal and moral restraints. At Texarkana in 1899, soldiers held off police with loaded rifles; the same year servicemen at Laredo assaulted a law officer after a policeman had severely beaten a comrade, and troops at Rio Grande City fired on the town after reports of a gathering mob. In 1900 enlisted men attempted to free an imprisoned soldier from the El Paso jail, killing a lawman and losing one of their own. In the mildest incident, troops flouted San Antonio's segregationist ordinances in 1911. More ominously, soldiers at Del Rio shot up a red-light district after a Texas Ranger killed an enlisted man during an arrest. The following year blacks from Camp MacArthur marched armed into Waco to avenge police abuse, eerily anticipating by days the so-called Camp Logan rising at Houston.[2]

An examination of each crisis reveals a dismal catalog of common ingredients pointing toward an explosive result. In every locality pre-existing racial norms, buttressed by personal bias in varying degrees, stymied the free movement of the soldiers. Considerations other than the conduct of the men determined the extent of community opposition to their presence.

Curiously, some causes suggested by chroniclers of military racial conflicts elsewhere held less applicability in these instances. Factors reportedly furthering race relations in garrison communities included locations of posts near large cities; proximity of racial groups held in low esteem, such as Chinese, Mexicans, and especially Indians; a vibrant black community in which the soldiers could interact; and a citizenry aware of economic and security benefits. Unfavorable factors supposedly abounded in isolated posts, towns with few blacks and no Indians, and communities with many drifters rather than a permanent population. Racial composition of the civilian population weighed relatively lightly. Texarkana, with a sizable black citizenry and Old South traditions, predictably reacted strongly to the bordello transgression, but scarcely more than Hispanic Laredo, Rio Grande City, or Del Rio. The viability of El Paso's black community may have moderated the city's stance toward black garrisons initially, but other factors predominated.[3]

Security ranked surprisingly low. Even against a threat of border revolution and banditry, South Texans opposed black troops so vehemently that the War Department temporarily closed Forts McIntosh and Ringgold. Unable to procure white garrisons to fill the vacated posts, due to the downsizing of the army, the citizenry belatedly protested its exposure to lawlessness. While El Paso publicly enunciated the security advantages of Fort Bliss, newspaper editorials and other pronouncements candidly acknowledged the economic profitability of a large permanent post.

El Paso, San Antonio, and Waco displayed the most patience in official circles during their crises. Significantly, the first two cities enjoyed long military traditions, and the third aspired to their status. The economies of El Paso and San Antonio, although diverse, depended heavily on military spending, frequently expanded through enlargements of Forts Bliss and Sam Houston. Waco early perceived the financial rewards of a National Guard encampment and the possibilities of a permanent base. While none of the three could repeal the Jim Crow laws or effect a sea change in the people's racial views, the city fathers diligently cooperated with the army to minimize tensions. Anything less might have jeopardized the lucrative relationship with the War Department and the United States Treasury. Pointedly, when one Waco newspaper overzealously but typically reported the Camp MacArthur affray, business leaders brought down their wrath on the repentant publisher. The press in each city, however, vented its journalistic spleen on the African Americans after their departure.

Each conflict, preceded by minor incidents, occurred soon after the troops arrived, an indication of immediate community hostility. At Texarkana only minutes separated the disembarkation of the 10th Cavalry and the commotion in the vice zone. In Waco jeering whites and brusque police measures precipitated the retaliation on the 24th Infantry's first night in town. Ninth Cavalrymen instantly took aim at the Alamo City's racial ordinances, and the violence at Brownsville and Houston exploded in the first weeks at the new stations.[4]

A strong sense of identity, consistent with isolated and proud groups, characterized the black military. Troops coalesced to protect a member from arrest at Texarkana, to liberate a barracks mate at El Paso, and to avenge injury to a comrade at Laredo, Del Rio, Waco, and, presumably, Houston. If one accepts the government's case against the Fort Brown garrison, documented harassment of individual soldiers united the men against the community. The Rio Grande City firing may have arisen from spontaneous rather than planned action, but the apparently indiscriminate shooting demonstrated widespread rejection of local conduct. Every incident involved a confrontation with peace officers and the use or display of arms by the soldiery, perhaps a natural recourse for military men but the source of acute anguish to a citizenry whose fear of armed blacks dated to slavery.[5]

If arrested, the errant soldier could expect little sympathy from either the public or its tribunals. Frequent punishments and fines were common at all garrison towns, a point often noted in army investigations. More than one inspecting officer believed that police seized black soldiers for offenses that went unpunished when committed by civilians or white troops. Although failing to indict, the Starr County grand jury flayed the Fort Ringgold garrison after the incident at Rio Grande City. Texas Rangers, though aided by black soldiers in suppressing the Salt War near El Paso and the rioting during a smallpox epidemic at Laredo, regularly showed contempt for them. Public opinion routinely supported the accusers, with governors, congressmen, and federal appointees joining the chorus for removal of the black garrisons. Newspapers, except when modulated by overriding concerns, skewed racial reporting to the point of distortion. Coupled with customary sensationalism in general racial reportage, press accounts of the military incidents strengthened and perpetuated the public's deepest fears about black soldiers.

The military itself offered scant solace to the men. Despite official reports decrying racial prejudice against the troops and an outwardly positive relationship between white officers and black commands, army discipline exacted harsh punishment. Garrison commanders, like their superiors, highly valued harmonious relations with the camp towns and their political representatives. A budgetarily starved military scarcely could afford to alienate a powerful congressman, as indicated in the hasty transfer of the 9th Cavalry from San Antonio after a demand by Representative Garner. Never considering itself a social laboratory or a community completely apart from the public that it served, the army expected its charges to comply with all civilian laws and norms, just or not. An institution harboring many prejudices of the general society would hardly risk its prestige or well-being for the sake of black activists. The prosecution in the Kipper trial considered Fort Bliss Commander Loughborough an ally. Evidently the army declined to investigate the Del Rio slaying of a soldier, while the provost guards at Waco obediently deferred to the police. Indeed, the War Department's practice of stationing Negroes in hostile settings and abandoning them to the worst elements of society contributed to the troops' sense of isolation. Lacking visible supporters, blacks fell into a "conspiracy of silence" when not forced to betray a comrade. To them military justice was the arbitrary discharge of 167 members of the 25th Infantry, who may have known nothing of the Brownsville raid.[6]

The object of both contemporary praise and scorn, the black units profited less from official commendations and published accounts than they suffered from notoriety. Campaign decorations and medals of valor, though widely publicized, accrued little sympathy in the garrison towns or, ultimately, at Washington. The cashiered Fort Brown garrison included six Medal of Honor winners and thirteen recipients of citations for bravery. The Brownsville affray and reaction severely undercut the prestige of the black military and appeared in virtually every press account of subsequent racial incidents, while the Camp Logan riot heightened preexisting tensions to a fever pitch. Racial demagoguery fed on the tragedies, as when Sen. Tom Connally of Texas cited the two events in opposing an antidiscrimination amendment to the Selective Training and Service Act of 1940. American blacks, proud of their uniformed role models, experienced a sense of betrayal from the public and government after Brownsville. Booker T. Washington, a loyal supporter of the Roosevelt administration, which expelled the three companies of the 25th Infantry, voiced the despondency of his people:

> I have never in all my experience with the race, experienced a time when the entire people have the feeling that they now have in regard to the administration. The race is not so much resentful or angry, perhaps, as it feels hurt or disappointed.[7]

Blacks correctly discerned the soldiers as natural leaders in their quest for equality. Uniformed and armed, the men symbolized defenders and agents of the United States government, a symbol that white supremacists despised. Independent of local employers and pressures, they could challenge restrictions that intimidated resident blacks. Far more than the general population, white or black, they had demonstrated their mettle in Cuba, the Philippines, and Mexico prior to the world war. They believed they had bought into the system with a social contract that promised them liberty in exchange for protection of the state, a bargain widely discussed and encouraged by government when wartime demands required their services.[8]

Ironically, the military that offered the soldiers a measure of independence also prevented them from articulating issues dear to them. The frustration proved unbearable when their sacrifices failed to grant them acceptance as full-fledged citizens. One need not condone the ghastly, if occasional, bursts of violence to recognize that soldiers might revert to training and combat experience under extreme stress. These excesses and more justifiable reactions shocked white America but in time melded into a larger and more controlled civil rights movement. The New Negro of the post–World War I period—assertive, decisive, and proud—was a younger cousin of the black fighting man.

That relationship lay far beyond the horizon in 1917. In a shameful disregard of the African Americans' combat record, the War Department kept the four regiments stateside throughout World War I and limited other black units primarily to service roles. Jim Crowism and prejudice stalked the new troops to Europe, where vindictive rumors challenged their courage and effectiveness despite acknowledged acts of heroism. Washington imposed grimly familiar restraints on black participation at the beginning of World War II, inspiring racial incidents at American bases in Australia, the South Pacific, England, and the United States. Black America's dismay at the government's treatment of its soldiers fueled the civil rights movement during and after the war. As partial compensation, President Harry Truman issued Executive Order 9981, July 26, 1948, mandating "equality of treatment and opportunity for all those who serve in our country's defense," well in advance of civil rights court decisions and legislation of the 1950s and 1960s. Appropriately, the order stemmed in great part from the insistence of black soldiers and veterans.[9]

Sadly, many of the earlier maligned soldiers who fought for their rights at home and abroad before the Great War failed to witness this long-sought triumph. When the government revoked the administrative discharges of the alleged Brownsville raiders in 1972, only one former garrison member remained. Survivor Dorsie Willis, describing the punishment as "a frame," mustered little enthusiasm for the upgraded discharge which now allowed him, at age eighty-six, to reenlist or obtain federal employment. A compassionate observer could only weep for the bitterness-turned-violence in that tormented time, for the malignancy of hatred that pitted citizens of a great nation against each other, and for the continuing injustices that fashioned the words of a civil rights activist two generations later.[10]

Notes

Introduction

1. Blacks served in a nonmilitary capacity, as servants, in the Mexican War. Jack Foner, *Blacks and the Military in American History,* p. 30.

2. Defense Department, *Black Americans in Defense of Our Nation,* pp. 22 (third quote), 58–65; James M. McPherson, *The Negro's Civil War: How American Negroes Felt and Acted during the war for the Union,* p. viii (first quote); Thomas Wentworth Higginson, *Army Life in a Black Regiment,* p. 194 (second quote); Irvin H. Lee, *Negro Medal of Honor Men,* pp. 90–94.

3. Marvin E. Fletcher, *The Black Soldier and Officer in the United States, 1891–1917,* pp. 26, 154; An example of Roosevelt's favorable, yet condescending, appraisal of black troops at Santiago: "No troops could have behaved better than the Colored Soldiers but . . . they were peculiarly dependent upon their officers. "Roosevelt to [Maj.] George W. Ford, Oyster Bay, New York, July 9, 1900, in Elting E. Morison, ed., *The Letters of Theodore Roosevelt,* 2:1351. Perry E. Gianakos, "The Spanish-American War and the Double Paradox of the Negro," *Phylon* 26, no. 1 (Spring, 1965): 34; James Robert Payne, "Afro-American Literature of the Spanish-American War," *Melus* 10, no. 3 (Fall, 1983): 19.

4. Black writers William Wells Brown, George W. Williams, and Joseph T. Wilson wrote of the black in the Civil War for nineteenth-century audiences. Dudley T. Cornish, *The Sable Arm: Negro Troops in the Union Army, 1861–1865,* pp. 316–18; Benjamin Quarles, *The Negro in the Civil War,* passim. William A. Dunning, *Reconstruction, Political and Economic, 1865–1877,* set the prosouthern tone of Reconstruction history for much of the first half of the twentieth century. John M. Carroll, ed., *The Black Military Experience in the American West,* p. xxi (first quote); William H. Leckie, *The Buffalo Soldiers, A Narrative of the Negro Cavalry in the West,* p. viii (second quote).

5. Kenneth M. Stampp, *The Era of Reconstruction, 1865–1877,* set the pace for revisionist Reconstruction history, which viewed blacks more favorably. John H. Nankivell, *History of the Twenty-fifth Regiment, United States Infantry, 1869–1926,* omits racial controversies. Richard O. Hope, *Racial Strife in the U.S. Military: Toward the Elimination of Discrimination,* p. 49.

6. Bernard C. Nalty and Morris J. MacGregor, eds., *Blacks in the Military: Essential Documents,* p. 47; Defense Department, *Black,* 15–23; Charles H. Wesley and Patricia W. Romero, *Negro Americans in the Civil War: From Slavery to Citizenship,* p. 55 (second quote); McPherson, *Negro's,* p. 161 (first quote).

7. The first West Point graduate, Henry O. Flipper, was expelled from the army under questionable financial allegations, overturned by the issue of an honorable discharge, posthumously, in 1976. John Alexander became a professor of military science at Wilberforce University. Charles Young reached the rank of lieutenant colonel before retirement. Department, *Black*, pp. 142–43. Racial bias is documented by Maj. Gen. J. M. Schofield, Superintendent, United States Military Academy, "The Freedman at West Point in the Army" in Nalty and MacGregor, *Blacks*, p. 52–53; Leckie, *Buffalo*, p. 8; Frank E. Vandiver, *Black Jack: The Life and Times of John J. Pershing,* (College Station, 1977), 1:150–51.

8. William L. Katz, *The Black West*, p. 202; Edward M. Coffman, *The Old Army: A Portrait of the American Army in Peacetime, 1784–1898*, p. 332; Willard B. Gatewood, Jr., *Black Americans and the White Man's Burden 1898–1903*, p. 42.

9. J. Evetts Haley, "Racial Troubles on the Conchos," in Carroll, *Black*, 462–68 (quote); Haley, *Fort Concho and the Texas Frontier*, pp. 235–37.

10. Arlen L. Fowler, *The Black Infantry in the West, 1869–1891*, pp. 58–59.

11. Defense, *Black*, pp. 64–65; Hope, *Racial*, pp. 14–15; Foner, *Blacks*, pp. 79–80. DuBois's philosophy is stated in his autobiographical work, W. E. B. DuBois, *Dusk of Dawn*.

12. Alwyn Barr, *Black Texans, A History of Negroes in Texas 1528–1971*, pp. 82, 84, 98; C. Vann Woodward, *The Strange Career of Jim Crow*, pp. 67–109; Martin Binkin and Mark J. Eitelberg with others, *Blacks and the Military*, p. 16; Willard B. Gatewood, Jr., "Negro Troops in Florida, 1898," *Florida Historical Quarterly* 49, no. 1 (July, 1970): 7–9, 12. For the soldiers' viewpoint see Gatewood, *"Smoked Yankees" and the Struggle for Empire: Letters from Negro Soldiers, 1898–1902.*

13. For the Brownsville raid, see John D. Weaver, *The Brownsville Raid*, and Ann J. Lane, *The Brownsville Affair: National Crisis and Black Reaction.* The most thorough treatment of the Houston riot is Robert V. Haynes, *A Night of Violence: The Houston Riot of 1917*. Also consult chapter end notes. Black military and civilians also clashed at Huntsville, Alabama (1898), Winnemuca, Nevada (1899), San Carlos Agency, Arizona (1899), Fort Niobrara, Nebraska (1904), and elsewhere during this period. U.S. Congress, Senate Committee on Military Affairs, "Affray at Brownsville, Texas," 60th Cong., 1st sess. (Serial 5252), document no. 402, part 2, 419. Urban riots occurred in East St. Louis, Philadelphia, Newark, and New York in the summer of 1917, Chicago in 1919, and Tulsa in 1921. Haynes, "The Houston Mutiny and Riot of 1917," *Southwestern Historical Quarterly* 74, no. 4 (April, 1973): 435; William M. Tuttle, *Race Riot: Chicago in the Red Summer of 1919;* Elliott M. Rudwick, *Race Riot at East St. Louis, July 2, 1917;* (Carbondale, 1964); Allen Grimshaw, ed., *Racial Violence in the United States;* Hugh Davis Graham and Ted Robert Gurr, eds., *The History of Violence in America.* "The tendencies toward retaliatory violence are correlated to a considerable extent with periods of gererally heightened militance among Negroes, and . . . the reasons . . . are to be found less in external circumstances than in the changing expectations of the black population of the United States." August Meyer and Elliott Rudwick, "Black Violence in the Twentieth Century: A Study in Rhetoric and Retaliation," in Graham and Gurr, *History*, p. 397.

1: The Road Back to Texas

1. S. W. Dunning, Captain, 16th Infantry, to the Adjutant General, 4th Army Corps, Huntsville, Alabama, Oct. 17, 1898, AGO file 2046322, RG 94, N.A. The Florida incidents are related in Jack D. Foner, *Blacks and the Military in American History,* pp. 76–77. Members of the 10th Cavalry were denied service at a barbershop and a soda fountain in Tampa, causing some troopers to fire their weapons into the air. A riot ensued when guardsmen from a white Ohio regiment used a black youth as a target in a shooting demonstration. Theodore Anderson Baldwin entered the army in New Jersey in 1862 and retired at the rank of brigadier general in 1903. Francis B. Heitman, *Historical Register and Dictionary of the United States Army,* 1:186.

2. Dunning to Adjutant General, Huntsville, Oct. 17, 1898, AGO file 2046322, RG 94, N.A.

3. Ibid.

4. S. L. Woodward, Captain, 10th Cavalry, to the Adjutant General, 4th Army Corps, Huntsville, Oct. 26, 1898, Ibid.

5. Ibid. Samuel Lippincott Woodward, of New Jersey, entered the Illinois cavalry in 1862 and was cited for meritorious service during the raid through Mississippi and for gallantry at Egypt Station, Mississippi, in the Civil War. Heitman, *Historical,* 1:1059.

6. Dunning to the Adjutant General, 4th Army Corps, Huntsville, Nov. 3, 1898. Samuel Wadsworth Dunning, from New York, graduated nineteenth in his class at the Military Academy in 1876, was promoted to major in 1903. Heitman, *Historical,* 1:389.

7. Ass't Adjutant General to Commanding Officer, 10th Cavalry, Huntsville, Nov. 5, 1898, 4th Endorsement; Woodward to Major General Chafee, Camp A. G. Forse, Nov. 8, 1898, 5th Endorsement, AGO file 2046322, RG 94, N.A.

8. Dunning to Adjutant General, Huntsville, Oct. 17, 1898; Ass't Adjutant General to the Provost Marshall, Huntsville, Oct. 29, 1898, 3rd Endorsement, ibid.

9. T. A. Baldwin, Lieut. Col. 10th Cavalry, Commanding, to the Adjutant General, United States Army, Fort Clark, Texas, Feb. 7, 1899, AGO file 184450, RG 94, N.A.

10. H. B. Dixon, 2d Lieutenant, 10th Cavalry, to Lieut. Col. T. A. Baldwin, Commanding Squadron, 10th Cavalry, Fort Clark, January [*sic*] 7, 1899, ibid. Henry Benjamin Dixon, of Iowa, transferred from the 4th to the 10th Cavalry in 1896 and was promoted to captain in 1901. Heitman, *Historical,* 1:375.

11. Houston *Daily Post* Feb. 1, 1899; Galveston *Daily News,* Feb. 1, 1899.

12. "Bowie County," *Texas Almanac and State Industrial Guide, 1904,* pp. 217–18.

13. Alwyn Barr, "The Texas 'Black Uprising' Scare of 1883," *Phylon* 41, no. 2 (Summer, 1980): 179–86.

14. B. H. Byrne, Captain, 6th Infantry, to the Adjutant, Fort Sam Houston, Texas, Feb. 13, 1899, AGO file 184450, RG 94, N.A.

15. Houston *Daily Post,* Feb. 1, 1899; Galveston *Daily News,* Feb. 1, 1899.

16. Galveston *Daily News,* Feb. 2, 1899.

17. Alwyn Barr, *Black Texans: A History of Negroes in Texas 1528–1971,* pp. 85, 138.

18. Houston *Daily Post,* Feb. 1, 1899; Galveston *Daily News,* Feb. 1, 1899.

19. Galveston *Daily News,* Feb. 5, 1899; Horace W. Vaughan, County Attorney

of Bowie County, Texas to Honorable Joseph D. Sayers, Governor, Texarkana, Texas, Feb. 3, 1899, AGO file 184450, RG 94, N.A.

20. Ibid.
21. Ibid.
22. Ibid.
23. Ibid.
24. Sayers to Vaughan, Austin, Feb. 4, 1899, Governors' Papers: Joseph D. Sayers Letter Press Books 2–11/420, vol. I, no. 197, Archives, Texas State Library, Austin; Sayers to Senators Roger Q. Mills and Horace Chilton, Austin, Feb. 6, 1899, ibid.
25. Houston *Daily Post,* Feb. 3, 1899.
26. Galveston *Daily News,* Feb. 3, 1899.
27. Houston *Daily Post,* Feb. 2, 1899.
28. Ibid.
29. Dixon to Baldwin, Jan. 7, 1899, AGO file 184450, RG 94, N.A.
30. Ibid.
31. Houston *Daily Post,* Feb. 3, 1889; Feb. 4, 1899.
32. Baldwin to Adjutant General, Feb. 7, 1899, AGO file 184450, RG 94, N.A.; R. A. Alger, Secretary of War, to the Honorable Attorney General, Washington, D.C., Mar. 3, 1899, ibid.
33. Alger to Governor of Texas, Washington, D.C., March 4, 1899, Sayers Correspondence 2–11/378, Austin; Sayers to Alger, Austin, Mar. 11, 1899, AGO file 184450, RG 94, N.A.
34. Byrne to Adjutant, Feb. 13, 1899, AGO file 184450, RG 94, N.A.
35. Ibid.
36. Ibid.
37. Ibid.
38. J. L. Fowler, Major, 10th Cavalry, to Regimental Adjutant, 10th U.S. Cavalry, Fort Sam Houston, Texas, Feb. 28, 1899, ibid. Joshua Lounsberry Fowler of New York was promoted to major in 1898 and died in July, 1899. Heitman, *Historical,* 1:433.
39. 6th Endorsement, S. M. Whitside, Colonel, Cavalry, Commanding Regiment, to the Adjutant General, Fort Sam Houston, Mar. 4, 1899, AGO file 184550-E, RG 94, N.A. Samuel Marmaduke Whitside enlisted in Canada in 1858 and attained the rank of brigadier general in 1902. Heitman, *Historical,* 1:1031.
40. 5th Endorsement, L. P. Hunt, Captain, 10th Cavalry, Respectfully returned, Fort Sam Houston, Feb. 24, 1899. Levi Pettibone Hunt from Missouri had served in the 10th Cavalry since 1870, four years after his enlistment in Missouri. He was promoted to major in 1901. Heitman, *Historical,* 1:556.
41. 9th Endorsement, C. G. Ayres, Captain, 10th Cavalry, to the Adjutant General, Fort McIntosh, Texas, Mar. 13, 1899. Charles Greenlief Ayres of New York transferred to the 10th Cavalry in 1875, one year after his enlistment at New York. He was promoted to captain in 1892 and major in 1901. Heitman, *Historical,* 1:177.
42. Mattingly, Mar. 30, 1899, AGO file 184550.

2: South to the Rio Grande

1. *Army and Navy Journal* 36 (Jan. 28, 1899): 511; (Sept. 9, 1899): 45.
2. "Webb County," *Texas Almanac and State Industrial Guide for 1912,* pp. 363–

64; "Laredo, Texas," *The Handbook of Texas* 2:28; "José de Escandon," ibid. 1:571; Gilberto Miguel Hinojosa, *A Borderlands Town in Transition: Laredo, 1755–1870,* pp. 3–4.

3. "Fort McIntosh," *Handbook.,* 1:628; Jerry Thompson, *Sabers on the Rio Grande,* pp. 181 (second quote), 184 (first quote); Joseph B. Wilkinson, *Laredo and the Rio Grande,* pp. 227–28; Edward M. Coffman, *The Old Army: A Portrait of the American Army in Peacetime, 1784–1898,* pp. 128, 186.
4. "Fort McIntosh," *Handbook,* 1:628.
5. Wilkinson, *Laredo,* pp. 331–33, 337.
6. Laredo," *Handbook,* 2:28; Wilkinson, *Laredo,* pp. 366–67.
7. Wilkinson, *Laredo,* 370–74; Coffman, *Old Army,* p. 218.
8. *United States Census Returns, 1910,* pp. 848–49; Wilkinson, *Laredo,* pp. 298, 312, 320, 324.
9. Thompson, *Sabers,* pp. 197–300; Galveston *Daily News,* Nov. 22, 1899.
10. Evan Anders, *Boss Rule in South Texas: The Progressive Era,* pp. 6, 10–11; David Montejano, *Anglos and Mexicans in the Making of Texas, 1836–1986,* pp. 89–90, 104–105; George B. Hufford to General Nelson A. Miles, Laredo, Texas, Nov. 22, 1899, AGO file 298752, RG 94, N.A. (quote).
11. Arlen L. Fowler, *The Black Military in the West, 1869–1891,* p. 19; Robert Wooster, *Soldiers, Sutlers, and Settlers: Garrison Life on the Texas Frontier,* pp. 203–204.
12. Wilkinson, *Laredo,* pp. 377–78; Walter Prescott Webb, *The Texas Rangers: A Century of Frontier Defense,* pp. 450–62.
13. Webb, *Texas Rangers,* ibid.
14. *Army and Navy Journal* 36 (Apr. 29, 1899): 830; 37 (Sept. 9, 1899): 45.
15. J. M. Campbell, 2d Lieutenant, 25th Infantry, to the Adjutant General, Department of Texas, Fort McIntosh, Texas, Oct. 20, 1899, AGO file 292843, RG 94, N.A; W. H. H. Crowell, Major, 6th Infantry, to Adjutant General, San Antonio, Texas, Oct. 31, 1899, ibid.
16. Ibid.; Galveston *Daily News,* Oct. 20, 1899; Dallas *Morning News,* Oct. 20, 1899; Wilkinson, *Laredo,* pp. 378–79.
17. Campbell to Adjutant General, Oct. 20, 1899, N.A.
18. Galveston *Daily News,* Oct. 20, 1899.
19. Ibid.
20. Ibid.
21. Ibid.
22. Ibid.; A.A.G. to Commanding Officer, San Antonio, Texas, Oct. 19, 1899, AGO file 292843, RG 94, N.A. (quote).
23. Campbell to Adjutant General, Oct. 20, 1899, N.A.
24. Ibid. Chambers McKibbin enlisted in Pennsylvania in 1862, reaching the rank of brigadier general thirty years later. He was cited for gallant service in the battle of North Anna River, Virginia, during the Civil War. Francis B. Heitman, *Historical Register and Dictionary of the United States Army,* 1:672. William Henry Harrison Crowell, a native Ohioan, enlisted in 1861, attaining the rank of major in 1888 before retiring in 1900. Ibid., 1:341.
25. Roberts, A.A.G., to Major Crowell, Inspector, San Antonio, Texas, Oct. 25, 1899, ibid.; Crowell to Adjutant General, Oct. 31, 1899, N.A.
26. A. E. Vidaurri, Mayor of Laredo, Texas to Hon. Joseph D. Sayers, Laredo, Texas, Oct. 26, 1899, AGO file 292843, RG 94, N.A.

27. Sayers to the Honorable Secretary of War, Austin, Texas, Oct. 31, 1899, ibid.

28. Sayers to the Commanding General of Fort Sam Houston, Austin, Texas, Nov. 9, 1899, ibid. (first quote); Roberts, A.A.G. to Commanding Officer, San Antonio, Texas, Nov. 9, 1899, ibid. (second quote). Cyrus Swan Roberts, of Connecticut, entered the New York state militia in 1862 and was cited for gallant and meritorious service in campaigns in West Virginia and the Shenandoah Valley. He became assistant adjutant general in 1898. Heitman, *Historical*, 1:835.

29. Pritchard, Commanding, to Adjutant General, Fort McIntosh, Texas, Nov. 9, 1899 (quote); Pritchard to Adjutant General, Fort McIntosh Texas, Nov. 10, 1899, AGO file 292843, RG 94, N.A.

30. Assistant Adjutant General to the Commanding General, San Antonio, Texas, Nov. 9, 1899, AGO file 292843, RG 94, N.A.

31. Crowell to Adjutant General, Oct. 31, 1899, ibid.

32. Ibid.

33. Ibid.

34. Chambers McKibbin, Commanding, to the Adjutant General, San Antonio, Texas, Nov. 13, 1899, ibid.

35. Ibid.

36. Ibid.

37. C. A. Culberson to the Secretary of War, Washington, D.C., Nov. 16, 1899, ibid.

38. Adjutant General to Hon. C. A. Culberson, Washington, D.C., Nov. 20, 1899, ibid (first quote).; McKibbin, Commander, to Adjutant General, U.S.A., San Antonio, Texas, Nov. 20, 1899; Hufford to Miles, Nov. 22, 1899, ibid. (block quote). Almost twenty years earlier, Miles had demonstrated leniency in presiding over the court martial of Cadet Johnson Chesnut Whittaker at West Point. John F. Marszalek, Jr., *Court-Martial: A Black Man in America*, p. 240. Nelson Appleton Miles enlisted in the Massachusetts infantry in 1861, cited for valor in the battle of Reams Station, Virginia. He received the medal of honor in 1892 for gallantry at Chancellorsville in 1863. Heitman, *Historical*, 1:708–709.

39. Galveston *Daily News*, Nov. 23, 1899 (quote); Dallas *Morning News*, Nov. 23, 1899; Austin *Daily Statesman*, Nov. 22, 1899.

40. McKibbin, Commanding, to Adjutant General, Fort Sam Houston, Texas, Nov. 25, 1899, AGO file 292843, RG 94, N.A.

41. Corbin, Adjutant General, to Commanding Officer, Department of Texas, Washington, D.C., Nov. 27, 1899, ibid.

42. Assistant Adjutant General to Col. Chambers McKibbin, Washington, D.C., Dec. 1, 1899, ibid.

43. Chambers McKibbin, 3rd Indorsement, Headquarters, Department of Texas, San Antonio, Texas, Dec. 16, 1899, ibid.; Galveston *Daily News*, Jan. 13, 1900.

44. "Rio Grande City, Texas," *Handbook*, 2:475; "Starr County," *Texas Almanac*, pp. 365–66.

45. "Rio Grande City, Texas," *Handbook*, 2:475; "Starr County," *Texas Almanac*, p. 366 (quote).

46. "Fort Ringgold," *Handbook*, 1:631.

47. *Army and Navy Journal* 36 (Jan. 28, 1899): 511; (Apr. 29, 1899): 830.
48. Leckie, *Buffalo Soldiers*, pp. 11, 98, 99; Lieutenant Grote Hutcheson, "The Ninth Regiment of Cavalry," in John Carroll, ed., *The Black Military Experience in the American West*, pp. 65–74.
49. Leckie, *Buffalo Soldiers*, pp. 108–12.
50. Galveston *Daily News*, Nov. 20, 1899; Lt. Col. C. S. Roberts to the Commanding Officer, Department of Texas, San Antonio, Texas, Dec. 3, 1899, AGO file 296983, RG 94, N.A.
51. Galveston *Daily News*, Oct. 20, 1899; Dallas *Morning News*, Oct. 20, 1899.
52. Galveston *Daily News.*, Oct. 23, 1899.
53. Affidavit of Pvt. William Turner, Troop D, 9th Cavalry, in Roberts to the Commanding Officer, Department of Texas, San Antonio, Texas, Dec. 3, 1899, AGO file 296983, RG 94, N.A.
54. Affidavit of Pvt. Thomas Nicholson, ibid.
55. Verbal Statement of Lt. E. H. Rubottom, 9th Cavalry, ibid.; Gary D. Ryan, Navy and Old Army Branch, Military Archives Division, to author, Washington, D.C., June 15, 1978. Letter in possession of author.
56. Verbal Statement of Rubottom, Dec. 3, 1899, N.A.
57. Ibid. (first quote); Affidavit of Pvt. Naudian J. Jones, ibid. (second quote).
58. Affidavit of Mary McPherson, ibid.
59. E. H. Rubottom to Adjutant General, Department of Texas, Fort Ringgold, Texas, Nov. 23, 1899, ibid. (first quote); Affidavit of Pvt. Albert Brodie, ibid. (second quote).
60. Affidavit of Pvt. George Harcoumbe, ibid.; Report of Acting Assistant Surgeon Percy N. Barnesby, U.S.A., ibid.
61. Verbal Statement of Rubottom (first quote); Rubottom to Adjutant General, Nov. 23, 1899, ibid. (second quote).
62. Ibid. (first quote in Rubottom to Adjutant General).; Written Statement of Ordnance Sgt. Frank Byrne, U.S.A., ibid.
63. Verbal Statement of Rubottom, ibid.
64. Galveston *Daily News*, Nov. 22, 1899.
65. Ibid.
66. Ibid.
67. Ibid.
68. Ibid.; Rubottom to Adjutant General, Nov. 23, 1899, N.A. (quotes).
69. Anders, *Boss Rule*, p. 44; Galveston *Daily News*, Nov. 22, 1899 (quotes); Austin *Daily Statesman*, Nov. 22, 1899.
70. Anders, *Boss Rule*, p. 51; Galveston *Daily News*, Nov. 22, 1899 (quotes).
71. Galveston *Daily News*, Nov. 22, 1899 (quotes); Dallas *Morning News*, Nov. 22, 1899.
72. Anders, *Boss Rule*, 54; Galveston *Daily News*, Nov. 22, 1899.
73. Roberts to Commanding Officer, Dec. 3, 1899, N.A.
74. Thomas Scurry, Adjutant General, to His Excellency, Joseph D. Sayers, Governor of Texas, Austin, Texas, Nov. 30, 1899, Texas State Archives (quote); Galveston *Daily News*, Nov. 26, 1899; "Thomas Scurry," *Handbook*, 2:584. Matthias Walter Day, of Ohio, graduated from the Military Academy in 1873, seventieth in his class. He was awarded the medal of honor in 1890 for service against Geronomino in 1879. Heitman, *Historical*, 1:392. George Bernard Pritchard, Jr., a native Georgian, graduated thirty-seventh

in his class from the Military Academy in 1891 and joined the 9th Cavalry in 1891. Ibid., 808; Adjutant General's Office, *Official Army Register* (Washington, 1950), 1:814.

75. Scurry to Sayers, Nov. 30, 1899, T.S.A.; Roberts to Commanding Officer, Dec. 3, 1899, N.A.; "Scurry," *Handbook*, 2:584.

76. Scurry to Sayers, Nov. 30, 1899, T.S.A.

77. Galveston *Daily News*, Nov. 23, 1899 (quotes); Dallas *Morning News*, Nov. 23, 1899.

78. Ibid.

79. Ibid., Nov. 24, 1899.

80. Galveston *Daily News*, Nov. 26, 1899.

81. Testimony of W. W. Shely in Scurry to Sayers, Nov. 30, 1899, T.S.A.; Anders, *Boss Rule*, pp. 20, 44.

82. First Statement of G. Duffy; Additional Statement of G. Duffy in Scurry to Sayers, Nov. 30, 1899, T.S.A.; Anders, *Boss Rule*, p. 47.

83. Statement of T. W. Kennedy, County Judge, in Scurry to Sayers, Nov. 30, 1899.

84. Statement of K. H. Merren, Deputy U.S. Marshall (first and second quotes); Affidavit of K. H. Merren (third and fourth quotes), ibid.

85. Scurry to Sayers, Nov. 30, 1899, N.A.

86. Ibid.

87. Ibid.

88. Ibid.

89. Roberts to Commanding Officer, Dec. 3, 1899, N.A.

90. Ibid.

91. Ibid.

92. Ibid.

93. Ibid.

94. Ibid.

95. Ibid.

96. McKibbin to Adjutant General, Dec. 4, 1899, N.A.

97. Galveston *Daily News*, Dec. 7, 1899.

98. McKibbin, Commanding, to Governor Sayers, Fort Sam Houston, Texas, Dec. 12, 1899, T.S.A.

99. R. H. Ward, Office Asst. Atty. Gen'l. to Hon. Joseph D. Sayers, Governor of Texas, Capitol, Dec. 14, 1899, T.S.A.

100. Ibid.

101. Chambers McKibbin to the Adjutant General, United States Army, San Antonio, Texas, Dec. 19, 1899, AGO file 296983, RG 94, N.A.

102. Galveston *Daily News*, Dec. 19, 1899.

103. "Fort McIntosh", Handbook, 1:628; *Army and Navy Journal* 37 (Feb. 17, 1900): 586; (Feb. 24, 1900): 597; (Mar. 24, 1900): 705.

3: At the Pass of the North

1. For El Paso see Cleofas Calleros, *El Paso, Then and Now;* Leon C. Metz, *City at the Pass: An Illustrated History of El Paso;* C. L. Sonnichsen, *Pass of the North: Four Centuries on the Rio Grande;* W. H. Timmons, *El Paso: A Borderlands History;* Owen White, *Out of the Desert: The Historical Romance of El Paso.* On Fort Bliss see Arthur Van Voorhis Crego, *City on the Mesa: The New*

Fort Bliss, 1890–1895; Richard K. McMaster, *Musket, Saber, and Missile: A History of Fort Bliss;* Leon C. Metz, *Fort Bliss: An Illustrated History.*

2. Walter Prescott Webb, ed., *The Handbook of Texas* (Austin, 1952), 1:561–62; El Paso *Times,* Aug. 1, 1889 (quote); Metz, *El Paso,* pp. 19, 39–41; Timmons, El *Paso,* pp. 79, 166.

3. Webb, *Handbook.* 1:620–21; Metz, *Fort Bliss,* pp. 48–52.

4. Allan W. Sandstrum, "Fort Bliss: The Frontier Years" (M.A. thesis, Texas Western College of the University of Texas, 1962), 175–76.

5. William H. Leckie, *The Buffalo Soldiers: A Narrative of the Negro Cavalry in the West,* pp. 190; El Paso *Times,* Apr. 30, 1899 (quote).

6. El Paso *Times,* July 13, 1903.

7. Marilyn T. Bryan, "The Economic and Political Social Status of the Negro in El Paso," *Password* 13, no. 3 (Fall, 1968): 83; See Timmons, *El Paso,* p. 162, for anti-Hispanic bias.

8. Bryan, "Economic," pp. 78–79.

9. John H. Nankivell, *History of the Twenty-Fifth Regiment, United States Infantry, 1869–1926,* pp. 83–84.

10. El Paso *Times,* Dec. 12, 1899; Dec. 24, 1899; Jan. 5, 1900.

11. Ibid., Nov. 22, 1899 (second quote); Nov. 24, 1899; Dec. 24, 1899; Feb. 13, 1900 (first quote).

12. Ibid., Sept. 8, 1899 (first quote); Lt. Col. Cyrus S. Roberts to the Adjutant General, Department of Texas, San Antonio, Texas, Feb. 28, 1900, AGO file 325267, RG 94, N.A. (second quote).

13. El Paso *Times,* Oct. 29, 1899.

14. Ibid., Nov. 3, 1899.

15. Ibid., Nov. 11, 1899; Nov. 18, 1899 (quote); El Paso *Herald,* Feb. 17, 1900.

16. El Paso *Herald,* Feb. 17, 1900. A reporter described Stewart's funeral, attended by uniformed police and volunteer firemen on February 20, as "one of the most impressive ceremonies of the kind El Paso shall have seen." *Ibid.,* Feb. 19, 1900.

17. El Paso *Herald,* Feb. 17, 1900; El Paso *Times,* Feb. 18, 1900.

18. El Paso *Herald,* Feb. 17, 1900; El Paso *Times,* Feb. 18, 1900.

19. Hull's corporal chevrons were missing from the fatigues, indicating an attempt to conceal the man's identity. The press described Hull, 25, with almost three years of army experience in the battalion, as "of tremendously powerful build, with a head like a bullet." El Paso *Herald,* Feb. 17, 1900.

20. El Paso *Times,* Feb. 18, 1900. Robert Henry Rose Loughborough, a Virginian, joined the 25th Infantry in his first year in the military, 1875. He attained the rank of captain in 1881 and major in 1900. Francis B. Heitman, *Historical Register and Dictionary of the United States Army,* 1:643.

21. El Paso *Times,* Feb. 18, 1900 (first quote); El Paso *Herald,* Feb. 17, 1900 (second quote).

22. El Paso *Herald,* Feb. 17, 1900.

23. Colonel Chambers McKibbin to the Adjutant General, San Antonio, Texas, Feb. 18, 1900, AGO file 325267, RG 94, N.A.; McKibbin to the Adjutant General, San Antonio, Texas, Feb. 19, 1900 (first quote), ibid.; McKibbin to the Adjutant General, San Antonio, Texas, Nov. 20, 1900 (second quote), ibid.

24. El Paso *Times*, Feb. 18, 1900.
25. Ibid., Feb. 20, 1900.
26. Ibid., Feb. 22, 1900.
27. Ibid., Feb. 23, 1900.
28. Roberts to Adjutant General, Department of Texas, Feb. 28, 1900, AGO file 325267, RG 94, N.A.
29. Ibid.
30. Ibid.
31. Ibid.
32. Ibid.
33. Ibid.
34. Ibid.
35. Ibid.
36. Ibid.
37. McKibbin to the Adjutant General, United States Army, Washington, D.C., Mar. 1, 1900, ibid.
38. Ibid.
39. H. R. H. Loughborough, Captain 25th Infantry, Commanding, to Adjutant General, Department of Texas, San Antonio, Texas, Mar. 2, 1900, ibid.
40. Ibid.
41. El Paso *Times*, Feb. 25, 1900; Mar. 1, 1900.
42. Ibid., Mar. 3, 1900 (first quote); June 3, 1900 (second quote).
43. Ibid., Mar. 4, 1900; Apr. 21, 1900; May 23, 1900.
44. See chapters on Waco and Houston, for example.
45. Ibid., May 5, 1900; El Paso *Herald*, Aug. 21, 1901 (quote).
46. El Paso *Times*, Aug. 6, 1890; El Paso *Herald*, Mar. 28, 1893; June 10, 1904; July 28, 1904; Aug. 20, 1909 (quote); Oct. 8, 1914; Aug. 23, 1932.
47. El Paso *Herald*, Oct. 25, 1902; Apr. 21, 1923; El Paso *Times*, Apr. 22, 1923.
48. El Paso *Times*, May 1, 1900.
49. Ibid., May 2, 1900; May 3, 1900.
50. Ibid., May 3, 1900.
51. Ibid., May 4, 1900.
52. Ibid.
53. Ibid., May 5, 1900.
54. Ibid.
55. Ibid.
56. Ibid.
57. Ibid.
58. Ibid., May 6, 1900.
59. Ibid.
60. El Paso *Herald*, Nov. 14, 1900; Nov. 16, 1900 (quote); Nov. 20, 1900.
61. Ibid., Aug. 9, 1900; Sept. 7, 1900 (quotes).
62. Ibid., July 2, 1900 (quote); Nov. 20, 1900. Texas provided more test cases on the right of blacks to serve as jurors than any other southern state. Still, by the turn of the century, relatively few blacks sat on grand or petit juries. Lawrence D. Rice, *The Negro in Texas, 1874–1900* (Baton Rouge, 1971), p. 256.
63. *Kipper v. State*, Court of Criminal Appeals of Texas, Apr. 10, 1901, *Southwestern Reporter* 62 (1901): 421–22.

64. El Paso *Herald,* Mar. 27, 1901 (quotes); Edward M. Coffman, *The Old Army: A Portrait of the American Army in Peacetime, 1784–1898,* pp. 360–61.

65. El Paso *Herald,* May 16, 1901 (second quote); July 15, 1901 (first quote); 1910 U.S. Census, Supplement for Texas, Federal Archives and Records Center, Fort Worth, Texas, 650.

66. J. M. Dean to Elihu Root, El Paso, Texas, June 21, 1900, AGO file 330323, RG 94, N.A.; Assistant Adjutant General to J. M. Dean, Washington, D.C., June 29, 1900, ibid. (quotes); Adjutant General to Commanding Officer, Department of Texas, Washington, D.C., Aug. 23, 1900, ibid.; Capt. R. H. R. Loughborough to Adjutant General, Department of Texas, Fort Bliss, Texas, Aug. 20, 1900, ibid.

67. Loughborough to Adjutant General, Department of Texas, Fort Bliss, Texas, Jan. 2, 1901, ibid.; McKibbin to Adjutant General, San Antonio, Texas, Feb. 28, 1901, ibid.

68. G. H. Liebe to Adjutant General, San Antonio, Texas, Mar. 27, 1901, ibid.

69. Memorandum for Carter, Miscellaneous Division, Adjutant General's Office, Mar. 22, 1901, ibid.; Roberts to Adjutant General, Department of Texas, Mar. 13, 1901, ibid. (quotes).

70. Roberts to Adjutant General, Department of War, San Antonio, Texas, Apr. 22, 1901, ibid.; Dean to Roberts, El Paso, Texas, Apr. 23, 1901, ibid.

71. M. W. Stanton to Roberts, El Paso, Texas, Apr. 23, 1901, ibid. (first quote); Dean to William Cary Sanger, El Paso, Texas, May 29, 1901, ibid. (second quote).

72. George Andrews to Dean, Washington, D.C., May 11, 1901, ibid.; Joseph D. Sayers to Adjutant General, Austin, Texas, May 11, 1901, ibid. (first quote); Andrews to Commanding Officer, Department of Texas, Washington, D.C., May 17, 1901, ibid. (second quote).

73. Sanger to Sayers, Washington, D.C., May 20, 1901, ibid.; Dean to Sanger, El Paso, Texas, May 29, 1901, ibid. (quote).

74. El Paso *Herald,* June 3, 1901 (quote); June 14, 1901; Stanton to Roberts, El Paso, Texas, June 14, 1901, AGO file 330323, RG 94, N.A.

75. El Paso *Herald,* June 29, 1901. The Dallas *Morning News,* the city's largest journal, offered no coverage.

76. Ibid., July 17, 1901; July 23, 1901; July 24, 1901; July 29, 1901 (quote); Aug. 2, 1901.

77. Ibid., Aug. 5, 1901.

78. Ibid., Aug. 15, 1901 (quote); Aug. 17, 1901.

79. Ibid., Aug. 6, 1901.

80. Ibid., Aug. 21, 1901.

81. Ibid., Aug. 23, 1901.

82. Ibid., Aug. 24, 1901.

83. *Kipper v. State,* Court of Criminal Appeals of Texas, Dec. 9, 1903, *Southwestern Reporter* 77 (1904): 61–62, 617–18 (quotes).

84. Conditional Pardon by the Governor of Texas, no. 11566, June 20, 1913, Texas Department of Corrections, Huntsville, Texas.

4: The Brownsville Legacy

1. John H. Nankivell, *History of the Twenty-fifth Regiment, United States Infantry, 1869–1926,* pp. 86, 112, 119–20. Andrew Sheridan Burt from Ohio joined

the Ohio infantry as a private in 1861, receiving a commission in the 18th Infantry the same year. He retired at the rank of brigadier general in 1902. He was cited for meritorious service in the Kentucky and Georgia campaigns of the Civil War. Francis B. Heitman, *Historical Register and Dictionary of the United States Army*, 1:267.

2. Nankivell, *History*, pp. 86, 112, 119–20. Charles Wilkinson Penrose, from Michigan, joined the 11th Infantry in 1884, later serving in the 23rd and 28th Infantries by 1902. Heitman, *Historical*, 1:783.

3. Nankivell, *History*, pp. 115, 120.

4. Col. Harold B. Simpson, ed., *Frontier Forts of Texas*, pp. 46, 57; Herbert M. Hart, *Old Forts of the Southwest*, p. 36 (first quote); Merle Elliott Tracy, "The Romance of the Lower Rio Grande," *Texas Magazine* 8, no. 2 (June, 1913): 117; Colonel M. L. Crimmins, "An Army Bride's Impressions of Fort Brown," *Frontier Times* 15, no. 9 (July, 1938): 419 (second and third quotes). The surgeon at Fort Brown attributed severe fevers at the fort to the "exceedingly unpleasant and by no means sweet scented effluence arising from the lagoon." Robert Wooster, *Soldiers, Sutlers, and Settlers: Garrison Life on the Texas Frontier*, 199. Randolph B. Marcy, Inspector General of the Army, shared Mrs. Viele's view: "This is one of the most beautiful and comfortable posts I have seen on the frontier. . . . the air resounds with the delightful music of thousands of birds." Jerry Thompson, *Sabers on the Rio Grande*, p. 187.

5. Elizabeth Petit Davenport, "Fort Brown," Walter Prescott Webb, ed., *Handbook of Texas*, 1:621; Simpson, *Frontier*, p. 44 (quote); Robert W. Frazer, *Forts of the West*, pp. 144–45. Jacob Brown joined the 11th Infantry as a private in 1812, receiving a commission in 1814. Promoted to major in 1843, he died in May, 1846, from wounds received in the defense of the fort later named Fort Brown. Heitman, *Historical*, 1:252.

6. Henry N. Ferguson, *The Port of Brownsville: A Maritime History of the Rio Grande Valley*, p. 122; Edward M. Coffman, *The Old Army: A Portrait of the American Army in Peacetime, 1784–1898*, pp. 215–16; Simpson, *Frontier*, p. xxii. William Crawford Gorgas, from Alabama, became an assistant surgeon in 1880, attaining the rank of major surgeon in 1898 and assistant surgeon general in 1903. Heitman, *Historical*, 1:466.

7. Antonio N. Zavaleta, "The Twin Cities: A Historical Synthesis of the Socio-Economic Interdependence of the Brownsville-Matamoros Border Community," in Milo Kearney, ed., *Studies in Brownsville History*, pp. 139–40; David M. Vigness, "Brownsville, Texas," *Handbook* 1:228–29; *Texas Almanac and Industrial Guide*, pp. 229–30; Anders, *Boss Rule*, p. xiii.

8. Ann J. Lane, *The Brownsville Affray: National Crisis and Black Reaction*, pp. 8–9; M. C. Scott, "The Lower Rio Grande Country," *Farm and Ranch*, 23, no. 17 (April 24, 1904): 1–2; Zavaleta, "Twin," pp. 141–43; David Montejano, *Anglos and Mexicans in the Making of Texas, 1836–1986*, pp. 42–43.

9. Zavaleta, "Twin," pp. 141–43; Montejano, *Anglos and Mexicans*, pp. 107–10.

10. Jack D. Foner, *Blacks and the Military in American History*, pp. 82, 95–96.

11. John D. Weaver, *The Brownsville Raid*, pp. 21–22; C. A. Culberson to Secretary of War, Dallas, Texas, Aug. 17, 1906. Hearings Before the Committee on Military Affairs, United States Senate, "Affray at Brownsville, Texas" (Washington, 1907), III, 2526.

12. Lane, *Brownsville*, p. 16; Weaver, *Brownsville*, pp. 26–27; Richard Young, "The Brownsville Affray," *American History Illustrated* 21, no. 6 (October, 1986): 11. The customs office was highly politicized at Brownsville, leading to charges of favoritism, collusion with smuggling elements, and disorderly behavior. Anders, *Boss Rule*, pp. 133–34.

13. Report of Maj. Augustus P. Blocksom, Investigation of the Conduct of United States Troops Stationed at Fort Brown, Texas (Washington, 1906), p. 6.

14. Ibid., pp. 6–7.

15. Ibid., p. 7.

16. Hearings, 2:939, 948, 1205–1207.

17. Major C. W. Penrose to Military Secretary, Fort Brown, Texas, Aug. 15, 1906, Investigation, 11–12.

18. Culberson and Bailey to Taft, Dallas, Texas, Aug. 15, 1906, Hearings, 3:2526, Ibid., 12.

19. Culberson to Secretary of War, Dallas, Texas, Aug. 17, 1906, ibid.

20. Houston *Post*, Aug. 15, 1906; Dallas *Morning News*, August 15, 1906; Austin *Statesman*, Aug. 15, 1906. These stories mirrored the reportage of the Brownsville *Herald*, Aug. 14, 1906. By contrast, the Houston *Chronicle* carried a brief notice August 14 on page 3 without a sensational headline.

21. Houston *Post*, Aug. 15, 1906.

22. Ibid., Aug. 16, 1906 (first quote); *Army and Navy Journal* 49, no. 1 (Sept. 1, 1906): 16 (second quote).

23. Houston *Post*, Aug. 16, 1906.

24. Austin *Statesman*, Aug. 16, 1906.

25. Houston *Post*, Aug. 15, 1906; C. W. Penrose to Capt. William Kelly, Fort Brown, Texas, Aug. 20, 1906, Investigation, 14–15; Blocksom, Aug. 28, 1906, ibid., 5 (quote). Augustus Perry Blocksom, of Ohio, graduated 22nd in his class at the Military Academy in 1873 and was promoted to major in 1903. He was cited in 1890 for gallant service against hostile Indians at Ash Creek, Arizona, in 1880. Heitman, *Historical*, 1:225.

26. Blocksom, Aug. 29, 1906, Investigation, pp. 5–10.

27. Ibid., pp. 6–10.

28. Ibid., p. 7.

29. Ibid., pp. 8–9. Edgar Augustus Macklin of North Dakota joined the 5th Artillery as a private in 1889. He was commissioned in 1898. Heitman, *Historical*, 1:674.

30. Blocksom, Aug. 29, 1906, Investigation, p. 9; Harold John Weiss, Jr., "'Yours to Command': Captain William J. 'Bill' McDonald and the Panhandle Rangers of Texas" (Ph.D. thesis, Indiana University, 1980), pp. 190–96.

31. William S. McCaskey to Headquarters, Southwestern Division, Oklahoma City, Oklahoma, Sept. 4, 1906, Investigation, 10 (quote); Hearings, I, Feb. 18, 1907, 562. William Spencer McCaskey from Pennsylvania entered the Pennsylvania infantry as a private in 1861, obtaining a commission in the 13th Infantry in 1866. He attained the rank of colonel in the 7th Infantry in 1900 and transferred to the 20th Infantry. Heitman, *Historical*, 1:654–55.

32. Weiss, "Yours," pp. 201–204; Blocksom, Investigation, pp. 9 (quotes), 10.

33. Weaver, *Brownsville*, pp. 78, 91 (quote). President Roosevelt transferred the fort to the Department of Interior, which converted it into an experimental

garden for spineless cacti. Scheduled for deactivation before the arrival of the 25th Infantry, it was reactivated in 1914. Webb, *Handbook,* 1:621.

34. Robert Oliver Shaw to Brigadier General E. A. Garlington, Washington, Oct. 4, 1906, Report of Brig. Gen. Ernest A. Garlington, Investigation, p. 107. Ernest Albert Garlington, of South Carolina, graduated 30th in his class from the Military Academy in 1872 and joined the 7th Cavalry. He received the medal of honor in 1893 for distinguished gallantry against the Sioux Indians at Wounded Knee Creek, South Dakota, in 1890, suffering a severe wound. Heitman, *Historical,* 1:447.

35. Garlington, Oct. 4, 1906, Investigation, pp. 108–11.

36. Lewis N. Wynne, "Brownsville: The Reaction of the Negro Press," *Phylon* 33, no. 2 (Summer, 1972): 155 (quotes); Emma Lou Thornbrough, "The Brownsville Episode and the Negro Vote," *Mississippi Valley Historical Review* 44 (December, 1957): 490. Critics pointed out that Secretary of War Taft earlier had intervened on behalf of white soldiers charged with shooting up Athens, Ohio. Wynne, "Brownsville," 158. The report of Lt. Col. Leonard A. Lovering, submitted Oct. 4, 1906, was the first to include sworn statements from the soldiers themselves. Message from the President of the United States, pp. 459–511. Leonard Austin Lovering, from Vermont, graduated 10th in his class from the Military Academy in 1872. He was assigned to the Inspector General's Department in 1903. Heitman, *Historical,* 1:644.

37. Lane, *Brownsville,* pp. 25–27.

38. James A. Tinsley, "Roosevelt, Foraker, and the Brownsville Affray," *Journal of Negro History* 41, no. 1 (January, 1956), 46 (quote): 50– 51. Foraker devoted three chapters, 96 pages, to Brownsville in his autobiography, *Notes of a Busy Life,* 2:231–327.

39. "The Black Battalion Speeches of Hon. Joseph B. Foraker of Ohio in the Senate of the United States, January 3, 16 and 17, 1907," p. 15.

40. Message from the President, December 19, 1906, Sen. Doc. 155, 59th Congress, 2nd session, in "Brownsville Affray," pp. 1–9; Hearings, 1:221–22. Charles James Truman Clarke entered the army as a private in the 22nd Infantry band in 1870. He was commissioned in 1882 and promoted to captain in 1898. Heitman, *Historical,* 1:306.

41. Tinsley, "Roosevelt," p. 64; Foraker, "Black," pp. 4–5, 34 (quote).

42. Foraker, "Black," 37.

43. Lane, *Brownsville,* p. 159; Weaver, *Brownsville,* p. 210 (quote). Foraker denied any misconduct. *Notes,* 2:328–54.

44. "The Brownsville Affray," Senate Doc. 389, 60th Congress, 1st sess., March 11, 1908, part 1, pp. 23–27, part 2, pp. 27–30.

45. Ibid., part 3, pp. 35–36.

46. Ibid., pp. 43–52.

47. Ibid., pp. 65–69, 71–76, 87–102.

48. Ibid.; Joseph Benson Foraker, "A Review of the Testimony in the Brownsville Investigation," *North American Review,* April, 1908, pp. 550–58. Foraker and Roosevelt both hired Herbert J. Browne, independently, believing him privy to information strengthening their position. Foraker stated that he dismissed the man for unreliability and discredited the report he made to Roosevelt. Lane, *Brownsville,* pp. 59–66.

49. Proceedings of a General Court-Martial, Capt. Edgar A. Macklin, pp. 247; Hearings, 2:2030.
50. Weaver, *Brownsville*, pp. 164, 168.
51. Five retired generals heard testimony on only eighty-two applicants and inexplicably stopped the hearings, leaving more than seventy unheard. Foner, *Blacks*, p. 102; Senate Doc. 430, 60th Congress, 2nd session, Apr. 8, 1908, pp. 1–125.
52. Weaver, *Brownsville*, p. 278.
53. An M.A. thesis by Lawrence Hugh Cook, "The Brownsville Affray of 1906" (University of Colorado, 1942), essentially argued the Foraker position; Tinsley, "Roosevelt," pp. 61–63. Historians' concentration on the dismissal, rather than culpability, of the troops continued in a series of articles. Emma Lou Thornhrough depicted the negative reaction of the black community to Roosevelt's order. African Americans remained loyal to the Republican party because the southern-white oriented Democratic party could not take advantage of the opportunity; Booker T. Washington minimized the damage; and the period of time between the dismissals and the presidential election allowed Roosevelt to rebuild his political base. Seth M. Scheiner, in 1962, interpreted Roosevelt's action as a conscious attempt to placate the South. Lewis N. Wynne, a decade later, denounced the summary discharge as "the blot on Roosevelt's humanitarian record," but conjectured that he had blundered and could not extricate himself gracefully. Subsequently, James E. Haney emphasized the importance of the South to Roosevelt in securing Taft's nomination. The Brownsville raid alienated many blacks from Taft's candidacy, but most finally supported him as Foraker's campaign stalled. Still, the issue divided the strident Roosevelt and the more reticent Taft and contributed to their confrontation in 1912. Thornbrough, "Brownsville," p. 493; Seth M. Scheiner, "President Roosevelt and the Negro, 1901–1908," *Journal of Negro History* 47 (July, 1962): 169–81; Wynne, "Brownsville," 160; James E. Haney, "Blacks and the Republican Nomination of 1908," *Ohio History*, 84, no. 4 (1975): 221.
54. Lane, *Brownsville*, pp. 97, 140, 161, 167.
55. Ibid., p. 166.
56. Weaver, *Brownsville*, 258.
57. New York *Times*, Sept. 29, 1972 (second quote). With most employment opportunities closed to him, Willis had retired from a career of shining shoes in Minneapolis when he received his honorable discharge on his eighty-seventh birthday. A native of Meridian, Mississippi, reared in Oklahoma, he died in 1977, survived by his wife, Ollie, and son, Reginald. Ibid., Aug. 25, 1977. Edward Warfield, the other remaining member of the discharged men, died previously in 1973. Ibid., Sept. 19, 1973; Hearings, 3:139 (first quote).
58. One man was a 26-year veteran; thirteen had been decorated for bravery; six were Medal of Honor recipients. Foraker, "Review," p. 551; Foner, *Blacks*, p. 98.
59. Message, p. 4.
60. Hearings, 2:1204–1207.
61. Ibid., 2:2782, 2809; Message, pp. 459–511. One may postulate a hypothesis of a narrow range of military guilt which is consistent with the testimony

of most of the soldiers. A smaller number of men than described by frightened and biased town witnesses could have escaped the observation of their comrades and officers. Sergeant Kipper's group managed as much at El Paso six years earlier. Employing nongovernmental weapons, perhaps modified to accept surplus ammunition left by the 26th Infantry or concealed from Fort Niobrara, they would have avoided the arms room. They could have jumped the wall in darkness and fired the shots from outside the reservation that Howard, Tamayo, Penrose, and others heard. They almost certainly would not have fired from the barracks as town witnesses reported. A few attackers and shots would have magnified exponentially in the minds of the residents. The culprits could have discarded the hastily used weapons without causing a search. The townspeople were looking for military weaponry and perhaps busily contriving evidence to confirm their impressions. Such a scenario would account for the clean weapons and accurate count of ammunition without impeaching the testimony of their barracks mates if the several men sneaked back to camp in the confusion and darkness. Given this speculative set of circumstances, Roosevelt's mass dismissals still stand unjustified.

62. C. W. Penrose to Military Secretary, Fort Reno, Oklahoma, Dec. 22, 1906, AGO file 1744, RG 94, N.A. (quote). Dallas *Morning News,* Dec. 23, 1906.

63. Records of the Office of the Judge Advocate General, General Court Martial of Edward Knowles, CM no. 52863, Preliminary Hearing, RG 153, N.A., 1–3, 25–29.

64. Ibid., pp. 1–3; B. J. Edger, Jr. to the Adjutant, Fort Reno, Oklahoma, Jan. 5, 1907, AGO file 1744, N.A.; Penrose to Military Secretary, Fort Reno, Dec. 22, 1906, ibid.; *Daily Oklahoman* (Oklahoma City), Dec. 22, 23, 1906; Dallas *Morning News,* Dec. 23, 29, 1906. Benjamin Jones Edger, Jr., of Pennsylvania was assigned Assistant Surgeon in 1899. Heitman, *Historical,* 1:397.

65. *Daily Oklahoman,* Jan. 8, 1907; Preliminary, pp. 14–16.

66. Physical Examination of Recruit Edward L. Knowles, Portland, Oregon, June 23, 1906, RG 94, N.A.; U.S. Register of Enlistments, vol. 95, p. 397, entry 1731, ibid.; vol. 119, p. 323, entry 398, ibid.; Preliminary, 3–5; *Daily Oklahoman,* January 9, 1907.

67. Court Martial of Edward Knowles, Proceedings, p. 1; Edward L. Knowles to Judge Advocate General, Leavenworth, Kansas, Nov. 6, 1910, AGO file 278665, RG 94, N.A.

68. Court Martial of Edward Knowles, Proceedings, pp. 4–6, 14.

69. Ibid., pp. 15, 122, 144, 150, 188.

70. Ibid., p. 309; Preliminary, p. 15.

71. Preliminary, p. 11; Proceedings, pp. 87, 133, "Exhibit H," pp. 2–3.

72. Memorandum Clemency Report in the Case of Edward L. Knowles, War Department, Washington, Nov. 10, 1908, AGO file 278665, RG 94, N.A.

73. Dallas *Morning News,* Jan. 8, 1907; Court Martial of Edward Knowles, Proceedings, pp. 144, 150, 188, 145–254, 269.

74. Proceedings, 162; *Daily Oklahoman,* Dec. 23, 1906.

75. Proceedings, 312; *United States Army and Navy Journal* 44 (June 8, 1907): 1115.

76. Memorandum Clemency Report, Oct. 15, 1913, Nov. 10, 1913, AGO file 278665, N.A. Apparently Knowles was discharged June 15, 1917, after re-

ceiving credit for good time. Warden Thomas W. Morgan to the War Department, Leavenworth, Kansas, Sept. 22, 1914, AGO file 2210441, RG 94, N.A.

77. Courts-martial traditionally exacted severe penalties on enlisted men, perhaps more so in the case of black soldiers. "Even the slightest breach of discipline could become the basis of a court-martial action, the number of army trials reaching staggering proportions. . . . During some years [in the late nineteenth century] there were almost as many cases before the courts as there were enlisted men. . . . If white soldiers received harsh sentences . . . Negro soldiers were given more severe punishments for the same offenses." Jack D. Foner, *The U.S. Soldier between Two Wars: Army Life and Reforms, 1865–1898,* pp. 33, 133. "Soldiers expected little justice when hauled before a court martial." Don Rickey, Jr., *Forty Miles a Day on Beans and Hay: The Enlisted Soldier Fighting the Indian Wars,* p. 141. "A Buffalo Soldier in the Ninth could expect little mercy at the hands of a court-martial, even for trivial offenses." Leckie, *Buffalo,* p. 56. After Brownville, "the army automatically assumed the soldiers were guilty if violence occurred as a result of discrimination. . . . Blacks were guilty and never could be proved innocent." Marvin E. Fletcher, *The Black Soldier and Officer in the United States Army, 1891–1917,* pp. 153, 158. "Punishment was almost inevitably severe. . . . Pvt. John Curtis, Ninth Cavalry, received two months' hard labor for telling his sergeant to 'go to Hell.'" Wooster, *Soldiers,* pp. 189.

5: Return to the Pass

1. El Paso *Times,* Nov. 8, 1905; Dec. 6, 1905; Dec. 11, 1905.
2. El Paso *Herald,* Jan. 8, 1906.
3. El Paso *Times,* Jan. 20, 1906 (quotes); Mar. 19, 1906; *Army and Navy Journal,* Feb. 3, 1906, p. 643. Joseph McDowell Trimble Partello from Ohio entered the service as a private in 1872 and attained the rank of major in 1903. Heitman, *Historical,* 1:773.
4. El Paso *Times,* Jan. 26, 1906; Apr. 16, 1906; El Paso *Herald,* June 27, 1906; Sept. 26, 1906.
5. El Paso *Times,* July 12, 1906; El Paso *Herald,* Nov. 27, 1906 (quote).
6. El Paso *Herald,* Aug. 15, 1906; Aug. 20, 1906; Aug. 22, 1906; Nov. 27, 1906; El Paso *Times,* Aug. 15, 1906; Aug. 17, 1906; Aug. 20, 1906. See chap. 4.
7. El Paso *Times,* Aug. 25, 1906; El Paso *Herald,* Dec. 6, 1906 (quote).
8. El Paso *Herald,* Dec. 4, 1906.
9. Ibid., Sept. 17, 1906; Sept. 25, 1906; Dec. 22, 1906; Jan. 28, 1907; Apr. 26, 1907; May 4, 1907; El Paso *Times,* Mar. 17, 1907.
10. El Paso *Herald,* Feb. 22, 1907; Feb. 23, 1907; Mar. 7, 1907 (quote).
11. El Paso *Times,* Aug. 17, 1906 (first quote); Aug. 20, 1906; (second quote) Aug. 29, 1906; (third quote) Dec. 30, 1906 (fourth quote).
12. El Paso *Herald,* Feb. 20, 1907.
13. El Paso *Times,* Sept. 20, 1906 (quote); Jan. 6, 1907; El Paso *Herald,* Mar. 27, 1907.
14. El Paso *Herald,* Mar. 7, 1907 (first quote); El Paso *Times,* June 13, 1907 (second quote).
15. El Paso *Herald,* June 12, 1907.

6: Something Inspiring to Behold

1. History of Ninth Cavalry, Year 1900, AGO file 1374702, RG 94, National Archives.
2. Ibid.
3. Ninth Cavalry, 1901, ibid.
4. Ninth Cavalry, 1902, ibid.
5. Ninth Cavalry, 1903, 1904, ibid. A U.S. officer marveled at the ability of 9th Cavalry interrogators to intimidate Filipino prisoners into divulging information by using threatening, but not violent, tactics. William Thaddeus Sexton, *Soldiers in the Sun: An Adventure in Imperialism,* p. 242.
6. Ninth Cavalry, 1907, ibid.
7. Ninth Cavalry, 1910, ibid.
8. Henry Bamford Parkes, *A History of Mexico,* pp. 316–20; Michael C. Meyer and William L. Sherman, *The Course of Mexican History,* pp. 492–503; Howard F. Cline, *The United States and Mexico,* pp. 121–22; Ramon Eduardo Ruiz, *The Great Rebellion: Mexico, 1905–1924,* pp. 139–48; El Paso *Times,* Dec. 3, 1910; Feb. 2, 1911; San Antonio *Express,* Mar. 8, 1911.
9. Walter Prescott Webb, ed., *The Handbook of Texas,* 2:540–42; Boyce House, *San Antonio: City of Flaming Adventure,* p. 190. David Emanuel Twiggs, a Georgian, entered the army in 1812 and attained the rank of major general in 1846. He was cited for gallantry in the Mexican War. He held that rank in the Confederacy until his death in 1862. Francis B. Heitman, *Historical Register and Dictionary of the United States Army,* 1:976.
10. Webb, *Handbook* 1:632; Leo Turner, *The Story of Fort Sam Houston, 1876–1936,* pp. 6–12; C. R. Howland, "Fort Sam Houston—Largest Army Post in the United States," *Texas Centennial Magazine,* September, 1935, pp. 3–4; Maj. E. A. Kindervater, *Fort Sam Houston: A Historical Sketch,* pp. 1–4; Col. M. L. Crimmins, *Historical Data on San Antonio and Fort Sam Houston,* p. 3; General Orders, No. 99, Headquarters of the Army, Adjutant General's Office, Washington, Sept. 11, 1890, Post Library, Fort Sam Houston, Texas (quote). Houston was the first elected president of the Texas Republic, but succeeded David G. Burnet. James Pinckney Henderson was the first governor of the state of Texas; Houston was one of the two first U.S. Senators from Texas and the eighth governor. Rupert N. Richardson, Ernest Wallace, and Adrian Anderson, *Texas, the Lone Star State,* pp. 127–28, 444.
11. Kindervater, *Fort Sam Houston,* pp. 1–2; House, *San Antonio,* pp. 190–93. Leonard Wood from New Hampshire entered the army as an assistant surgeon in 1886. He was awarded the Medal of Honor in 1898 for distinguished conduct in an Apache campaign in 1886. He was promoted to brigadier general in 1901. Heitman, *Historical,* 1:1055.
12. Sherwin R. Mills, "The Army Maneuvers in Texas, *Texas Magazine,* 3, no. 1 (May, 1911): 11. William Harding Carter from Tennessee graduated thirty-fifth in his class from the Military Academy in 1868. He was awarded the medal of honor in 1891 for bravery in the Apache campaign at Arizona in 1881. He attained the rank of brigadier general in 1902. Heitman, *Historical,* 1:288.
13. Webb, *Handbook,* 2:540–42; *Texas Almanac and Industrial Guide, 1911* p. 255; United States Census Report, 1910, Texas, pp. 853–54.
14. San Antonio *Express,* Apr. 15, 1911; House, *San Antonio,* p. 193 (quote).

15. 1910 Census, pp. 853–54; *Texas Republic,* Mar. 25, 1911; Apr. 8, 1911. San Antonio newspapers emphasized the economic, strategic, and prestigious value of the troops, never expressing fear of an invasion. San Antonio *Express,* Mar. 9, 1911.

16. San Antonio *Express,* Mar. 8, 1911.

17. Ibid.

18. Ibid., Mar. 13, 1911; 9th Cavalry, 1911.

19. San Antonio *Express,* Mar. 14, 1911 (first quote); Apr. 16, 1911 (second and fourth quotes); San Antonio *Light,* Mar. 16, 1911 (third and fifth quotes); 9th Cavalry, 1911.

20. San Antonio *Light,* Mar. 23, 1911; May 6, 1911; San Antonio *Express,* Mar. 13, 1911; Apr. 1, 1911.

21. *Texas Republic,* Mar. 25, 1911.

22. Ibid.

23. Arthur Ruhl, "The Gallery at San Antonio," *Collier's* 47 (April 29, 1911): 14.

24. San Antonio *Express,* Apr. 1, 1911.

25. Ibid., Apr. 4, 1911; San Antonio *Light,* Apr. 4, 1911.

26. San Antonio *Express,* Apr. 4, 1911.

27. Carter to Adjutant General, San Antonio, Texas, Apr. 3, 1911, AGO file 1766391, RG 94, N.A.; McLean, Adjutant General, to Commanding General, Department of Texas, Washington, Apr. 4, 1911, ibid.

28. San Antonio *Express,* Apr. 4, 1911.

29. John Francis Guilfoyle, of Maryland, graduated fortieth in his class at the Military Academy in 1872. He was cited in 1881 for gallantry against Indians at White Sands, New Mexico in 1880. Heitman, *Historical,* 1:483; Dallas *Morning News,* Apr. 5, 1911 (quotes).

30. Ibid.; San Antonio *Light,* Apr. 10, 1911.

31. A. G. Peterson to Hon. W. H. Taft, San Antonio, Texas, Apr. 4, 1911, AGO file 1769561, RG 94, N.A.

32. San Antonio *Express,* Apr. 7, 1911.

33. Ibid., Apr. 6, 1911 (first and second quotes); Apr. 7, 1911 (third quote).

34. San Antonio *Express,* Apr. 6, 1911; Apr. 8, 1911 (quote).

35. Ibid., Apr. 7, 1911; [Chief of Staff] Memorandum to the Adjutant General, Washington, AGO file 1766391, RG 94, N.A. (quote).

36. San Antonio *Express,* Apr. 6, 1911 (fifth and sixth quotes); Apr. 7, 1911 (first through fourth quotes).

37. San Antonio *Light,* Apr. 7, 1911 (first through fourth quotes); *Texas Republic,* Apr. 8, 1911 (fifth and sixth quotes).

38. *Texas Republic,* Apr. 8, 1911 (first quote); Apr. 15, 1911 (second quote).

39. San Antonio *Express,* Apr. 7, 1911 (first quote); Apr. 10, 1911; June 1, 1911 (second quote).

40. Ibid., Apr. 11, 1911; San Antonio *Light,* May 17, 1911 (second quote).

41. San Antonio *Express,* Apr. 7, 1911.

42. Ibid.

43. Ibid., Apr. 15, 1911.

44. Ibid. (first and second quotes); San Antonio *Light,* Apr. 18, 1911 (third quote); May 6, 1911 (fourth quote); Mills, "Army Maneuvers," 13.

45. San Antonio *Express,* Apr. 15, 1911.

46. Ibid., Apr. 8, 1911; July 1, 1911; *Texas Republic,* June 24, 1911 (quote). Hermann Augustus Sievert entered the army from Ohio as an enlisted man in 1888. He was promoted to captain in the 9th Cavalry in 1902. Heitman, *Historical,* 1:886.
47. San Antonio *Express,* Apr. 9, 1911; Apr. 13, 1911; June 8, 1911; San Antonio *Light,* July 11, 1911.
48. Parkes, *History,* p. 321; Meyer and Sherman, *Course,* pp. 503–504; Ruiz, *Great,* pp. 148–49; Ninth Cavalry, 1911; San Antonio *Light,* July 12, 1911 (quote).
49. Webb, *Handbook,* 1:632; Kindervater, *Fort,* pp. 4–10; Dallas *Morning News,* June 25, 1916; San Antonio *Express,* July 25, 1916. For a differing view of the second San Antonio controversy, see Chicago *Defender,* July 29, 1916.
50. Kindervater, *Fort,* p. 7.

7: A Hero's Welcome

1. El Paso *Times,* June 21, 1916; Houston *Chronicle,* June 29, 1916; New York *Times,* June 30, 1916.
2. Ibid.; El Paso *Times,* June 22, 25, 1916; Houston *Chronicle,* June 27, 1916; Historical Sketch of the 10th U.S. Cavalry, AGO file 1195363, RG 94, N.A.; Clarence Clendenen, *Blood on the Border: The United States Army and the Mexican Irregulars,* pp. 303–10; Marvin E. Fletcher, *The Black Soldier and Officer in the U.S. Army, 1891–1917,* pp. 56–59; Jack D. Foner, *Blacks and the Military in American History,* p. 107. John Joseph Pershing from Missouri graduated thirtieth in his class from the Military Academy in 1882. His familiarity with black troops dated to his service as a first lieutenant in the 10th Cavalry in 1892. Francis B. Heitman, *Historical Register and Dictionary of the United States Army,* 1:785.
3. Houston *Chronicle,* June 27, 1916 (quote); El Paso *Times,* June 30, 1916.
4. Houston *Chronicle,* June 29, 1916 (quote); El Paso *Times,* June 30, 1916. George Bell, Jr., of Maryland graduated from the Military Academy forty-third in his class in 1876. Heitman, *Historical,* 1:207.
5. El Paso *Herald,* Apr. 10, 1916; El Paso *Times,* July 7, 1916.
6. Lieutenant H. W. Hovey, "The Twenty-fourth Regiment of Infantry," in John M. Carroll, ed., *The Black Military in the American West,* pp. 78–87; William H. Leckie, *The Buffalo Soldiers: A Narrative of the Negro Cavalry in the West,* pp. 217–29; Paul Carlson, "'Pecos Bill' Shafter: Scouting the Llano Estacado," *Military History of Texas and the Southwest* 16, no. 1 (1980): 39; Paul Carlson, "'Pecos Bill' Shafter Campaigning in Mexico," ibid., no. 4 (1980): 225; Douglas C. McChristian, "Grierson's Fight at Tinaja de Las Palmas— An Episode in the Victoria Campaign," *Red River Valley Historical Review* 7, no. 1 (Winter, 1982): 50; Rosemary Whitehead Jones, Jr., ed., *La Hacienda: An Official Bicentennial Publication,* pp. 429–56; Robert V. Haynes, *A Night of Violence: The Houston Riot of 1917,* pp. 9–11.
7. Historical Sketch of the 24th U.S. Infantry from Apr. 20, 1898 to Dec. 31, 1904, AGO file 966421-A, RG 94, N.A.
8. Ibid. A correspondent called the Siboney hospital "a terrible one" with "practically no ambulances;" Richard H. Titherington, *A History of the Spanish American War of 1898,* p. 264.
9. Historical Sketch of the 24th U.S. Infantry from Apr. 20, 1898 to Dec. 31, 1904, AGO file 966421-A, RG 94, N.A.

10. Ibid. from June 22, 1899 to Aug. 1, 1902, AGO file 966421, RG 94, N.A.
11. History, 24th Infantry, 1916, ibid.; Clendenen, *Blood*, pp. 303–10.
12. 24th Infantry, 1916, N.A.
13. Axie C. Seale, "Del Rio, Texas," in Walter Prescott Webb, ed., *The Handbook of Texas*, 1:485–86; Seale, "Val Verde County," ibid., 2:828–29.
14. Ibid.; Fred I. Meyers, "Prosperous Del Rio," *Texas Magazine* 2, no. 3 (July, 1910): 83–84.
15. Population—Texas, *United States Census, 1910*, pp. 848–49; Meyers, "Prosperous," pp. 83–84.
16. Meyers, "Prosperous," pp. 83–84.
17. Ibid. (quotes); "Val Verde County," *Texas Almanac and State Industrial Guide, 1914* p. 341.
18. *Texas Almanac*, p. 23; Jones, *La Hacienda*, pp. 420; 504; Austin *Statesman*, Mar. 20, 1916.
19. Herbert M. Hart, *Old Forts of the Southwest*, p. 188. Camp Del Rio remained active from 1876 to 1891 and from 1914 to 1922. Its antecedent, Camp San Felipe, dated from the 1850s; Robert Wooster, *Soldiers, Sutlers, and Settlers: Garrison Life on the Texas Frontier*, p. 10.
20. The county name derived from H. H. Sibley's Confederate victory in New Mexico during the Civil War. Seale, "Val Verde," *Handbook*, 2:828. Racial conservative John Nance Garner represented the district in Congress. San Antonio *Express*, Apr. 10, 1916.
21. 24th Infantry, 1916, N.A.
22. Houston *Post*, Apr. 10, 1916.
23. Ibid.; San Antonio *Express*, Apr. 10, 1916; Dallas *Morning News*, Apr. 10, 1916; El Paso *Herald*, Apr. 10, 1916; El Paso *Times*, Apr. 10, 1916; New York *Times*, Apr. 10, 1916.
24. San Antonio *Express*, Apr. 10, 1916.
25. Ibid.
26. Ibid.
27. Ibid.
28. El Paso *Times*, Apr. 10, 1916; San Antonio *Express*, Apr. 10, 1916; New York *Times*, Apr. 10, 1916; El Paso *Herald*, Apr. 10, 1916.
29. Ibid.; Vann is cited as observer in San Antonio *Express*.
30. Ibid.; The INS account in the El Paso *Times* confused the regiment with the 25th Infantry.
31. First Lt. A. W. Chilton, 24th Infantry, to the Commanding Officer, Camp Del Rio, Texas, Apr. 10, 1916, AGO file 2389649, RG 94, N.A.; Alexander Wheeler Chilton from Minnesota graduated from the Military Academy in 1907. He retired as a lieutenant colonel in 1930. The Adjutant General's Office, Washington, D.C., *Official Army Register*. Vol. I, United States Army Active and Retired Lists 1 Jan. 1950, p. 678. William Newman from Tennessee graduated thirty-eighth in his class from the Military Academy in 1888. He attained the rank of captain in 1901. Heitman, *Historical*, 1:745.
32. Chilton to Commanding Officer, Apr. 10, 1916. James Arthur Wilson of Michigan graduated from the Army Medical School in 1909. He retired in 1935 with the rank of colonel. Adjutant, *Official*, 1:874.
33. Chilton to Commanding Officer, Apr. 10, 1916.
34. Ibid.

35. Ibid.
36. Ibid.
37. Ibid.
38. San Antonio *Express,* Apr. 10, 1916 (quote); Julian Samora, Joe Bernal, and Albert Pena, *Gunpowder Justice: A Reassessment of the Texas Rangers,* pp. 1–7; Walter Prescott Webb, *The Story of the Texas Rangers,* pp. 133, 140; John L. Davis, *The Texas Rangers: Their First 150 Years,* p. 91; C. L. Douglas, *The Gentlemen in the White Hats: Dramatic Episodes in the History of the Texas Rangers,* p. 7; David Montejano, *Anglos and Mexicans in the Making of Texas, 1836–1986,* pp. 126–27. The Plan of San Diego, an attempt to return Texas to Mexico, and the Zimmerman Telegram, raising the specter of a German-Mexican alliance, further embittered relations along the border. Don M. Coerver and Linda B. Hall, *Texas and the Mexican Revolution. A Study in State and National Border Policy, 1910–1920,* pp. 106–108, 118–19.

Contrary to press accounts, Barler's official records show him entering the Rangers on Apr. 9, 1915, and a native of Llano, Texas, not Edwards County. He listed his occupation as "ranchman," his age as forty-one, his height 5' 8", his hair and complexion "light," eyes blue, and marital status as married. He was promoted to captain, Aug. 24, 1917. Interestingly, on Dec. 9, 1915 Ranger Barler arrested a black man, W. H. Wells, thirteen miles west of Del Rio on a rape charge and turned him over to the deputy sheriff, apparently without harm. See Oath of Members, Ranger Force, Monthly Returns, State of Texas, Jan. 1, 1917 to Dec. 31, 1918, Texas State Archives.

39. Report of Ranger Investigating Committee, Feb. 18, 1919, Journal of the House of Representatives of the Regular Session of the Thirty-Sixth Legislature, T.S.A., p. 537.
40. Davis, *Texas,* 91; Michael J. Dabrishus, Archivist, T. S. A., to author, Austin, Texas, Jan. 20, 1983. Letter in possession of author. See State of Texas Adjutant General's Department Warrant of Authority and Descriptive List, W. L. Barler, T.S.A. On Oct. 11, 1918, then Sergeant Timberlake, evidently Barler's associate on the night of Wade's death, was killed "in the line of duty." Biennial Report, 61.
41. See for examples Galveston *Daily News,* Nov. 22, 1899; Nov. 23, 1899; El Paso *Herald,* June 13, 1907.
42. Joseph Jones District Judge, C. C. Belecher, Dist. Atty., John W. Ammond Sheriff to John N. Garner, Del Rio, Texas, Apr. 9, 1916, AGO file 2389649, RG 94, N.A.
43. Houston *Post,* Apr. 11, 1916 (first quote); El Paso *Times,* Apr. 10, 1916 (second and third quotes).
44. Houston *Post,* Apr. 11, 1916; El Paso *Herald,* Apr. 10, 1916; 24th Infantry, 1916, N.A.
45. 24th Infantry, 1916, N.A.; Adjutant General's, *Official,* p. 678.

8: The Very Best Type of Manhood

1. David M. Kennedy, *Over Here: The First World War and American Society,* p. 29.
2. New York *Times,* June 17, 1917.
3. C. Wilbur Coons, "Waco—A Typical Texas City: Her Past, Her Present, Her Future," *Texas Magazine* 1, no. 6 (April, 1910): 66–68; Dayton Kelley, ed.,

The Handbook of Waco and McLennan County, Texas, pp. 212, 287–88; Waco *Sunday Tribune-Herald*, July 28, 1936.

4. Kelley, *Handbook*, p. 212.
5. William H. Curry, *A History of Early Waco with Allusions to Six Shooter Junction*, pp. 82, 88; Waco *Times-Herald*, Aug. 12, 1905; July 13, 1917; Dec. 14, 1921; Waco *Morning News*, May 16, 1916; James M. SoRelle, "'The Waco Horror': The Lynching of Jesse Washington," *Southwestern Historical Quarterly* 86, no. 4 (April, 1983): 517–19.
6. SoRelle, "Waco," p. 527.
7. Waco *Times-Herald*, Aug. 12, 1905 (first and third quotes); July 13, 1917 (second quote); Waco *Morning News*, May 16, 1916.
8. Waco *Times-Herald*, Aug. 10, 1905; SoRelle, "Waco," p. 529 (quote).
9. Waco *Times-Herald*, June 11, 1917; Aug. 12, 1917; Waco *Morning News*, June 12, 1917; Waco *Sunday Tribune-Herald*, June 28, 1936; New York *Times*, June 20, 1917; El Paso *Times*, June 15, 1917.
10. Waco *Times-Herald*, June 11, 1917 (quote); Waco *Morning News*, June 12, 1917.
11. Waco *Times-Herald*, June 11, 1917 (first quote); Waco *Morning News*, June 12, 1917 (second quote).
12. Waco *Times-Herald*, June 11, 1917; June 20, 1917 (quote); New York *Times*, June 19, 1917; June 20, 1917.
13. Waco *Times-Herald*, June 19, 1917; July 20, 1917; July 21, 1917.
14. Ibid., July 15, 1917; Aug. 1, 1917; Aug. 2, 1917; Aug. 3, 1917; Aug. 6, 1917; Aug. 19, 1917; Waco Board of Commissioners, Aug. 23, 1917, Waco City Council Minutes.
15. New York *Times*, May 17, 1917; July 24, 1917; Aug. 17, 1917; James Parker, Brigadier General, U.S. Army, Commanding, to the Adjutant General of the Army, San Antonio, Texas, Aug. 4, 1917, AGO file 25021, RG 407, N.A.; Waco *Times-Herald*, Aug. 6, 1917. James Parker from New Jersey graduated thirty-first in his class from the Military Academy in 1872. He was awarded the Medal of Honor in 1902 for gallantry in the defense of Vigan Luzon in the Philippines. Francis B. Heitman, *Historical Register and Dictionary of the United States Army*, 1:770.
16. Waco *Times-Herald*, Aug. 6, 1917 (quote); Aug. 10, 1917; Waco *Morning News*, Aug. 10, 1917 (Editorial); Curry, *Early*, p. 129; Board of Commissioners, Aug. 23, 1917, Minutes; Margaret Davis, "Harlots and Hymnals: An Historic Confrontation of Vice and Virtue in Waco, Texas," *Waco Heritage and History* 9, no. 3 (Fall, 1978): 15.
17. Waco *Tribune-Herald*, Oct. 30, 1949; Oct. 26, 1975; Mar. 22, 1980; Aug. 9, 1982.
18. Tasker Bliss, Major-General, to the Adjutant General, Washington, D.C., Aug. 25, 1917, AGO file 25021, RG 407, N.A.; Waco *Times-Herald*, July 30, 1917; Robert V. Haynes, *A Night of Violence: The Houston Riot of 1917*, pp. 60–62; Houston *Post*, Apr. 10, 1916.
19. Waco *Times-Herald*, July 23, 1917; Parker to Mr. Penland, San Antonio, Texas, July 24, 1917, AGO file 25021, RG 407, N.A. (quote).
20. J. M. Penland to Brig. Gen. Parker, Waco, Texas, July 25, 1917, AGO file 25021, RG 407, N.A.
21. Kelley, *Handbook*, pp. 101, 229, 284, 288.

22. Waco *Times-Herald*, July 23, 1917; July 25, 1917 (quotes).

23. Ibid., July 28, 1917.

24. Ibid., Statement of Capt. C. F. Andrews, 24th Infantry, to Colonel G. O. Cress, July 30, 1917, AGO file 25021, RG 407, N.A.

25. Memorandum by order of Captain Andrews, aboard troop train, July 27, 1917, AGO file 25021, RG 407, N.A.

26. Statement of Andrews, July 30, 1917, ibid.

27. Ibid.; Waco *News Tribune*, July 31, 1964. James Aloysius Higgins from Pennsylvania entered the signal corps as an enlisted man in 1898. He became a second lieutenant in 1899 and retired as a colonel in 1931. The Adjutant General's Office, *Official Army Register*, 1:740. Eugene Warren Fales was born in New York in 1887. He rose to the rank of major general at retirement in 1946. Ibid.

28. Col. G. O. Cress to Commanding General, Southern Department, Fort Sam Houston, Texas, Aug. 1, 1917, AGO file 25021, RG 407, N.A.

29. Statement of Higgins, July 31, 1917, ibid.; Direct Examination of Capt. James A. Higgins, 24th Infantry, Record of Trial by General Court-Martial of Pvts. James H. Johnson and Howard hood, et al., Camp MacArthur, Waco, Texas, Aug. 21, 1917, GCM 105553, RG 153, N.A. Higgins was promoted to major, Aug. 23, 1917. The Adjutant General's Office, Washington, D.C., *Official Army Register*, vol. 1, United States Army Active and Retired Lists, Jan. 1, 1950.

30. Statement of Higgins, July 31, 1917, AGO file 25021, RG 407, N.A.; Statement of Private Howard Hood, Waco, Texas, July 31, 1917, ibid. (quotes).

31. Waco *Morning News*, July 30, 1917; Waco *Times-Herald*, July 30, 1917.

32. Waco *Morning News*, July 31, 1917; Statement of Andrews, Waco, Texas, July 30, 1917, AGO file 25021, RG 407, N.A.

33. Waco *Morning News*, July 31, 1917.

34. Waco *Times-Herald*, July 30, 1917.

35. Ibid.

36. Cress to Commanding General, Aug. 1, 1917, AGO file 25021, RG 94, N.A.

37. Ibid.

38. Ibid.

39. Waco *Times-Herald*, Aug. 5, 1917; Aug. 19, 1917.

40. Ibid., Aug. 3, 1917; Aug. 26, 1917.

41. Ibid., Aug. 5, 1917; Aug. 20, 1917.

42. Proceedings of a Board of Officers Convened Pursuant to the Following Order: Headquarters Camp MacArthur Texas, GCM 105553, RG 153, N.A., pp. 1–9.

43. Statement of Andrews, July 30, 1917, N.A.; Cress to Commanding General, Aug. 1, 1917, N.A.

44. Report on General Prisoner 12077, James E. Mitchell, United States Penitentiary, Leavenworth, Kansas, Sept. 23, 1919, GCM 105553, N.A.; Report on General Prisoner 12076, Walter Lusk, ibid.; Report on General Prisoner 12075, Willie Lewis, ibid.

45. Report on General Prisoner 12061, Luther Briggs, ibid.

46. Record of Trial, Aug. 21, 1917, N.A., pp. 1–3.

47. Ibid., 4–5.

48. Ibid., 13–24; Procccdings of a Board, pp. 1–8 (quotes).

49. Record of Trial, pp. 22–30.
50. Ibid., p. 34.
51. Ibid., pp. 34–38; Office of the Judge Advocate General Memorandum for General Kreger, Washington, D.C., Mar. 21, 1919, ibid.; Report on General Prisoner 12061, ibid.
52. Houston *Post,* Aug. 24, 1917; Waco *Times-Herald,* Aug. 25, 1917 (first quote); Aug. 26, 1917 (second quote).
53. Statement of Andrews, July 30, 1917, N.A.; Testimony of Sgt. W. M. Lomax, Waco, Texas, July 31, 1917, AGO file 25021, RG 407, N.A.
54. Waco *Times-Herald,* Aug. 26, 1917 (quote); "A Letter of Appreciation of Waco," *Chamber of Commerce News* 1, no. 1 (May, 1919): 5. Camp Mac-Arthur closed in 1919, a year after the end of the war. Waco *Tribune-Herald,* Mar. 22, 1980.

9: Hell Has Broken Loose
1. Ray Miller, *Ray Miller's Houston,* pp. 68–105; David G. McComb, *Houston: A History,* pp. 11–15, 65–85; Marguerite Johnston, *Houston: The Unknown City, 1836–1946,* pp. 9–12, 92–97, 136–48, 184–87.
2. Marvin Hurley, *Decisive Years for Houston,* pp. 47–50.
3. Practically level, it included approximately two thousand acres in the campsite proper and remount station; eight hundred acres of rifle ranges; two thousand acres in the machine gun and artillery ranges; and some twenty-eight hundred acres in drill grounds. It afforded convenient access to the M. K. & T. and H. & T. C. lines and the Hillendahl highway, a county tarvia road. W. P. Rothrock, Captain, Engineers, U. S. R., "Completion Report of Camp Logan," Houston, January 14, 1918, War Department, Houston Metropolitan Research Center.
4. Houston *Chronicle,* July 23, 1917 (first quote); July 24, 1917; Houston *Post,* July 26, 1917; Houston *Press,* July 23, 1917.
5. James Martin SoRelle, "'The Darker Side of Heaven': The Black Community in Houston, Texas," Ph.D. diss. (Kent State University, 1980), pp. iv–v; McComb, *Houston,* pp. 108–10; Clifton P. Richardson, Sr., "Houston's Colored Citizens' Activities and Conditions among the Negro Population in the 1920s," in Howard Beeth and Cary D. Wintz, eds., *Black Dixie: Afro-Texan History and Culture in Houston,* pp. 129–33 (quote).
6. Ben S. Davison," Introductory to Chief of Police Davison's Annual Report," *The Detective* 32, no. 370 (1916): 17 (first quote); Martha Gruening, "Houston, an N.A.A.C.P. Investigation," *The Crisis* 15, no. 1 (November, 1917): 17 (second quote); Louis J. Marchiafava, "The Houston Police, 1878–1948," *Rice University Studies* 63, no. 2 (Spring, 1977): 11–13; Houston *Post,* Aug. 22, 1978.
7. See chapter one for Houston article and incident. For the East St. Louis race riot, see Elliott M. Rudwick, *Race Riot at East St. Louis, July 2 1917.* White mobs invaded black neighborhoods, killing at least forty. The Illinois National Guard and city police encouraged the rioters. Robert V. Haynes, *A Night of Violence: The Houston Riot of 1917,* pp. 58–59. For black migration northward see David M. Kennedy, *Over Here: The First World War and American Society,* pp. 279–80.
8. Houston *Press,* July 28, 1917; Houston *Post,* July 29, 1917; Houston *Chronicle,* July 29, 1917.

9. *U.S. v. William C. Nesbit, Sergeant, Company I, 24th Infantry, et al.*, Fort Sam Houston, Texas, Nov. 1, 1917, Judge Advocate General's Office, U.S. War Department, RG 153, N.A. The marchers took the southward route, August 23.

10. Houston *Chronicle*, Aug. 26, 1917.

11. Johnston, *Houston*, pp. 200; Houston *Chronicle*, Aug. 17, 1917; Aug. 26, 1917.

12. C. D. Waide, "When Psychology Failed," *Houston Gargoyle*, May 15–June 12, 1928, p. 6; Houston *Post*, Aug. 23, 1976; *U.S. v. Nesbit*.

13. Houston *Chronicle*, July 30, 1917; Houston *Post*, July 31, 1917; Houston *Press*, Aug. 3, 1917; Aug. 7, 1917.

14. Houston *Press*, Aug. 1, 1917; Aug. 3, 1917; Aug. 7, 1917 (quote).

15. Houston *Chronicle*, Aug. 2, 1917 (first quote); Aug. 4, 1917; Houston *Press*, Aug. 22, 1917 (second quote).

16. Houston *Press*, July 30, 1917; Aug. 21, 1917; Houston *Chronicle*, Aug. 20, 1917 (quote).

17. Houston *Post*, Aug. 15, 1917; Houston *Press*, Aug. 21, 1917.

18. Houston *Chronicle*, July 30, 1917.

19. Report of Col. G. O. Cress, A.I.G. to Commanding General, Sept. 13, 1917, Southern Department General Correspondence File 370.61, N.A.; Thomas Richard Adams, "The Houston Riot of 1917," M.A. thesis (Texas A&M University, 1972), p. 27.

20. *U.S. v. Nesbit*; Phocion Samuel Park, Jr., "The Twenty-fourth Infantry Regiment and the Houston Riot of 1917," M.A. thesis (University of Houston, 1971), p. iii; Edgar A. Schuler, "The Houston Race Riot, 1917," *Journal of Negro History* 29, no. 3 (July, 1944): 314–15.

21. Gruening, "Houston," p. 15.

22. Ibid.; Tamara Miner Haygood, "Use and Distribution of Slave Labor in Harris County, Texas, 1836–60," in Beeth and Wintz, *Black*, pp. 37.

23. *U.S. v. Nesbit*; Gruening, "Houston," p. 16.

24. *U.S. v. Nesbit* (quote); Major K. S. Snow, Infantry to Brig. Gen. John S. Hulen, Report of Circumstances Attending the Rioting, Aug. 24, 1917, HMRC. Kneeland Sparrow Snow entered the army from Ohio as a private in the hospital and signal corps in 1900. He obtained a commission in 1901. Francis B. Heitman, *Historical Register and Dictionary of the United States Army*, 1:906.

25. *U.S. v. Nesbit*; Snow to Hulen, Aug. 24, 1917.

26. *U.S. v. Nesbit*; Cress to Commanding General, Sept. 13, 1917.

27. Cress to Commanding General, Sept. 13, 1917 (quotes); Houston *Chronicle*, Aug. 24, 1917; Houston *Press*, Aug. 24, 1917; Houston *Post*, Aug. 24, 1917. A Houston realtor recalled as a boy planning to meet Earl Findley and Freddie Schofield in downtown Houston to drive to a party in the west end. While waiting, young William fell asleep in a movie theater, missing the fatal ride that killed Findley and seriously wounded Schofield. William A. Bernrieder to Dr. Robert V. Haynes, Aug. 23, 1977, Houston, Texas, HMRC. Obviously, if the soldiers had fired truly indiscriminately and at will, the carnage would have exceeded the actual count.

28. *U.S. v. Nesbit*; Houston *Chronicle*, Aug. 24, 1917; Houston *Press*, Aug. 24, 1917; Houston *Post*, Aug. 24, 1917.

29. *U.S. v. Nesbit*; Houston *Chronicle*, Aug. 24, 1917; Houston *Press*, Aug. 24, 1917; Houston *Post*, Aug. 24, 1917.

30. Snow to Hulen, Aug. 24, 1917 (first and third quotes); Cress to Commanding General, Sept. 13, 1917 (second quote).

31. Cress to Commanding General, Sept. 13, 1917.

32. Ibid.; Houston *Chronicle*, Aug. 24, 1917; Houston *Press*, Aug. 24, 1917; Houston *Post*, Aug. 24, 1917.

33. Houston *Chronicle*, Aug. 24, 1917; Houston *Post*, Aug. 24, 1917; Houston *Press*, Aug. 24, 1917.

34. *U.S. v. Nesbit*; Houston *Chronicle*, Aug. 24, 1917; Houston *Press*, Aug. 24, 1917; Houston *Post*, Aug. 24, 1917.

35. Houston *Chronicle*, Aug. 24, 1917.

36. Houston *Post*, Aug. 25, 1917 (first quote); Houston *Press*, Aug. 27, 1917 (second quote); Aug. 31, 1917 (third quote).

37. Houston *Chronicle*, Aug. 24, 1917; Aug. 26, 1917 (quote); Houston *Post*, Sept. 6, 1917.

38. Houston *Chronicle*, Aug. 25, 1917.

39. Ibid.

40. Ibid., Aug. 29, 1917; Aug. 30, 1917.

41. Houston *Press*, Aug. 28, 1917; Houston *Post*, Aug. 25, 1917; Houston *Chronicle*, Aug. 26, 1917 (quotes). Contrast the reporting in *The Crisis*, Gruening, "Houston," pp. 14–19.

42. Houston *Post*, Sept. 13, 1917; Houston *Press*, Sept. 11, 1917.

43. Houston *Chronicle*, Aug. 23, 1917 (first quote); Sept. 11, 1917 (second and third quotes); Sept. 12, 1917 (fourth quote); Houston *Post*, Sept. 12, 1917.

44. Houston *Chronicle*, Sept. 12, 1917; Houston *Post*, Sept. 2, 1917; Houston *Press*, Aug. 31, 1917; Sept. 11, 1917.

45. Gruening, "Houston," 17 (first quote); "Houston," *The Crisis* 14, no. 6 (October, 1917): 285 (second quote).

46. Cress to Commanding General, Sept. 13, 1917.

47. Ibid.

48. Ibid.

49. Houston *Chronicle*, Aug. 28, 1917; Sept. 1, 1917; Sept. 4, 1917 (first quote); Sept. 8, 1917; Houston *Post*, Sept. 5, 1917 (second quote); Sept. 13, 1917.

50. Houston *Chronicle*, Sept. 2, 1917; Houston *Post*, Sept. 6, 1917; Sept. 10, 1917; Houston *Press*, Sept. 6, 1917; Mrs. W. M. Baines, ed., *Houston's Part in the World War*, pp. 91–99; Haynes, *Night*, pp. 204.

51. *U.S. v. Nesbit*; *U.S. v. Corporal John Washington et al.*; *U.S. v. Corporal Robert Tillman et al.* George King Hunter of Ohio graduated sixty-seventh in his class from the Military Academy in 1873. He served in the 4th Cavalry, 3rd Cavalry, and 15th Cavalry. Heitman, *Historical*, 1:557. Benjamin Andrew Poore from Alabama graduated thirty-third in his class from the Military Academy in 1882. He served in the 12th Infantry, 10th Infantry, and 6th Infantry. Ibid., 1:797. John Adley Hull of Iowa served as a major and lieutenant colonel in the volunteers in 1898–1899 and was commissioned a major in the army in 1901. Ibid.

52. *U.S. v. Nesbit*.

53. Ibid.

54. Ibid.
55. Ibid.
56. Ibid.
57. Ibid.
58. Ibid.
59. Ibid.
60. Ibid.; Haynes, *Night,* pp. 254–96.
61. *U.S. v. Nesbit; U.S. v. Tillman.* The condemned men requested death by firing squad, but the army considered them unworthy. Every account had them dying courageously, while maintaining their innocence. Houston *Chronicle,* Dec. 2, 1917; San Antonio *Light,* Dec. 7, 1975.
62. *U.S. v. Washington.*
63. Ibid.
64. Ibid.
65. Ibid.; Haynes, *Night,* pp. 301–302; Houston *Chronicle,* Sept. 4, 1918; San Antonio *Light,* Dec. 7, 1975.
66. Houston *Chronicle,* Dec. 12, 1917; Houston *Press,* Dec. 11, 1917.
67. "Houston and East St. Louis," *The Crisis* 15, no. 6 (April, 1918): 269.
68. Mary F. Berry and John W. Blassingame, *Long Memory: The Black Experience in America,* p. 316; "Riot of United States Negro Soldiers at Houston, Tex.," Senate Report No. 235, 66th Congress, lst sess., Oct. 1, 1919; "Houston Riot Cases," House Report No. 503, 67th Congress, 2nd sess., Dec. 9, 1921. The author as a child in Houston heard hushed rumors of past and pending unprovoked black riots. Celeste Walker, author of the play *Camp Logan,* stated, "I had always heard bits and pieces of the Camp Logan Story." See Rosalind Alexander, "Houston's Hidden History," *Texas Observer* 81, no. 7 (April 7, 1989): 18–20.
69. A series of articles that appeared in a Houston magazine in 1928 served as the closest kin to a formal history until the mid-1940s. The series, by Edgar A. Schuler for the *Journal of Negro History,* relied heavily on local newspapers, thereby validating the hometown version of the story. Waide, "When", May 15–June 12, 1928; Schuler, "Houston," pp. 300–38; Park, "Twenty-fourth"; Adams, "Houston"; Haynes, "The Houston Mutiny and Riot of 1917," *Southwestern Historical Quarterly* 76 (April, 1973): 418–39; Haynes, *Night.* For continued interest, see W. C. Weltz to Editor, "Dialogue," *Texas Observer* 81, no. 11 (June 2, 1989): 2; John Minton, *The Houston Riot and Courts-Martial of 1917.*
70. Arthur E. Barbeau and Florette Henri, *The Unknown Soldiers: Black American Troops in World War One,* p. 27; Berry and Blassingame, *Long,* pp. 315–17. The army established one black officer training school at Des Moines, which attracted over sixty noncommissioned officers from the 24th Infantry. Haynes, *Night,* p. 248; Kennedy, *Over,* p. 159 (quote); Edward M. Coffman, *The War to End All Wars: The American Military Experience in World War I,* p. 58; Garna L. Christian, "Newton Baker's War on El Paso Vice," *Red River Valley Historical Review* 5, no. 2 (Spring, 1980): pp. 55–67.
71. Snow to Hulen, Aug. 24, 1917 (first quote); *U.S. v. Nesbitt;* Cress to Commanding General, Sept. 13, 1917 (second and third quotes). Credible arguments that fear, and possible existence, of a white mob produced the shootings are found in C. Calvin Smith, "On The Edge: The Houston Riot

of 1917 Revisited," *The Griot* 10, no. 1 (Spring, 1991): 3–17 and "The Houston Riot of 1917, Revisited," *Houston Review* 13, no. 2 (1991): 84–101.

72. *U.S. v. Nesbit* (first quote); Smith, "Houston," p. 95 (second quote); Snow to Hulen, Aug. 24, 1917 (third quote).

73. *U.S. v. Nesbit.* Disobedience of direct orders in wartime, as the prosecution emphasized in the Camp MacArthur courts-martial, carried punishment, including death, at the discretion of the court. Every soldier knew the possible consequences.

74. Ibid.

75. Snow to Hulen, Aug. 24, 1917; Review of record of trial by a general court-martial convened at Headquarters, Southern Department, Fort Sam Houston, Texas, on Nov. 1, 1917, War Department, Office of the Judge Advocate General, Washington, Jan. 29, 1918, RG 153, N.A.; Haynes, *Night,* pp. 164–66 (quote).

76. Houston *Post,* Aug. 24, 1917; Houston *Chronicle,* Aug. 24, 1917; Houston *Press,* Aug. 24, 1917 (first quote); Aug. 28, 1917 (second quote).

77. Sworn statement of Lincoln Kennerly to J. M. Ray, J. P. and ex-officio coroner, Harris County, Texas, Aug. 24, 1917, Harris County Texas Records Center. The author is indebted to Douglas Olefke for locating and providing inquest material on Henry and Private Watson.

78. J. R. Richardson to Maj. B. M. Chiperfield, Judge Advocate, 33d Division, U.S.A. in re Inventory of Effects Found on the Body of Sgt. Vida Henry, deceased, Sept. 22, 1917, RG 153, N.A. (first quote); Statement of H. D. Goldstein to Ray, Aug. 24, 1917, HCTRC (second quote). Henry's personal effects consisted of one leather belt, five face towels, two civilian shirts, one kimona, two handkerchiefs, one table cover, one safety razor, one fountain pen, one tobacco pouch, one leather purse, and one pair of black shoes, which brought $6.10 at sale.

79. Inquest reports on Vida Henry and Bryant Wilson, HCTRC.

80. Testimony of Major Snow to Board of Officers, Columbus, New Mexico, Sept. 26, 1917, RG 153, N.A.

81. Board of Officers report, ibid.

82. Texas State Board of Health, Bureau of Vital Statistics, Standard Certificate of Death, Sgt. Vida Henry, Sept. 13, 1917, ibid.

83. Houston *Chronicle,* Aug. 25, 1917.

84. Henry and Watson were buried in College Park Cemetery in Houston on Aug. 26, 1917, the U.S. government paying the expenses. The Houston *Press* carried the item under the headline "Unwept, Unhonored, and Unsung, Two Negro Soldiers Are Buried," Aug. 28, 1917.

85. Shortly before his execution, twenty-four-year-old Pvt. T. C. Hawkins, claiming presence on a picket line at camp during the riot, wrote his parents: "When this letter reaches you I will be beyond the veil of sorrow . . . in heaven with the angels. . . . I am not guilty of the crime that I am accused of[,] but Mother it is God's will that I go now in this way." Menton, *Houston,* p. 25. Contemporary criticism of the prosecution of the riot centered on the swiftness of punishment, the harshness of justice in comparison to white violence, and the possibility of individual innocence.

10: Last Muster

1. Newsfilm Collection, Mississippi Department of Archives and History, Jackson, Mississippi, by courtesy of Dan Den Bleyker, Audio-Visuals Records Curator.

2. San Antonio blacks boycotted the city's trolley cars in 1904, following the ordinance segregating the cars in 1903. Although more peaceful than the soldiers' resistance, six boycotters were arrested for pulling a youth from a car. Houston also passed a segregation ordinance for trolley cars in 1903, producing protests three years before the passage of the state law. August Meier and Elliott Rudwick, "The Boycott Movement against Jim Crow Streetcars in the South, 1900–1906," *Journal of American History* 55, no. 4 (March, 1969): 757–63.

3. Admittedly, the analyses centered on late nineteenth-century garrison towns. See Jack D. Foner, *Blacks and the Military in American History*, p. 57; Marvin E. Fletcher, *The Black Soldier and Officer in the U.S. Army 1891–1917*, p. 25; Frank N. Schubert, "Black Soldiers on the White Frontier: Some Factors Influencing Race Relations," *Phylon* 32, no. 4 (Winter, 1971): 411–15.

4. "Discipline: The Brownsville Affray," Annual Report of the Secretary of War, 1906, in Bernard C. Nalty and Morris J. MacGregor, eds., *Blacks in the Military: Essential Documents*, p. 60; Memorandum, Col. G. C. Gross, assistant inspector general, to commanding general, Southern Department, Sept. 13, 1917, in ibid., p. 68.

5. Southern whites' fear of armed blacks contributed to their exclusion from the state militia in the early 1900s. Texas legislated an all-white militia in 1906. Alwyn Barr, "The Black Militia of the New South: Texas as a Test Case," *Journal of Negro History* 63, no. 3 (July, 1978): 209–19.

6. "By the late 1870s, the army, like the civilian society it mirrored, was less concerned for the black man than it had been earlier." Arlen L. Fowler, *The Black Infantry in the West, 1869–1891*, p. 135. Most white officers accepted assignment to black units reluctantly. Foner, *Blacks*, p. 60.

7. Richard O. Hope, *Racial Strife in the Military: Toward the Elimination of Discrimination*, pp. 15; U.S. Congress, Senate, Congressional Record, 76th Congress, 3rd sess., 1940, in Nalty and MacGregor, *Blacks*, p. 100; Booker T. Washington to Secretary of War William Howard Taft, Tuskegee, Alabama, Nov. 20, 1906, in ibid., pp. 61–62 (quote). Popular literature celebrated the black soldier's role in the Spanish-American War, sometimes condescendingly, and included significant contributions of black authors. Perry E. Gianakos, "The Spanish-American War and the Double Paradox of the Negro," *Phylon* 26, no. 1 (Spring, 1965): pp. 34–49; Robert B. Rackleff, "The Black Soldier in Popular American Magazines, 1900–1971," *Negro History Bulletin* 34, no. 8 (December, 1971), p. 185; James Robert Payne, "Afro-American Literature of the Spanish-American War," *Melus* 10, no. 3 (Fall, 1983): 19–32.

8. "Negroes had little at the turn of the century to help sustain our faith in ourselves except the pride that we took in the Ninth and Tenth Cavalry, the Twenty-fourth and Twenty-fifth Infantry." Rayford W. Logan, *The Betrayal of the Negro from Rutherford B. Hayes to Woodrow Wilson*, p. 335; John F. Marszalek, Jr., "The Black Man in Military History," *Negro History Bulletin* 36, no. 6 (October, 1973): 122–25.

9. The army created the 92nd and 93rd Divisions, which participated in both world wars. The two cavalry regiments served in the 2nd Cavalry Division in World War II. See Department of Defense, *Black Americans in Defense of Our Nation*, pp. 29, 34; Foner, *Blacks*, p. 160; Hope, *Racial*, p. 24; David M. Kennedy, *Over Here: The First World War and American Society*, pp. 162, 176, 199–200. "In the future the whites would emphasize the failure of the 368th in the Argonne and forget the achievements of the four separate Negro infantry regiments. On the very days in late September that the 368th had its difficulties, the Negroes in the 369th, 370th, 371st, and 372nd were carrying out successfully their missions in general attacks with the French in Champagne and the Oise-Aisne sectors. And the 370th was officered largely by Negroes. The French praised these regiments but white Americans chose to remember the 368th." Edward M. Coffman, *The War to End All Wars: The American Military Experience in World War I*, p. 320. Truman's order did not technically end segregation in the armed forces, which finally occurred in 1954. Defense, *Black*, p. 42.

10. New York *Times*, Sept. 29, 1972; Dec. 31, 1971 (quote). Continued racial discrimination prompted the Gesell Committee Report of 1964, which noted unbalanced grade distribution of blacks, token integration and exclusionary practices in the National Guard and reserves, and racial discrimination on military installations and in surrounding communities. Martin Binkin and Mark J. Eitelberg with others, *Blacks and the Military*, pp. 31–32.

Bibliography

Documents and Collections

Adjutant General's Office. *Official Army Register.* 3 vols. Washington, D.C.: Government Printing Office, 1956.

Adjutant General's Office, 1780s-1917. General Correspondence, 1890–1917. Record Group 94. National Archives and Records Service, Washington, D.C.

Adjutant General's Office, 1917-. Record Group 407. National Archives and Records Service, Washington, D.C.

"Affray at Brownsville, Texas." Hearings before the Committee on Military Affairs, United States Senate. 6 vols. Washington, D.C.: Government Printing Office. 1907.

Biennial Report of the Adjutant General of Texas, from January 1, 1917 to December 31, 1918, Texas State Archives, Austin, Texas.

"The Black Battalion Speeches of Hon. Joseph B. Foraker of Ohio in the Senate of the United States, January 3, 16 and 17, 1907." Washington, D.C.: Government Printing Office, 1907.

"The Brownsville Affray." Senate Document no. 389. 60th Congress, 1st sess. Washington, D.C.: Government Printing Office, 1907.

Conditional Pardon by the Governor of the State of Texas, no. 11566. June 20, 1913. Texas Department of Corrections, Huntsville, Texas.

General Court Martial no. 105553. Record Group 153. Adjutant General's Office. National Archives and Records Center, Washington, D.C.

Governors' Papers: Joseph D. Sayers. Texas State Archives, Austin, Texas.

Heitman, Francis B. *Historical Register and Dictionary of the United States Army.* 2 vols. Washington, D.C.: Government Printing Office, 1903.

"Houston Riot Cases." House Report No. 503. 67th Congress, 2nd sess., December 9, 1921.

Inquest Reports of Harris County Texas Records Center, Houston, Texas, 1917.

Investigation of the Conduct of United States Troops Stationed at Fort Brown, Tex. Washington, D.C.: Government Printing Office, 1906.

Investigation of Riot at Rio Grande City and Fort Ringgold by Thomas Scurry, Adjutant General of Texas, November 30, 1899. Texas State Archives, Austin, Texas.

Judge Advocate General's Office. Record Group 153. National Archives and Records Service, Washington, D.C.

Nalty, Bernard C., and Morris J. MacGregor, eds. *Blacks in the Military: Essential Documents.* Wilmington, Del.: Scholarly Resources, 1981.

Newsfilm Collection. Mississippi Department of Archives and History. Jackson, Mississippi.

Proceedings of a General Court-Martial, Capt. Edgar A. Macklin. Washington, D.C.: Government Printing Office. 1907.

Ranger Force Monthly Returns, Texas State Archives, Austin, Texas.

Ranger Investigating Committee, February 18, 1919. Journal of the House of Representatives of the Regular Session of the 36th Legislature. Texas State Archives, Austin, Texas.

"Riot of United States Negro Soldiers at Houston, Tex." Senate Report No. 235. 66th Congress, 1st sess., October 1, 1919.

Rothrock, W. P. "Completion Report of Camp Logan." Department of War. Washington, D.C.: Government Printing Office, 1918.

Southwestern Reporter, vols. 62, 77. St. Paul, Minn.: West Publishing Co., 1901, 1904).

United States Census, 1910. Supplement for Texas. Federal Archives and Records Center, Fort Worth, Texas.

United States Continental Commands, 1821–1920. Record Group 393. National Archives and Records Service, Washington, D.C.

Waco City Council. Minutes. Texas Collection. Baylor University, Waco, Texas.

Warrant of Authority and Descriptive List. Texas Adjutant General's Department. Texas State Archives, Austin, Texas.

Books

Anders, Evan. *Boss Rule in South Texas: The Progressive Era.* Austin: University of Texas Press, 1987.

Baines, Mrs. W. M., ed. *Houston's Part in the World War.* Houston, 1919.

Barbeau, Arthur E., and Florette Henri. *The Unknown Soldiers: Black American Troops in World War One.* Philadelphia: Temple University Press, 1974.

Barr, Alwyn. *Black Texans: A History of Negroes in Texas, 1528–1971.* Austin: Jenkins, 1973.

Beeth, Howard, and Cary D. Wintz, eds. *Black Dixie: Afro-Texan History and Culture in Houston.* College Station: Texas A&M University Press, 1992.

Berry, Mary F., and John W. Blassingame. *Long Memory: The Black Experience in America.* New York: Oxford University Press, 1982.

Binkin, Martin, and Mark J. Eitelberg with Alvin J. Schexnider and Marvin N. Smith. *Blacks and the Military.* Washington, D.C.: Brookings Institution, 1982.

Calleros, Cleofas. *El Paso, Then and Now.* El Paso: American Printing, 1959.

Carroll, John M., ed. *The Black Military Experience in the American West.* New York: Liveright, 1971.

Chatfield, Lieutenant W. H. *The Twin Cities of the Border and the Country of the Lower Rio Grande.* New Orleans: E. P. Brandao, 1893.

Clendenen, Clarence. *Blood on the Border: The United States and the Mexican Irregulars.* New York: Macmillan, 1969.

Cline, Howard F. *The United States and Mexico.* Cambridge: Harvard University Press, 1965.

Coerver, Don M., and Linda B. Hall. *Texas and the Mexican Revolution: A Study in State and National Border Policy, 1910–1920.* San Antonio: Trinity University Press, 1984.

Coffman, Edward M. *The Old Army: A Portrait of the American Army in Peacetime, 1784–1898.* New York: Oxford University Press, 1986.

——————. *The War to End All Wars: The American Military Experience in World War I.* New York: Oxford University Press, 1968.

Conger, Roger N. *Frontier Forts of Texas.* Waco: Texian Press, 1966.

Cornish, Dudley T. *The Sable Arm: Negro Troops in the Union Army, 1861–1865.* New York: W. W. Norton and Company, 1966.

Crego, Arthur Van Voorhis. *City on the Mesa: The New Fort Bliss, 1890–1895.* Fort Bliss, Tex., 1969.

Cummins, [Col.] M. L. *Historical Data on San Antonio and Fort Sam Houston.* San Antonio, n.d.

Curry, William H. *A History of Early Waco with Allusions to Six Shooter Junction.* Waco: Texian Press, 1968.

Davis, John L. *The Texas Rangers: Their First 150 Years.* San Antonio: Institute of Texan Cultures, 1975.

Defense Department. *Black Americans in Defense of Our Nation.* Washington, D.C.: Government Printing Office, 1985.

DuBois, W. E. B. *Dusk of Dawn.* Millwood, New York: Kraus-Thomson, 1975.

Douglas, C. L. *The Gentlemen in the White Hats: Dramatic Episodes in the History of the Texas Rangers.* Dallas: Southwest Press, 1934.

Dunning, William A. *Reconstruction, Political and Economic, 1865–1877.* New York: Harper and Brothers, 1907.

Dupuy, [Col.] Richard Ernest. *The Compact History of the United States Army.* New York: Hawthorn Publishers, 1973.

Ferguson, Henry N. *The Port of Brownsville: A Maritime History of the Rio Grande Valley.* Brownsville: Springman-King Press, 1976.

Fletcher, Marvin E. *The Black Soldier and Officer in the U.S. Army, 1891–1917.* Columbia: University of Missouri Press, 1974.

Foner, Jack D. *Blacks and the Military in American History.* New York: Praeger, 1974.

——————. *The United States Soldier between Two Wars: Army Life and Reforms, 1865–1898.* New York: Humanities Press, 1970.

Foner, Philip S. *History of Black Americans: From the Emergence of the Cotton Kingdom to the Eve of the Compromise of 1850.* Westport, Conn.: Greenwood Press, 1983.

Foraker, Joseph B. *Notes of a Busy Life.* Cincinnati: Stewart and Kidd Company, 1916. 2 vols.

Fowler, Arlen L. *The Black Infantry in the West, 1869–1891.* Westport, Conn.: Greenwood, 1971.

Frazer, Robert W. *Forts of the West.* Norman: University of Oklahoma Press, 1965.

Gatewood, William B., Jr. *Black Americans and the White Man's Burden, 1893–1903.* Urbana: University of Illinois Press, 1975.

——————, comp. *"Smoked Yankees" and the Struggle for Empire: Letters from Negro Soldiers, 1898–1902.* Urbana: University of Illinois Press, 1971.

Graham, Hugh Davis, and Ted Robert Gurr, eds. *The History of Violence in America.* New York: Praeger, 1969.

Grimshaw, Allen, ed. *Racial Violence in the United States.* Chicago: Aldine, 1969.

Haley, J. Evetts. *Fort Concho and the Texas Frontier.* San Angelo: San Angelo Standard Times, 1952.

Harris, Fred R. *America's Democracy: The Ideal and the Reality.* Glenview, Ill.: Scott, Foresman and Company, 1980.

Hart, Herbert M. *Old Forts of the Southwest.* Seattle: Superior, 1964.

Haynes, Robert V. *A Night of Violence: The Houston Riot of 1917.* Baton Rouge: Louisiana State University Press, 1977.

Higginson, Thomas Wentworth. *Army Life in a Black Regiment.* East Lansing: Michigan State University, 1960.

Hinojosa, Gilberto Miguel. *A Borderlands Town in Transition: Laredo, 1755–1870.* College Station. Texas A&M University Press, 1983.

Hope, Richard O. *Racial Strife in the Military: Toward the Elimination of Discrimination.* New York: Praeger, 1979.

House, Boyce. *San Antonio, City of Flaming Adventure.* San Antonio: Naylor, 1949.

Hurley, Marvin. *Decisive Years for Houston.* Houston: Houston Chamber of Commerce, 1966.

Johnston, Marguerite. *Houston: The Unknown City, 1836–1946.* College Station: Texas A&M University Press, 1991.

Jones, Rosemary Whitehead, Jr., ed. *La Hacienda: An Official Bicentennial Publication.* Urbana: University of Illinois Press, 1976.

Katz, William Loren. *The Black West.* Garden City, N.Y.: Doubleday, 1971.

Kearney, Milo, ed. *Studies in Brownsville History.* Brownsville: Pan American University, 1986.

Kelley, Dayton, ed. *The Handbook of Waco and McLennan County, Texas.* Waco: Texian Press, 1972.

Kennedy, David M. *Over Here: The First World War and American Society.* New York: Oxford University Press, 1980.

Kindervater, [Maj.] E. A. *Fort Sam Houston: A Historical Sketch.* n.p., 1936.

Lane, Ann J. *The Brownsville Affair: National Crisis and Black Reaction.* Port Washington, N.Y.: Kennikat Press, 1971.

Leckie, William H. *The Buffalo Soldiers, A Narrative of the Negro Cavalry in the West.* Norman: University of Oklahoma Press, 1967.

Lee, Irvin H. *Negro Medal of Honor Men.* New York: Dodd, Mead and Company, 1967.

Livermore, Seward L. *Politics Is Adjourned: Woodrow Wilson and the War Congress, 1916–1918.* Middletown, Conn: Wesleyan University Press, 1966.

Logan, Rayford W. *The Betrayal of the Negro from Rutherford B. Hayes to Woodrow Wilson.* New York: Collier Books, 1965.

McComb, David G. *Houston: A History.* Austin: University of Texas Press, 1981.

McMaster, Richard K. *Musket, Saber, and Missile: A History of Fort Bliss.* El Paso: Complete Printing and Letter Service, 1962.

McPherson, James M. *The Negro's Civil War: How American Negroes Felt and Acted during the War for the Union.* New York: Pantheon Press, 1965.

Marcus, Robert D., and David Burner, eds. *America since 1945.* New York: St. Martin's Press, 1981.

Marszalek, John F., Jr. *Court-Martial: A Black Man in America.* New York: Scribner, 1972.

Metz, Leon. *City at the Pass: An Illustrated History of El Paso.* Woodland, Calif.: Windsor Publication, 1980.

—————. *Fort Bliss: An Illustrated History.* El Paso: Mangan Books, 1981.

Meyer, Michael C., and William L. Sherman. *The Course of Mexican History.* New York: Oxford University Press, 1983.

Miller, Ray. *Ray Miller's Houston.* Houston: Cordovan Press, 1984.

Minton, John. *The Houston Riot and Courts-Martial of 1917.* San Antonio, n.d.

Montejano, David. *Anglos and Mexicans in the Making of Texas, 1836–1986.* Austin: University of Texas Press, 1987.

Morison, Elting E., ed. *The Letters of Theodore Roosevelt.* 8 vols. Cambridge: Harvard University Press, 1951–1954.

Nankivell, John H. *History of the Twenty-fifth Regiment, United States Infantry, 1869–1926.* New York: Negro Universities Press, 1969.

Parkes, Henry Bamford. *A History of Mexico.* Boston: Houghton Mifflin, 1969.

Quarles, Benjamin. *The Negro in the Civil War.* Boston: Little, Brown and Company, 1953.

Rice, Lawrence D. *The Negro in Texas, 1874–1900.* Baton Rouge: Louisiana State University Press, 1971.

Richardson, Rupert N., Ernest Wallace, and Adrian Anderson. *Texas, the Lone Star State.* Englewood Cliffs, N.J.: Prentice-Hall, 1988.

Rickey, Don, Jr. *Forty Miles a Day on Beans and Hay: The Enlisted Soldier Fighting the Indian Wars.* Norman: University of Oklahoma Press, 1963.

Rudwick, Elliott M. *Race Riot at East St. Louis, July 2, 1917.* Carbondale: Southern Illinois University Press, 1964.

Ruiz, Eduardo. *The Great Rebellion: Mexico, 1905–1924.* New York: W. W. Norton and Company, 1980.

Samora, Julian, Joe Bernal, and Albert Pena. *Gunpowder Justice: A Reassessment of the Texas Rangers.* Notre Dame, Ind.: Notre Dame University Press, 1979.

Scobee, Barry. *Old Fort Davis.* San Antonio: Naylor, 1947.

Sexton, William Thaddeus. *Soldiers in the Sun: An Adventure in Imperialism.* Harrisburg, Penn.: The Military Service Publishing Co., 1939.

Singletary, Otis. *Negro Militia and Reconstruction.* Austin: University of Texas Press, 1957.

Sonnichsen, C. L. *Pass of the North: Four Centuries on the Rio Grande.* El Paso: Texas Western Press, 1968.

Stampp, Kenneth M. *The Era of Reconstruction, 1865–1877.* New York: Alfred A. Knopf, 1965.

Texas Almanac and State Industrial Guide. Galveston and Dallas: A. H. Belo and Company, 1904, 1911, 1912, 1914.

Thompson, Jerry. *Sabers on the Rio Grande.* Austin: Presidial Press, 1974.

Timmons, W. H. *El Paso: A Borderlands History.* El Paso: University of Texas at El Paso, 1990.

Titherington, Richard H. *A History of the Spanish-American War of 1898.* Freeport, N.Y.: Books for Libraries Press, 1971.

Toulouse, Joseph H., and James R. Toulouse. *Pioneer Posts of Texas.* San Antonio: Naylor, 1936.

Turner, Leo. *The Story of Fort Sam Houston, 1876–1936.* San Antonio: Leo Turner, 1936.

Tuttle, William M., Jr. *Race Riot: Chicago in the Red Summer of 1919.* New York: Atheneum, 1970.

Vandiver, Frank E. *Black Jack: The Life and Times of John J. Pershing.* 2 vols. College Station: Texas A&M University Press, 1977.

Weaver, John D. *The Brownsville Raid.* New York: W. W. Norton and Company, 1970.

Webb, Walter Prescott, ed. *The Handbook of Texas.* 2 vols. Austin: Texas State Historical Association, 1952.

————. *The Texas Rangers: A Century of Frontier Defense.* Boston: Encino Press, 1955.

Wesley, Charles H., and Patricia W. Romero. *Negro Americans in the Civil War: From Slavery to Citizenship.* New York: Publishers Company, 1968.

White, Owen. *Out of the Desert: The Historical Romance of El Paso.* El Paso: McMath, 1923.

Wilkinson, Joseph B. *Laredo and the Rio Grande.* Austin: Jenkins, 1975.

Williams, George W. *A History of Negro Troops in the War of the Rebellion, 1861– 1865.* New York: Harpers and Brothers, 1888.

Woodward, C. Vann. *The Strange Career of Jim Crow.* New York: Oxford University Press, 1966.

Woolridge, Ruby A., and Robert B. Vezzetti. *Brownsville: A Pictorial History.* Norfolk, Va.: Donning, 1982.

Wooster, Robert. *Soldiers, Sutlers, and Settlers: Garrison Life on the Texas Frontier.* College Station: Texas A&M University Press, 1987.

Zinn, Howard. *Postwar America: 1945–1971.* Indianapolis and New York: Bobbs-Merrill, 1973.

Articles and Theses

Adams, Thomas Richard. "The Houston Riot of 1917." M.A. thesis, Texas A&M University, 1972.

Alexander, Rosalind. "Houston's Hidden History." *Texas Observer* 81, no. 7 (April 7, 1989): 18–20.

Barr, Alwyn. "The Black Militia of the New South: Texas as a Test Case." *Journal of Negro History* 63, no. 3 (July, 1978): 209–19.

————. "The Texas 'Black Uprising' Scare of 1883." *Phylon* 41, no. 2 (Summer, 1980): 179–86.

Billington, Monroe. "Black Soldiers at Fort Selden, New Mexico, 1866–1891." *New Mexico Historical Review* 62, no. 1 (January, 1987): 65–80.

Bryan, Marilyn T. "The Economic and Political Social Status of the Negro in El Paso." *Password* 13, no. 3 (Fall, 1968): 90–97.

Carlson, Paul. "'Pecos Bill' Shafter: Campaigning in Mexico 1876–1877." *Military History of Texas and the Southwest* 16, no. 4 (1980): 223–45.

————. "'Pecos Bill' Shafter: Scouting the Llano Estacado." *Military History of Texas and the Southwest* 16, no. 1 (1980): 34–53.

Christian, Garna L. "The Brownsville Raid's 168th Man: The Court Martial of Corporal Knowles." *Southwestern Historical Quarterly* 93, no. 1 (July, 1989): 45–59.

————. "The El Paso Racial Crisis of 1900." *Red River Valley Historical Review* 6, no. 2 (Spring, 1981): 28–41.

————. "Newton Baker's War on El Paso Vice." *Red River Valley Historical Review* 5, no. 2 (Spring, 1980): 55–67.

————. "The Ordeal and the Prize: The 24th Infantry and Camp MacArthur." *Military Affairs* 50, no. 2 (April, 1986): 65–70.

————. "Rio Grande City: Prelude to the Brownsville Raid." *West Texas Historical Association Year Book* 62 (1981): 118–32.

————. "Sword and Plowshare: The Symbiotic Development of Fort Bliss and El Paso, Texas, 1849–1918." Ph.D. thesis, Texas Tech University, 1977.

————. "The Twenty-fifth Regiment at Fort McIntosh: Precursor to Retaliatory Violence." *West Texas Historical Association Year Book* 55 (1979): 149–61.

————. "The Violent Possibility: The Tenth Cavalry at Texarkana." *East Texas Historical Review* 23, no. 1 (Spring, 1985): 3–15.

Cook, Lawrence Hugh. "The Brownsville Affray of 1906." M.A. thesis, University of Colorado, 1942.

Coons, C. Wilbur. "Waco—A Typical Texas City: Her Past, Her Present, Her Future." *Texas Magazine* 1, no. 6 (April, 1910): 66–68.

Cornish, Dudley T. "The Union Army as a Training School for Negroes." *Journal of Negro History* 37 (October, 1952): 368–82.

Cottrol, Robert J. "Heroism and the Origins of Afro-American History." *New England Quarterly* 51, no. 2 (June, 1978): 256–63.

Crimmins, Col. M. L. "An Army Bride's Impressions of Fort Brown." *Frontier Times* 15, no. 9 (July, 1938), 419–23.

Dalfiume, Richard M. "The Forgotten Years of the Negro Revolution." *Journal of American History* 55, no. 1 (June, 1968): 90–106.

Davis, Margaret. "Harlots and Hymnals: An Historic Confrontation of Vice and Virtue in Waco, Texas." *Waco Heritage and History* 9, no. 3 (Fall, 1978): 1–39.

Foraker, Joseph Benson. "A Review of the Testimony in the Brownsville Investigation." *North American Review,* April, 1908, 550–58.

Gatewood, Willard B., Jr. "Negro Troops in Florida, 1898." *Florida Historical Quarterly* 49, no. 1 (July, 1970): 1–15.

Haney, James E. "Blacks and the Republican Nomination of 1908." *Ohio History* 84, no. 4 (1975): 207–21.

Haynes, Robert V. "The Houston Mutiny and Riot of 1917." *Southwestern Historical Quarterly* 76, no. 4 (April, 1973): 418–39.

Howland, C. R. "Fort Sam Houston—Largest Army Post in the United States." *Texas Centennial Magazine* (September, 1935): 3–4.

"A Letter of Appreciation of Waco." *Chamber of Commerce News* 1, no. 1 (May, 1919): 5.

McChristian, Douglas C. "Grierson's Fight at Tinaja de Las Palmas: An Episode in the Victoria Campaign." *Red River Valley Historical Review* 7, no. 1 (Winter, 1982): 45–63.

Marchiafava, Louis J. "The Houston Police: 1878–1948." *Rice University Studies* 63, no. 2 (Spring, 1977): 8–23.

Marszalek, John F., Jr. "The Black Man in Military History." *Negro History Bulletin* 36, no. 6 (October, 1973): 122–25.

Meier, August, and Elliott Rudwick. "The Boycott Movement Against Jim Crow Streetcars in the South, 1900–1906." *Journal of American History* 55, no. 4 (March, 1969): 756–75.

Meyers, Fred T. "Prosperous Del Rio." *Texas Magazine* 2, no. 3 (July, 1910): 83–84.

Mills, Sherwin R. "The Army Maneuvers in Texas." *Texas Magazine* 3, no. 1 (May, 1911): 7–14.

Park, Phocion Samuel, Jr. "The Twenty-fourth Infantry Regiment and the Houston Riot of 1917." M.A. thesis, University of Houston, 1971.

Payne, James Robert. "Afro-American Literature of the Spanish-American War." *Melus* 10, no. 3 (Fall, 1983): 19–32.

Rackleff, Robert B. "The Black Soldier in Popular American Magazines, 1900–1917." *Negro History Bulletin* 34, no. 8 (December, 1971): 185–89.

Ruhl, Arthur. "The Gallery at San Antonio." *Collier's* 47 (April 29, 1911): 13–14+.

Scheiner, Seth M. "President Roosevelt and the Negro, 1901–1908." *Journal of Negro History* 47 (July, 1962): 169–81.

Schubert, Frank N. "Black Soldiers on the White Frontier: Some Factors Influencing Race Relations." *Phylon* 32, no. 4 (Winter, 1971): 410–15.

Schuler, Edgar A. "The Houston Race Riot, 1917." *Journal of Negro History* , no. 3 (July, 1944): 300–338.

Scott, M. C. "The Lower Rio Grande Country." *Farm and Ranch* 23, no. 17 (April 24, 1904): 1–2.

Smith, C. Calvin. "The Houston Riot of 1917 Revisited." *Houston Review* 13, no. 2 (1991): 84–101.

—————. "On the Edge: The Houston Riot of 1917 Revisited." *The Griot* 10, no. 1 (Spring, 1991): 3–12.

SoRelle, James Martin. "'The Darker Side of Heaven': The Black Community in Houston, Texas." Ph.D. dissertation, Kent State University, 1980.

—————. "'The Waco Horror': The Lynching of Jesse Washington." *Southwestern Historical Quarterly* 86, no. 4 (April, 1983): 517–36.

Thompson, Erwin N. "The Negro Soldiers on the Frontier: A Fort Davis Case Study." *Journal of the West* 7, no. 2 (April, 1968): 217–35.

Thornborough, Emma Lou. "The Brownsville Episode and the Negro Vote." *Mississippi Valley Historical Review* 44 (December, 1957): 469–93.

Tinsley, James A. "Roosevelt, Foraker, and the Brownsville Affray." *Journal of Negro History* 41 (January, 1956): 43–65.

Tracy, Merle Elliott. "The Romance of the Lower Rio Grande." *Texas Magazine* 8, no. 2 (June, 1913): 114–17.

Waide, C. D. "When Psychology Failed." *Houston Gargoyle,* May 15, 1928, pp. 5–6; May 22, 1928, pp. 5–6; May 22, 1928, pp. 10–11; May 29, 1928, pp. 11–12; June 12, 1928, pp. 10–11.

Weiss, Harold John, Jr. "'Yours to Command': Captain William J. 'Bill' McDonald and the Panhandle Rangers of Texas." Ph.D. thesis, Indiana University, 1980.

Wynne, Lewis N. "Brownsville: The Reaction of the Negro Press." *Phylon* 33, no. 2 (Summer, 1972): 153–60.

Young, Richard. "The Brownsville Affray." *American History Illustrated* 21, no. 6 (October, 1986): 10–17.

Index